Divine Design
For The
Family

Second Edition

Ray M. Wenger

Trust in the Lord with all your heart, and lean not on your own understanding. In all your ways acknowledge Him, and He shall direct your paths.

Proverbs 3:5-6

Plumb Line Press
8720 Unionville Rd.
Plain City, OH 43064

Cover design: Ray M. Wenger
                  Feinberg Design (consultant)

Copyright © 1990. Ray M. Wenger.
Second Edition 1992.

ISBN 0-9634616-0-5

Printed in USA

Contents

Foreword...4

Preface 5

Introduction...7

Foundations for the Family

1. Whom Shall We Believe?...11
2. Faith Determines Family Action...17
3. Marriage Credentials...29
4. Wisdom For a Happy Family 49

The Role of Parents

5. Parents Advancing the Kingdom of God 67
6. Dealing With Depravity 83
7. Godly Parenthood...91
8. Godly Fatherhood...115
9. Godly Motherhood...125

Training Your Child

10. Spiritual Training...135
11. Leading Children to Faith in Christ......................................153
12. Principles of Discipline 167
13. Developing Delightful Children...201

Bibliography...223

Foreword

Ray Wenger's *Divine Design for the Family* is a worthwhile contribution to the Christian home. When, nearly twenty years ago, I wrote *Christian Living in the Home,* there was relatively little in the area available that was of a biblical nature. There were a few books—psychologically, rather than biblically oriented. Since then, floods of materials on the family have poured forth from Christian publishers. So vast has been the output that the average person is overwhelmed by the array of titles in a well-stocked Christian bookstore.

So then—why another? There is one simple answer to that question: among all the offerings, there are still relatively few that are biblically-based rather than psychologically or experience-oriented.

Let me commend this book to you as one that not only sets forth basic biblical truth about marriage and the family but also introduces some new insights as well. Every Christian's home shelf should have a copy.

J. E. Adams
Escondido, CA
1988

Preface

The Scriptures provide the key to effective living. The Creator of the Universe tells us how to live as families, how to experience joy and fulfillment. As we apply God's principles, we experience blessing.

Some years ago David Foote, who frequently visited in our home, began telling me I should write a book on child training. I wondered who would read it, and just laughed at his suggestion. However, after months of his persistent prodding, and encouragement from two professors at Grace Theological Seminary, I finally made arrangements to work on the manuscript as a project during my seminary studies.

Professor David R. Plaster worked with me on this project. He evaluated the basic outline, studied the manuscript, and made valuable comments and suggestions. Many other people reviewed portions of it and made helpful suggestions: John C. Whitcomb, Ivan French, George Zemek, Tracy Howard, Larry Kayser, Allen Roth. John D. Martin was especially helpful in giving editorial assistance. David Foote went over the manuscript in detail during the final stages. Jay E. Adams graciously provided a forward.

The foundation for this work began with the teaching my wife and I received from our own parents. We were taught the importance of obedience to the Scriptures. We were taught to obey our parents. We grew up in homes that established wholesome patterns of living.

My immediate family has had a vital part in this work, and our interactions together have been the source for the majority of the examples in this book. My wife and children have loved me and been patient with me as I have been learning how to be an effective husband and father. My wife Rhoda has exhibited the wisdom of the virtuous woman in Proverbs 31, and has offered many helpful suggestions and ideas, as well as assisting in editorial work. We have eight children, and I list them here with their birth year: Rachelle (1975), Renee (1977), Roland (1979), Rosalyn (1982), Rolanda (1984), Rhonda (1986), Raphael (1988), Ryan (1991). Rachelle gave me free access to her personal journals for anecdotal material, and also helped with proofreading and editing.

As the book was in the final stages for the first printing, we began family discussions regarding how to illustrate each chapter with a pencil drawing. We had a wonderful time discussing both the content and composition of those pictures. During the summer of 1988,

Rachelle and Renee worked hard to produce the illustrations for each chapter.

By the time we received the first copy of the printed books in the spring of 1990, the girls' artistic skills had greatly improved. Rachelle exclaimed, "Those pictures! If we ever reprint the book, we'll have to draw new pictures!"

The response to the first edition was very encouraging. Although many families are being overwhelmed by a culture setting itself against God, there are still many people who want to hear what God says, even if it means costly changes in their lifestyle.

In this second edition, the basic content and format is the same as the first. We have made editorial changes, rearranged the order of the chapters, and added material for clarification, interest, or amplification. We printed the book in a larger font to increase readability. Again we discussed thematic, compositional, and artistic details as Rachelle and Renee worked to provide the illustrations.

We pray that God may be glorified, that His Word may be given its rightful place as the sufficient and comprehensive guide for effective family living, and that Christ may be exalted as the only One who can provide the power to fulfill God's righteous standards.

Ray M. Wenger
Lancaster County, PA
1992

Introduction

Our society and even our churches are filled with perplexity regarding the family. Is it possible to train a child with confidence? What can be done to have a happy home?

God has provided His Word and His Spirit to answer the perplexities of human experience. God's wisdom is sure where others can only conjecture. His promises do not fail. His message gives hope and confidence to every family that chooses to obey Him.

The arena of experience confirms this confidence. During five years of teaching in Christian schools, my observations of parents, children, and teachers clarified root issues that desperately needed to be addressed. I became painfully aware of the failure of many parents in training their children. This was very sobering to me as a beginning parent. How could I avoid in my own family the results I saw in my high school classroom? As I considered these things, I realized that many teenage problems could have been solved with relative ease when the child was two or three years old.

I began to apply God's principles in my own family, and we experienced His blessing. Obedience channeled the outpouring of His grace which brought further understanding of His ways for the family. Living and learning with eight children of my own has refined this understanding. Because we have always home-schooled our children, the blessing of interacting with them has been enhanced and intensified. Presenting seminars on how to have a happy family has provided opportunities to discuss these issues with many people.

Parents can have happy families if they really want them. Such families are not available as packages of instant ingredients. Such families are not produced by merely reading books on how to have a happy family. Such families are available to parents who obey God.

The solution is so easy, and yet so difficult. God's answers are easy to understand, but often difficult to obey. Those who want a happy family must be willing to obey God, even if that means difficult changes in living patterns.

It may involve apology to a spouse. It may involve getting up early to have more time to do the important things. It may involve choosing a lower living standard in order to invest in the lives of children.

This book is not intended to be a collection of fancy formulas for instant results. The goal is to clarify God's principles for raising a

7

vibrant family. God's principles give confidence to parents. By obeying God, parents can learn how to creatively apply His principles to fit their particular situation.

The book is divided into three major sections. The first section deals with foundational issues for the family. Chapter 1 raises the question of authority. Whom shall we believe? Where do we get our answers to family problems? Chapter 2 explains God's definition of faith as found in Hebrews 11, and shows how parents who exhibit this kind of faith provide the basis for their children to love God. Chapter 3 discusses the credentials required of husbands and wives if they want a model family. Chapter 4 explains the major emphasis of the book of Proverbs for each member of the family.

The second section analyzes the role of parents. Chapter 5 shows their responsibility to shape their children into a vital force for God's kingdom. Chapter 6 discusses depravity and how it affects both parents and children. Chapter 7 formulates a proper philosophy of godly parenthood. Chapter 8 on fatherhood gleans instruction by focusing on the perfect Fatherhood of God. Chapter 9 deals with motherhood as portrayed in the Scriptures.

The third section of the book deals specifically with child training. Chapter 10 deals with the principles of spiritual training. Chapter 11 discusses the spiritual status of children, and how parents should lead their children to active faith in Christ. Chapter 12 gives extensive treatment to the principles of discipline. Chapter 13 provides some practical suggestions on how to implement the principles discussed in this book—how to develop delightful children, children who are fun to live with. Since there is a grand total of thirteen chapters, the book could be used as a resource for a Sunday School lesson quarter.

This book is designed to help the reader understand God's message to the family. It should be read with a Bible close at hand. In particular it is addressed to Christian parents. However, to the extent any parent applies these principles, he will reap rewards in his family.

Foundations for the Family

In vain would boasting reason find
   The path to happiness and God:
Her weak directions leave the mind
   Bewildered in a doubtful road.

The various forms that men devise
   To shake my faith with treacherous art
I scorn as vanity and lies,
   And bind Thy Gospel to my heart.

—Anne Steele, 1760

"It Is Not in Man . . . To Direct His Own Steps" (Jer 10:23)

1

Whom Shall We Believe?

Questions haunt the minds of parents: Will discipline damage my child's personality? What if I disagree with the way my spouse handles the children? How should I deal with a strong-willed child? Can parents survive the teenage years? What about a child who always makes excuses? What if my child is hyperactive? Is my child just "going through a stage"? Should a child with emotional problems be required to obey? How should a parent cope with "The Terrible Twos"?

We live in a society that has an abundance of information. On practically every subject, the amount of knowledge available is many times what it was a century ago. Many vitally important areas of study were only begun in recent decades. Computer analysis and access to data provides instant information at our fingertips.

We live in a society that is flooded with information, but is arrogant in its ignorant shortage of wisdom. This arrogance is fueled by the fact that our magnificent technological expertise has nothing to do with wisdom. Wisdom is living life in the fear of God. Wisdom is living life in His Presence. Wisdom is living life the way God intended it to be lived.

Contemporary Voices

Today's parents are bombarded with counsel on how to raise their children. This advice comes from many sources, and is based on many different philosophies. The result is a set of contradictory opinions, each proclaimed loudly by its own herd of experts.

The end product of this advice has not been encouraging. The contemporary family is a scene of chaos and domestic disaster. Faced with such a scenario, many parents give up in despair and grimly hope for the best, wondering if they would have been better off without children.

Even Christian parents are faced with confusing advice. Many counsellors are peddling a mixture of humanistic psychology and Biblical principles. These counsellors love to emphasize, "All truth is God's truth." They point out, "The Bible does not tell how to build an airplane, or how to do dental work." They conclude, "Gold is where you find it," and therefore any information is valuable fodder for Christian consumption. Their analysis ignores the fact that mathematics, physics, and chemistry are disciplines which in themselves do not address the basic issues of spiritual existence.

Much of their advice appears Christian, but is based on a system in direct opposition to God: humanistic psychology, which is not a science, but a religion. This pseudo-scientific religion was founded by men who proposed non-Biblical alternatives to the great issues of existence addressed by the Scriptures: man's origin, basic nature, destiny, sin, and resolution of guilt.   Many contemporary advisors mix these ingredients with a smattering of clinical studies,[1] and cover it with a thin icing of Bible verses.   The whole package appears spiritually respectable, but is a recipe for confusion.

God does not want His people to explore the abyss of darkness in order to gain a few tidbits of understanding (Rom 16:19b).   Satan appears as an angel of light, gladly dispensing insight as bait to entice the unwary to destruction.

Ageless Wisdom

Wisdom for the demanding task of parenting does not emanate from the transient and humanistic philosophies of men in opposition to God. Neither does it reside within the parent himself (Jer 10:23). The source of wisdom is Jesus Christ, through His Word.

The Maker of the Universe provides the remedy to the uncertainty and chaos of contemporary families. His Word gives the Divine Design for the family, guiding our homes into havens of delight. Any parent can apply this design with confidence. The credentials for success in God's program are very simple.   Parents do not need extensive education, or brilliant intelligence, or large amounts of money. The only requirement is an unswerving obedience to the principles of God.

God's Word is clear, and has always been a great contrast to human philosophy. Our age is no different from that of the ancient prophet Isaiah. Human philosophy can only whisper and mutter in spiritual incoherence. Any philosophy of parenthood which does not correspond to the total perspective of Scripture is worse than worthless, ultimately bringing only confusion ending in anguish (Isa 8:19-22).

God's Word has precedence over any and every philosophy of men. One who has Jesus Christ as Lord will reject all advice contradicting what God has said in the Bible. He will be careful that no one takes him captive through "philosophy and empty deceit, according to the tradition of men, according to the basic principles of the world, and not according to Christ" (Col 2:8).

Because Christ is omniscient, the principles of Scripture are a sufficient guide for successful parenthood. God's Word is light: clear insight for effectiveness and joy. It gives understanding even to the simple (Psa 119:130).

---

[1]Even the clinical studies must be viewed with caution. Much of the supposed neutral analysis of child behavior is erroneous because it is based on observations of untrained children. God's standard is a trained child. He intended for children to be trained and for such children to be the norm.

A mother of teenagers was once asked, "Are you an expert on how to raise teenagers?" She replied, "No, because every teenager is different." Her apparent humility actually indicated a serious deficiency. She did not understand the importance of the Scriptures for the task of child training. All parents can be experts, to the extent of their diligent study and appropriation of God's principles for raising children. These principles apply to all parents and all children. Expertise in parenthood is measured by the degree to which the parent has learned and applied the principles of Scripture.

The parent who truly loves God's principles will meditate upon them and obey them. Since he is then following the instructions of the Creator of the Universe, he will have more understanding than the most sophisticated of teachers, and more wisdom than the most revered of authorities. He will learn to hate every philosophy opposing what God has said (Psa 119:97-104).

The parent who obeys God will become like Christ who confounded the intelligentsia of His own day with God's wisdom not learned in schools (John 7:15-17). God's instructions enable an inexperienced couple to be skillful in the raising of children.

A young lady once worked as a baby-sitter for a Ph.D. professor of anthropology, whose wife was working on her Ph.D. in sociology. Their three-year-old son was very bright, and had an amazing vocabulary. He was also undisciplined and difficult for his parents to manage. When he disliked something his mother did, he felt free to slap her in the face. She would respond in gentle anguish, "What's wrong? What have I done to upset you?" When the father wanted to make an important phone call, he would spend ten minutes begging his son to stay downstairs lest he disturb the conversation.

In contrast, the baby-sitter firmly insisted on proper behavior. The boy knew what she expected and was secure in their relationship. After several months, the father said to her, "I can't understand it. Our son is so calm and so happy after he has been with you." Even without children of her own, principles of Scripture made this young lady wiser than highly educated parents.

The parent who seeks God's answers illustrates the dynamics of the fiftieth chapter of Isaiah. Since he learns from God, he will be able to speak to his own household with amazing learning, giving a word in season to a child who is disappointed or a spouse who is weary (Isa 50:4). Like a flint he has set his face for obedience to Christ regardless of the cost (Isa 50:5-7), convinced that truth administered in God's way will ultimately be vindicated, and that all opposing philosophies will be destroyed (Isa 50:8-9). At times of difficulty he resolutely follows what God has said, knowing pseudo-light ultimately brings even greater trouble (Isa 50:10-11).

Many voices clamor for attention, but God's voice is superior to all others and guarantees parental wisdom for anyone who will listen: "Trust in the Lord with all your heart, and lean not on your own understanding; in all your ways acknowledge Him, and He shall direct your paths" (Prov 3:5-6). The One who created the universe and instituted the family invites us to come to Him for supernatural insight.

Personal Application to the Parent

Commitment to the principles of Christ transforms every area of family life, both personally and corporately. The parent who has Jesus Christ as Lord will be personally open to the impact of truth in his life. He will be willing to change his behavior when shown it does not measure up to the standard of God's Word, even if this is a very painful and costly process. He knows the alternative is even more costly.

He will deal with his own deficiencies (such as selfishness) as he sees them mirrored in his children. In the process he becomes a more effective parent, is more pleasant to live with, and is a better example for the family.

When he wrongs his spouse or children, he will ask their forgiveness. He will not try to hide behind a facade of his own supposed superiority, but will allow family interactions to mold his own character more completely into the image of Christ. Awareness of his own sin and his own need for forgiveness, helps him avoid harshness by combining a spirit of mercy with the discipline necessary for child training.

The bedrock foundation of an effective family is Jesus Christ. "Unless the Lord builds the house, they labor in vain who build it" (Psa 127:1). This means husband and wife must individually have a proper relationship with Jesus Christ as Lord of their personal lives. Unless submission to Christ governs the parent, his own selfishness will sabotage his attempts to build his family.

Corporate Application to the Family

Obedience to the Lordship of Christ means the family is determined to live according to Biblical patterns, even when this contradicts contemporary "wisdom." Members of such a family will rejoice in serving one another. Individuals will not expect commendation for merely fulfilling their duty (cf Luke 17:5-10). Work has a new significance as it is done for the glory of God and for His reward (Col 3:23-24). The husband will not generate bad attitudes in the family by complaining about the unpleasantness of his own work. The wife will not neglect God's assignment at home in preference to some other work of her own choosing. Parents will teach children to perform their tasks cheerfully.

The family committed to the Lordship of Christ will give extra attention to those areas of life that the Scriptures indicate as needing special diligence. Wives must submit to their own husbands as is appropriate in the Lord. Husbands must love their wives and conquer the temptation to be bitter against them. Children must obey their parents in all things. Fathers must be careful not to provoke their children, lest they become discouraged (Col 3:18-21). Each member of the family is given specific direction for the area in which he is most likely to be deficient.

Families committed to Christ as Lord do not regard this as an affront, or demeaning, or unfair. They realize God's plan is best, that these commandments have been given for their own good, and that any departure from them is destructive to the family. They recognize areas of weakness as opportunities to diligently apply God's principles and God's grace. Therefore, they heed these instructions carefully, with a joy the world cannot understand. The result is a family blessed by God.

Noah's Faith Produced Nonconformity to the World

2

Faith Determines Family Action

Many Christians want their children to be "in the faith," but have only a vague notion of what this means. They want them to be members of their own denomination. They want them to believe the propositions of orthodox Christianity. They want them to live good moral lives.

Such parents teach sound moral principles. They faithfully take their children to church. They send their children to Christian schools, hoping they will obtain a solid foundation of orthodox beliefs. Everyone is horrified when one of the children grows up to reject it all as being worthless.

In many cases, this rejection is rooted in the religious experience of the parents. The child has seen them busy in church activity. He has seen their emphasis on good moral conduct. He has heard the arguments for religious orthodoxy. But he has never seen his parents *live* their faith in direct opposition to the popular philosophies swirling around them. Why should he choose a religious system producing no fundamental difference in the *goal* of daily living? The parents have had an inadequate concept of faith. The child has never seen or experienced faith in *God*. No wonder he discards the external forms of religion.

What Is Faith?

Universality of Faith

Faith is a universal characteristic of humanity. God has given everyone the gift of faith as part of his natural human endowment. People act differently because their common gift of faith is not focused on the same object.

Some trust in themselves: their good looks, their physical strength, their intellectual brilliance, their money, their reputation. Others trust human achievements to answer every dilemma: science, technology, economic theory, political action. Some trust in other people: their friends, their spouse, their children, their leaders. Others trust in institutions: their government, their political party, or even their church.

None of these are adequate objects of faith. At some point all of them will fail. All of them will disappoint us at a crucial moment.

17

Only God is completely trustworthy, completely adequate for every circumstance, always working for our ultimate good.

Thousands of years ago, the prophet Jeremiah clearly described the disaster of trusting in man instead of in God. Apparent initial success inevitably succumbs to stunted spiritual experience. The contrast is one who trusts in the Lord. Even in the harshest and most difficult of times, he will continue to prosper, bringing benefits to others.

> Cursed is the man who trusts in man, and makes flesh his strength, whose heart departs from the Lord. For he shall be like a shrub in the desert, and shall not see when good comes, but shall inhabit the parched places in the wilderness, in a salt land which is not inhabited. Blessed is the man who trusts in the Lord and whose hope is the Lord. For he shall be like a tree planted by the waters, which spreads out its roots by the river, and will not fear when heat comes; but her leaf will be green, and will not be anxious in the year of drought, nor will cease from yielding fruit (Jer 17:5-9).

The next verses describe how the human heart is desperately wicked, apt to convince itself it is trusting in God when it is actually trusting in human schemes. God graciously tests us with stern circumstances (drought times) so we can know clearly where our faith is founded (Jer 17:9-10).

Demonstrated By Action

How then can we describe a family who lives by faith? A family who carefully participates in the activities and program of its church? A family who has a precise and correct understanding of theology? A family who prays and receives a check in the mail at exactly the time it is needed?

Certainly, faith may involve these things. But the kind of faith pleasing to God is much more comprehensive than any one of them. Faith which pleases God goes beyond mere intellectual assent to a certain set of axioms. True faith always produces actions demonstrating that faith (Jas 2:14-26).

God emphasizes the point in the eleventh chapter of Hebrews. Instead of giving a multifaceted definition of faith, He shows how faith affected the way people lived. This picture of families living by faith enlightens our understanding of what faith is, and helps us see how living by faith is an essential ingredient for leading a child into active participation in God's program. Faith defines the actions of the family. Only when parents live by faith in what the Unseen God has said can they expect their children to live by faith in the same God.

Faith in God Required for Pleasing Him

Hebrews 11 is a grand exhibit of saints who lived by faith in God. The chapter begins with a simple statement: "Now faith is the substance of things hoped for, the evidence of things not seen" (v 1). By definition, faith in *God* demands total trust in what *cannot be seen.* After mentioning the faith of Abel and Enoch, the writer makes an arresting statement: "Without faith it is impossible to please Him, for he who comes to God must believe that He is, and that He is a rewarder of those who diligently seek Him" (Heb 11:6).

Faith is mandatory because man really has only two choices: trust in God, or trust in something else. When confronted with a difficulty, we can either trust God to work a miracle upon our obedience to Him, or we can take the way of natural reasoning based upon our faith in something other than God. A man who has faith in God bases his actions on what God has said, even when it seems like nonsense to the natural mind.

Without faith in God, man's only recourse is to take the way of natural reasoning. This reasoning works in opposition to God (Rom 8:7-8), and therefore inevitably displeases Him. Much of the contemporary advice for families is merely following the dictates of the natural mind and runs in direct opposition to what God has said.

Faith Produces Nonconformity to the World

Noah is a great example of a man whose faith dramatically affected his family. "By faith Noah, being divinely warned of things not yet seen, moved with godly fear, prepared an ark for the saving of his household, by which he condemned the world and became heir of the righteousness which is according to faith" (v 7).

Faith produces nonconformity to the world. Noah experienced this in at least two areas: 1) obedience to God even if it involved things never heard of before, and 2) obedience to God which automatically made him and his family different from everyone else.

By Obedience Involving Incomprehensible Reality

Noah obeyed even when his obedience involved things never heard of before. When God warned of judgment coming on the earth, Noah could have objected. "What? Do you mean there is enough water in the sky to cover all the hills and mountains? In the history of the world, water has never come down from the sky. Besides, how would I get the animals into the ark? How will I keep them from fighting once they are inside?"

Like the Apostle Paul (1 Cor 4:10), Noah was willing to be regarded a fool because of his allegiance to God. Imagine the newslines after Noah had been working for decades on the ark, preaching the judgment to come. "Today is the thirty-fifth anniversary of when Old Fogey Noah began building his ark. Any competent observer can see there have been no meteorological changes during all these years; there is no more need for an ark now than on the day he started. As we review the size of his project and the pace he is proceeding, we predict it will take at least another seventy years for him to complete it. Some young entrepreneurs have even set up a booth nearby to provide tourist information for those who want to tour this supreme example of archaic religious folly. Old Noah and his sons will provide us with lots of humor for many decades."

True wisdom is folly to the natural mind. "The natural man does not receive the things of the Spirit of God, for they are foolishness to him; nor can he know them, because they are spiritually discerned" (1 Cor 2:14). The preaching of the Cross is foolishness to those who are perishing (1 Cor 1:18). In fact, anyone who regards the demands of the Cross as foolish has simply marked himself as one of those headed for destruction. Those who have faith in God obey Him, even when it involves things never heard of before.

By Obedience Which Makes the Believer an Anomaly

Faith is being obedient, even if it means being different from everyone else. Sometimes Christians speak of how the world is getting worse and worse. However, it is not yet as bad as it was in the days of Noah. Then there was only one righteous family on the earth. Everyone except Noah's family was wicked. His relatives were wicked. All the religious and secular leaders were wicked. Noah and his family were alone.

Probably even Noah's family was bending under the pressure. When God described the certainty of coming judgment upon the wicked kingdom of Judah, he mentions three great saints: Noah, Daniel, and Job. He repeatedly insists that even if these three men were in Judah, they would deliver neither sons nor daughters, but only their own souls by their righteousness (Ezek 14:12-20).

Apparently Noah's family was preserved because of the faith of their father. Although Noah's obedience in building the ark resulted in his inheriting righteousness and condemning the world, the focus of Noah's action was to save his family. "By faith Noah . . . prepared an ark for the saving of his household." Noah's action preserved his family from drifting to destruction. His example is a great encouragement to parents who by faith desire to preserve their families in the midst of a corrupt world.

Faith Focuses on Long-term Benefits

In verses eight to ten, Abraham's example shows how faith has its focus on long-term benefits, not short-term gains. Faith looks beyond the present because it anchors life in what God has said about the future.

By Obedience Without Knowing the Results

Clearly Abraham illustrates this attitude. "By faith Abraham obeyed when he was called to go out to the place which he would afterward receive as an inheritance. And he went out, not knowing where he was going" (v 8).

Abraham was both wealthy and prominent. He could have asked all the usual questions. "How will I be able to traverse hostile terrain amid the dangers of vagabonds and thieves? What if after I get there I find the land unsuitable for flocks? Will the inhabitants there be hostile to strangers?" God did not provide advance answers for these kinds of questions. He expected Abraham to trust Him and start going. Abraham obeyed, not knowing where that obedience would lead.

Living by faith in the Twentieth Century requires the same kind of commitment. Some may lament, "If I take God's Word literally in that area, I don't know where it will lead!" But such is always the walk of faith. God gives commands and provides grace and strength for immediate obedience, not advance notice for every possible contingency.

If we are unwilling to obey God without knowing the results, we are not really allowing God to lead us. We are merely leading ourselves according to our own best judgment and preferences.

Living by faith means the same kind of commitment exhibited in traditional wedding vows. We promise fidelity and love, not knowing what may happen. In prosperity or adversity, in poverty or wealth, in sickness or health we will delight in one another. Living by faith is a continual expression of the same kind of allegiance to God: obedience, not knowing what is ahead.

Such a lifestyle has an unforgettable impact on children. The difficulties and pressures Abraham faced in his venture of faith were platforms for God to reveal His grace and power. Such experiences impacted his family in ways they could never forget.

By a Pilgrim Lifestyle

This kind of obedience automatically produces a pilgrim lifestyle. "By faith he sojourned in the land of promise as in a foreign country, dwelling in tents with Isaac and Jacob, the heirs with him of the same promise" (v 9). Even though he lived in the land of promise, his lifestyle was like that of an alien in a foreign country.

After living there for years, he did not even have enough land to bury his wife when she died. He needed to make a special bargain with the sons of Heth to procure a burial plot (Gen 23:4).

During his entire life he never did obtain this land of promise as his personal possession. When Stephen recounted the history of this great patriarch he observed, "God gave him no inheritance in it, not even enough to set his foot on" (Acts 7:5). Obedience to God automatically meant living as a pilgrim, not as a permanent resident.

By a Focus on Invisible Reality

Life as a pilgrim is made possible by a focus on Invisible Reality. Otherwise the pilgrim life is utter folly. Abraham could contentedly sojourn in the land of promise because "he waited for the city which has foundations, whose builder and maker is God" (v 10).

By implication, all other cities do not have foundations. Paris, Tokyo, New York, London, Peking. All their splendor, magnificence, power, and wealth will one day crumble into ashes. Only the unshakable city built by God will remain. Such a place can really be called home (v 14). The vision of the unseen grants power for fearless action (cf v 27).

Caleb illustrates this kind of spiritual vision. All twelve spies saw the beautiful land and its spectacular fruit. All twelve saw the giants peering down from their high-walled cities. But Caleb saw more. He realized the giants would be a benefit rather than a hindrance to God's program. They would actually be a blessing for Israel, like bread for consumption (Num 14:9). By faith Caleb saw beyond the obvious to reality. Even after a forty-year delay, Caleb did not lose the vision. He specifically requested Hebron as his inheritance—the haunt of the most notorious of the giants (Josh 14:12).

Such faith is the true meaning of setting the affection on things above (Col 3:1): not merely wishing for an eternal reward and longing for ease, but living now according to the dictates of heavenly affection.

By Alignment With Promises Not Personally Received

One of the tests of the long-term focus is the ability to continue to trust God, and to embrace His promises, even when we do not personally receive them. These saints of the Old Testament gave us a magnificent example. "These all died in faith, not having received the promises, but having seen them afar off were assured of them, embraced them, and confessed that they were strangers and pilgrims on the earth" (v 13).

Abraham could have complained, "Nothing ever panned out since I left Mesopotamia. All I did was wander over a pile of rocks which was supposed to be mine, but which I never received."

Before Elizabeth Elliot married Jim, she worked on developing the linguistic background to translate the New Testament into the language of a South American Indian tribe. Fortunately, she found someone who knew both Spanish and the target language, enabling the work to progress rapidly. One day she heard a scuffle outside. To her horror, this key linguistic person had been shot. The brains holding the information she so desperately needed were spilled uselessly on the ground. Didn't the Lord care about His work?

When she moved to a different task, she gave her careful handwritten notes to someone else. Later the suitcase holding those notes was stolen from the top of a bus. Didn't the Lord care about his work? For Elizabeth Elliot, the answer was a greater understanding of what faith really is:

> Faith's most severe tests come not when we see nothing, but when we see a stunning array of evidence that seems to prove our faith vain. . . .
> To be a follower of the Crucified means, sooner or later, a personal encounter with the Cross. And the Cross always entails loss. . . . We are not by nature inclined to think spiritually. We are ready to assign almost any other explanation to the things that happen to us. There is a certain reticence to infer that our little troubles may actually be the vehicles to bring us to God.[1]

---

[1]Elisabeth Elliot, *These Strange Ashes* (New York: Harper and Row, 1975), pp. 110, 129.

Living by faith means embracing the promises not received because we are ultimately confident in the Unseen Giver of those promises, knowing that He is doing a work beyond what we could ask or think.

By Burning Bridges to the Past

He who lives by faith deliberately turns his mind away from previous life goals and patterns. He does not continually remind himself of the melons and garlics back in Egypt. Such resolution reduces the temptation to forsake one's confidence in God. Many people falter along the way because they have never "burned the bridges behind them" that lead back to their old life. At the first difficulty they are ready to repudiate God and wallow in old sins. Refusal to look back reduces temptation, and is one of the keys to focusing on long-term benefits: it increases one's desire for heaven. "And truly if they had called to mind that country from which they had come out, they would have had opportunity to return. But now they desire a better, that is, a heavenly country" (v 15).

God graciously identifies Himself with such persons, and prepares a special dwelling place for them. "Therefore God is not ashamed to be called their God, for He has prepared a city for them" (v 16).

Faith Obeys the Details of God's Program

Faith in God exhibits a careful obedience to the details of God's program. It is not enough just to be a child of God and to serve in His kingdom. One who is living by faith will be scrupulous in implementing God's program in the precise manner God requires. Ends do not justify means. God is glorified only when the believer uses God's methods to accomplish God's goals. Living by faith is trusting in God's power rather than relying on schemes of the flesh.

By Appropriating God's Power to Do the Impossible

Abraham's wife Sarah had learned hard lessons in the folly of fleshly schemes. Her attempts to help God accomplish His purposes through Hagar had only precipitated perpetual rivalry. So by faith she appropriated God's power to do the impossible for her family. She had been barren all her life. She had already gone through menopause. There was absolutely no hope of ever conceiving a child—except for one thing: God's word that she was to be the mother of the promised son.

By faith she received strength to conceive, and gave birth to a son. Because of *her* faith ("therefore," v 12), Abraham became the father of a great multitude. Sarah's faith was a key ingredient in the fulfillment of the impossible in the life of Abraham and his descendants.

The experience of Ezekiel illustrates the importance of appropriating God's power to do the impossible. God had set him in the midst of a valley full of dry bones and had asked, "Can these bones live?" Very wisely Ezekiel answered, "O Lord God, you know." Then God said, "Prophesy to these bones!" Ezekiel could have responded, "Lord, I don't want to waste my gifts doing things that are absolutely useless!"

Instead, Ezekiel obeyed. The result was a great and powerful army (Ezek 37:1-10).

God tests our faith by asking us to believe He will do the impossible. When king Asa acted in faith, God routed an enemy army of one million men. In later years, Asa succumbed to the temptation to rely on the arm of flesh rather than trust in God. God sent a prophet who reminded him of the previous victory from the Lord, and defined for us God's characteristic mode of operation: He wants a heart who trusts so that God can show *Himself* mighty on behalf of that person. "For the eyes of the Lord run to and fro throughout the whole earth, to show Himself strong on behalf of those whose heart is loyal to Him" (2 Chr 16:9).

By Obedience That Seems Absolutely Senseless

Faith means obedience, even when that obedience makes absolutely no sense to the natural mind. It is not for us to argue whether God's program will best be promoted in the way He stipulates. Faith believes God's ways are wiser than the best schemes we could devise. Even when God's commands seem strange or unnecessary, faith obeys.

Abraham could have complained that repeatedly God made demands that seemed absolutely senseless. At the beginning God asked him to go to some undisclosed place. Abraham got up and went.

After he got into the land, God told him to circumcise his entire household as a sign of their covenant relationship. Abraham could have argued, "What is spiritual about that? Even I could find a better symbol!" Instead, Abraham obeyed. That very same day he circumcised his entire household (Gen 17:10,22,23), in spite of the strategic risks involved.[2]

Worst of all was the startling announcement, "Go offer your son Isaac." Abraham had waited long years for a son. His wife had been barren. She finally had passed through menopause. Then beyond all hope, God had blessed them with a miracle son whom they named Isaac. Now God makes the most preposterous of all His demands: destroy the son for whom you have waited and prayed so long.

Again Abraham exhibited his true colors. No wonder he is called the father of the faithful. He arose early the next morning and began traveling with Isaac to the place of sacrifice. This "senseless" obedience dramatically affected the family. The events on that sacrificial hill made an impression Isaac could never forget.

By Willingness to Sacrifice Dearest Treasure

Faith means being willing to sacrifice the dearest thing in your life to God. When God approached Abraham, He gave clear direction so

---

[2]Years later, two of his great-grandsons, incensed that a Canaanite had defiled their sister, bargained with the offender to have his entire city circumcised. Three days later when everyone was in pain, these two men came in and single-handedly slaughtered all the men of the city (Gen 34:25).

there could be no mistake. "Take now your son, your only son Isaac, whom you love . . . and offer him" (Gen 22:2). Not just any son would do. Not the son of some servant. Not Ishmael. But Isaac, the son of promise, Abraham's most precious possession. Nothing in the world was dearer to the heart of Abraham.

"By faith Abraham, when he was tested, offered up Isaac" (Heb 11:17). The writer of the epistle uses the perfect tense: Abraham actually offered his son. Although God stopped him before he killed Isaac, Abraham had completely offered him in his heart. He was resolutely obeying every detail God had commanded. He built the altar. He prepared the wood. He bound Isaac and laid him on the wood. He took the knife to kill his son.

At the last possible moment, God stopped Abraham. If he had waited another minute, Isaac would have been dead. God said, "Now I know that you fear God, since you have not withheld your son, your only son, from Me" (Gen 22:12). Willingness to sacrifice our dearest treasure to God is the acid test of whether we really fear God. He who holds anything back does not fear God.

Total surrender lifestyle is the essential meaning of offering ourselves as living sacrifices (Rom 12:1). A sacrifice has no rights or privileges. Its only purpose is to be consumed on the altar. Because of God's great redemptive action on our behalf (Rom 1-11), offering ourselves completely for His disposal is our only reasonable service.

By Obedience That Requires a Miracle

Faith is obedient even if that obedience requires a miracle. Many people refuse to obey because they correctly realize there is no hope for success from a natural standpoint. Abraham's experience on Mount Moriah is his supreme exhibition of faith. It is the culmination of all the elementary tests God had used to strengthen his faith in the preceding years.

Abraham knew God had promised, "In Isaac your seed shall be called" (v 18). Then he heard an equally clear statement, "Go offer Isaac as a burnt offering." He knew the God Who had made both statements. There was no question about what God had said. Lesser men would have passed it off as a contradiction and refused to obey. Abraham knew better. He knew both statements must be true. The only way they could both be true would be for God to raise Isaac from the dead.

Whenever there is an apparent contradiction between God's commands and His promises, the commands must take precedence. It is our job to obey the commands, trusting God to fulfill His promises.

Abraham took Isaac to Mount Moriah. He verbalized his faith to his servants, "Stay here with the donkey; the lad and I will go yonder and worship, and we [plural] will come back to you" (Gen 22:5). Imagine the turmoil in the father's soul when Isaac wondered why they had brought wood and fire but no lamb. By faith Abraham told his son, "God will provide for Himself the lamb for the burnt offering" (Gen 22:8), not having the heart to tell him explicitly who the lamb would be.

By faith Abraham fully intended to kill his son and burn him to ashes, believing God would raise him from the dead in order to fulfill His promise. "By faith Abraham, when he was tested, offered up Isaac, and he who had received the promises offered up his only begotten son, of whom it was said, 'In Isaac your seed shall be called,' accounting that God was able to raise him up, even from the dead, from which he also received him in a figurative sense" (Heb 11:17-19). Faith obeys, even when that obedience requires God to work a miracle.

Faith Actively Enlists Descendants

In Infancy
Sometimes people are afraid to bring a child into a world so filled with evil. Such fears need the example of Moses' parents, who certainly lived in evil days. The king had commanded the midwives to kill every Hebrew boy before the mother knew what happened. When they refused to follow orders, he commanded every Hebrew boy to be thrown into the river. But Moses parents' were not afraid of the king's commandment, and they hid their son for three months (v 23). They were not intimidated by those who were antagonistic toward God.

Finally, by faith Moses' mother did put him into the river—but in a little basket which she had prepared. She deliberately placed him where she knew the princess would come for her religious bathing ritual. Undoubtedly she prayed for God's intervention. God answered gloriously. He used the baby's cry to touch the heart of the princess. He moved the quick wit of an older sister to arrange a bargain to pay the real mother for raising her child.

Jochebed's faith and teaching produced an outstanding son. Moses realized there was a greater power than the Egyptian court. He refused the rights of Egyptian royalty, considering them insignificant in comparison to being a servant to the God of Heaven (v 24).

He understood reality, and therefore made amazing choices, choices that are nonsense to the natural mind. By faith he knew affliction was better than pleasure, and the reproach of Christ was more valuable than all earthly treasures.

> By faith Moses, when he became of age, refused to be called the son of Pharaoh's daughter, choosing rather to suffer affliction with the people of God than to enjoy the passing pleasures of sin, esteeming the reproach of Christ greater riches than the treasures in Egypt, for he looked to the reward (vv 24-26).

A Final Legacy
Faith reaches beyond our own experience to the lives of others. Faith actively directs one's descendants into personal participation in God's program, a participation going beyond our own lifetime. He who

lives by faith does not endorse the passive nonsense called "letting his children choose."

> By faith Isaac blessed Jacob and Esau concerning things to come. By faith Jacob, when he was dying, blessed each of the sons of Joseph, and worshipped, leaning on the top of his staff. By faith Joseph, when he was dying, made mention of the departure of the children of Israel, and gave instructions concerning his bones (vv 20-22).

When these men neared the end of their lives, they personally directed their descendants to participate in God's program. They helped their children understand how God's purposes encompass grandeur far beyond their own lifetimes. They wanted their children never to forget their great privileges as people of God.

Beyond Death

Joseph's example is particularly instructive. As ruler of Egypt, he could have had a magnificent tomb. At the very least, if he wanted to be buried in Canaan, he could have had a grandiose funeral similar to the one he arranged for his own father—such a splendid display that the Canaanites named a location in honor of the event (Gen 50:11).

Joseph had a much higher goal in mind. He chose instead a small coffin, small enough to be carried. Instead of immediate burial he stipulated that this coffin be carried to Canaan when Israel left Egypt as a nation four centuries later.

In the meantime this coffin would be a dramatic object lesson. It would continually remind the Israelites, "You do not belong in Egypt. This is not really your home. One of these days God is going to lead you out of here. When you go, take these bones and bury them in that Promised Land." At the end of his life, Joseph took steps to insure the faithfulness of his descendants four centuries later. Who of us is thinking about how we can influence our descendants in the year 2400?

Conclusion

Faith for the family means basing our entire lifestyle on the things the Unseen God has said. It means embracing those promises, and taking action in daily living, actions which may seem strange to the people around us—even to the people of our own church.

But the goal is an unseen city, one that has foundations. Those who go to that city will be a demonstration of what it means to please God: following His principles when those principles directly oppose the "wisdom" of the natural mind.

Children who see this kind of lifestyle in their parents will be the kind of children who understand what faith in God really is. The life of the family has centered on the supreme glory of unseen reality. Faith in God then becomes the only reasonable choice. Such children have a basis for choosing to suffer affliction rather than enjoy the pleasures of sin for a season, and for esteeming the reproach of Christ greater riches than all the magnificent treasures of the present age.

Love Lifts a Wife to New Levels of Glory

3

Marriage Credentials

Suppose a gentlemen dressed in a three-piece suit rang your doorbell and announced, "You have just been awarded the sweepstakes grand prize dream house. It is the perfect place for your family. It has four bedrooms, a modern kitchen, three baths, a family room, a formal dining room, and a living room. An additional room can be used as a study or a library. A two-car garage has automatic door openers, and includes enough side space for a workshop. The basement is fully finished, and panelled with real wood. Other features include skylights, wooden decks, heat pump, hardwood floors, curved stairway, and built-in microwave.

"The lawn is spacious and shaded by large trees. To the east you have an uncluttered view of the mountains. On the west is three hundred feet of lake frontage. One side of the property includes four acres of woodland and open fields, giving ample space for gardens, orchards, and hideouts for the children to explore. The paved driveway faces a quiet neighborhood, which is only minutes from interstate access. Do you want it?"

The place is beyond your wildest dreams. You respond quickly, "Of course we want it. When can we have it?" The next day you meet the gentleman at the real estate office to receive the award. He is apologetic. "I'm terribly sorry, but there was a computer foul-up. The sweepstakes award actually belongs to someone else, although it does not include the property I told you about yesterday. That property is still available to you, but not as a grand prize. It can be yours for $700,000. You still want it, don't you?"

Most people would still like to have it, but few would be willing to pay the price for it. This story is a parable of how people commonly view the family. They would like to have a model family. They would like to have a devoted wife or an outstanding husband. They would like to have model children who are exemplary in behavior and a joy to live with. They would like all this and more. But they are unwilling to pay the price to obtain it. Model families are not available as sweepstakes awards. They go to husbands and wives who are willing to pay the price to have them.

The price required is obedience to God's recipe for an outstanding family. That recipe begins with the husband-wife relationship. Many parents would like to have model children, but have not concerned themselves with being model spouses. Only by being a good husband and a good wife can a couple expect to have good children. The Scriptures define the husband and wife credentials required for a model family.

Husband: Loving Authority

The fundamental credential of every effective husband is loving leadership. He must be the leader in the family. He must shoulder the responsibility for decisions. He must exercise loving authority in directing his wife and children into their maximum potential. He must guide the family to a life of fulfillment, social responsibility, and spiritual maturity.

Male Chauvinism?

Many women in Western culture find these statements repulsive and demeaning. They falsely believe such concepts are remnants of a reprehensible male chauvinism needing to be exterminated at all costs. They ignore the facts of history—how Christianity has elevated woman from a slaving piece of property to a person of dignity and worth. Their unbelief prefers their own unenlightened sophistication instead of God's clear direction for their benefit.

The Creator and Ruler of the Universe is not only omnipotent, He is also good, without a shadow of unkindness or evil. Therefore His directions to His children are always purposed for their best interest. Any deviation from those directives plants the seeds of disaster in the lives of the disobedient. Obedience to God creates an environment where each member of the family can experience maximum personal development.

Basis For Authority

The husband's role as leader is not a product of social evolution or male chauvinistic domination. His leadership is founded on the invincible authority of Him who does everything well, and before Whom every knee will eventually bow. The Bible emphatically teaches the husband to exercise authority in the husband and wife relationship. Just as God the Father is the Authority over Christ, the husband is to be the authority over his wife. "The head of every man is Christ, the head of the woman is man, and the head of Christ is God" (1 Cor 11:3).

The metaphor of "head" is suggestive. The head is at the top of the body, and provides the vision and sets goals. It sees needs, and implements solutions to problems. It provides protection for the body, and coordinates activities.

The strong New Testament emphasis on the wife submitting to her husband assumes he is to be her authority. God has given him the responsibility to make the final decisions in the family.

The Bible expects the husband to be the leader in spiritual matters. It assumes he will be able to answer his wife's questions regarding spiritual truth and issues in the church (1 Cor 14:35).

When the Apostle Paul discusses the relationships between the sexes (1 Cor 11:3,8,9; 1 Tim 2:13), he emphasizes the original Creation Order, with man being created first. Therefore, the Creation account given in the book of Genesis is foundational to a proper understanding of male leadership.

The first chapter of Genesis contains a general chronological account of the creation events. In the creation of Man, the emphasis is that both the male and the female were created in God's image (Gen 1:27-29). There is no elaboration of the functional relationship between the sexes.

The second chapter provides an expanded account of Man's creation, and emphasizes functional relationships: relationships to each other, to God, and to creation. A hierarchical relationship is simply assumed.[1]

Specific details in the Garden of Eden clarify the role distinctions between man and woman. 1) Man was created first (2:7), giving him seniority in the relationship. 2) The man was designated as "Adam," a term which was also used to refer to the entire race (Gen 1:27). 3) The narrative events assigned Adam with leadership and responsibility before Eve was created: he must keep the Garden and must refuse to eat from the Tree of the Knowledge of Good and Evil. 4) Adam immediately exercised his authority by naming the animals. 5) Adam's need for a helper emphasized his role in leadership. 6) Adam's exercise of authority in naming the woman further illustrates his headship. 7) God's commandment for a man to leave father and mother and cleave to his wife (Gen 2:24; Matt 19:4-5) places upon the man the responsibility of the relationship. The command does not say a woman should leave her father and mother and cleave to her husband. Rather, the man initiates the relationship. 8) After the Fall, the Lord addressed the man when He began the interrogation regarding sin (Gen 3:9,11).

The conclusion is inescapable. God deliberately arranged the details of the Creation events in order to make a dramatic point. The man is to be the authority in the family.

Satan soon interrupted the tranquility of the Garden. He came to Eve and slandered God as selfishly withholding something wonderful by prohibiting the fruit of that one tree. Since God gave the restriction to the man before Eve was created, she likely knew about the prohibition through Adam's instruction. Therefore, both her taking of the fruit, and her leading him to also partake, were acts of insubordination. Part of Adam's sin was his failure to provide leadership for Eve. The sin of the first couple involved role reversal. It involved insubordination on her part, and lack of leadership on his part—a problem which has continued to afflict households down through the centuries.

---

[1]For a helpful treatment of male/female relationships, see Michael F. Stitzinger, "Genesis 1-3 and the Male/Female Role Relationship," *Grace Theological Journal 2* (Spring 1981):23-44.

By creating Adam first, God emphasized that the subordination of woman was part of His original plan. However, as a result of the Fall certain changes were necessary. Woman would have a great increase in sorrow and conception. Her role in child-bearing would be include pain. The husband she desired would rule over her (Gen 3:16).

The Fall did not *create* the need for subordination; it changed its complexion. Because of the Fall, man is now depraved, and therefore abuses his role in headship. He exploits the woman's natural inclination toward him by dominating her. This abusive domination of woman is actually a symptom of man's fallen nature.[2] The woman is caught in the dilemma of having a tremendous desire for a husband, even though such a relationship will involve domination and the pains of child-bearing.

Sometimes an appeal is made to Galatians 3:28, "In Christ there is neither male nor female," as if to prove that redemption lifts woman above submission. However, this text is describing access to Christ, and has absolutely nothing to do with the functional relationship between the sexes. In other places the epistles deal with functionality and clearly refute any notion of administrative equality.

Besides, the first three chapters of Genesis make it clear that the subordination of woman is instituted from the beginning of Creation, not merely because of the Fall. Only the abuses and limitations associated with subordination are linked back to the Fall. Subordination itself is not cancelled by redemption. Instead, the abuse of headship is rectified by the new relationship in Christ. The Apostle Paul warns Christian men against abusively dominating their wives (Eph 5:25-30; Col 3:19; 1 Cor 11:11-12). Only by loving his wife can a husband exercise proper authority over her.

What Is Love?

When the Apostle Paul gives direction to each member of the family, he focuses on lack of love as the major deficiency of husbands. "Husbands, love your wives and do not be bitter toward them" (Col 3:19). The husband must use those occasions which tempt him to bitterness and lack of love as opportunities for loving his wife.

Why would a husband need to be told to love his wife? Wouldn't love be the most natural thing in the world, especially for Christian husbands? Unfortunately not. Simple observation of marriages makes it abundantly clear: many husbands do not really love their wives. The Bible underscores the fact by giving this point more emphasis than any other instruction to husbands. Repeatedly God speaks to husbands in the area where they tend to be most deficient: loving their wives. This emphasis makes it clear that men do not naturally love their wives according to God's definition of love.

---

[2]F. F. Bruce, "Women in the Church: a Biblical Survey," *Christian Brethren Review* 33 (1982):8-9.

The Apostle clarifies this point in the fifth chapter of Ephesians. Love is the key to the husband's responsibility. This love is an act of the will, and is exercised whether or not the husband feels a "surge of warm emotion" toward his wife. This love is defined by the example of Christ. The husband is to love his wife *in the same way* that Christ loved the Church (Eph 5:25).

Christ did not merely decide to do a "good deed" in eternity by an intermittent or temporary expression of love for the Church. His goal was to build something glorious by loving something intrinsically unlovely. Therefore, He loved the Church and gave[3] Himself for it (v 25). His love was so great that "while we were still sinners, Christ died for us" (Rom 5:8). His love was not merely theoretical, but included the giving of His very life. This love and giving of self became the basis from which Christ could sanctify and cleanse the Church from uncleanness (v 26).

Sometimes husbands feel justified for not loving their wives. They see faults, failures, blemishes, and ugliness. "If you had to live with her, you would have a hard time loving her!" Such excuses carry no weight when measured by the kind of love Christ had for the Church. He loved us while we were dead in trespasses and sins, full of all kinds of wretchedness and uncleanness. Such love is the definition of how a husband is to love his wife. The husband is to sacrificially love her in order to make her into a glorious person.

The marriage relationship is not merely for convenience or for companionship. It is not enough to live in the same house, eat at the same table, and sleep in the same room. The goal for the husband is to develop his wife into a woman who is more glorious than the one he married.

A husband may want a glorious wife without loving her first. By sheer authority he attempts to bulldoze through her deficiencies. Without loving his wife, he embarks on a program to straighten her out. The log in his own eye makes it dangerous for him to try to remove the speck in hers. His attitude forfeits the fragrance of God's approval.

Every husband should ask himself, "How did Jesus win our *voluntary* submission?" Christ's example with the Church is the pattern for leadership in the home. The husband must love his wife and give himself unreservedly to her in order to accomplish great things in her life. His love and unselfish devotion make it possible for him to elevate her to new levels of glory.

This love is the platform for dealing effectively with her deficiencies. He helps her become a better servant of God, one whose love is focused first on God, then on her husband (v 26a). His devotion to her sets her apart for himself, making her completely satisfied with him, having no

---

[3]The root word for "gave" in Greek is *paradidomi*, and is used repeatedly to describe Judas' betrayal of Christ in giving Him over to His enemies. Giving of self is not a superficial experience.

desire for any other man. He tenderly leads her to experience cleansing in those areas where holiness is lacking (v 26b).

His actions are not founded upon his own subjective whims, but are based on the Word of God (v 26c). By refusing to use his authority to bully his wife, the husband actually gains a much greater authority. He becomes the channel for God's authority through His Word.

In order for him to teach her from the Word, this message must first cleanse his own life. As the husband is personally washed, he then is in a position to apply God's Word to his wife's experience. The goal is to produce a glorious bride without spot, wrinkle, or blemish (v 27).

Who benefits from this glorious result? The husband himself (v 27)! The wonderful bride who is being developed is *his own* wife. It therefore becomes clear why a husband who loves his wife as his own body actually loves himself (v 28). His love for her produces a better wife for himself. If you want a better wife, help her become one by loving her like Christ loved the Church, not by being a dictator.

Paul amplifies his argument by giving it an additional twist. "For no one ever hated his own flesh, but nourishes and cherishes it, just as the Lord does the church" (v 29). The parallelism of this verse demonstrates that nourishing and cherishing one's own flesh is speaking about more than the care a man gives to his physical body. It is also speaking about the care a loving husband gives to his wife—in just the same way Christ cares for the Church. The tenderness and care of our Lord is a delight to His Church: "For we are members of His body, of His flesh and of His bones" (v 30). Only as a man loves and cherishes his wife does he really become "one flesh" with her in the complete sense.

The "one flesh" experience does involve a physical, sexual union. However, in marriage the idea of "one flesh" suggests unity encompassing more than the physical. Someone has aptly said, "You marry a person, not a body." The couple has unity of purpose, attitude, and interests. They experience mutual delight, and enjoy special benefits received from the other which no one else on earth can give. The physical relationship is especially beautiful and exciting as it becomes a climactic symbol of this exclusive relationship.

The idea of being "one flesh" hammers home a very significant point. A wife is not a slave to be used and abused. She is part of her husband. When he cares for her, he is caring for himself. When he serves her, he is serving himself. His oneness with her makes service to her more rewarding to his own personal development than any other ministry.

Sometimes husbands get this confused. They can be ever so exemplary when they appear in public and wax eloquent as they exhort others to obey the Bible, while at home they treat their wives like dogs. The contrast is the husband who nourishes and cherishes his wife like his own flesh. Someone once wrote a tribute to a pastor: "We watched your wife's face as she listened to you preach, and we knew you were an honest man."

The reason a man leaves his own father and mother and cleaves to his wife is to accomplish the grand result of building her into a glorious person (v 31). He is following the pattern of Christ Who has done the same thing for the Church—a great mystery incomprehensible to the world (v 32).

For example, many people find mathematics a mystery. Suppose someone said, "Arrange the coefficients of a set of linear equations into a rectangular matrix, and calculate the associated eigenvalues. Use a computer to iteratively calculate the solution to the equations. If every eigenvalue has magnitude less than one, no matter what is used for an initial guess, the iteration will be guaranteed to converge to the solution." Most people would be perplexed. They would understand sentences composed of English words, but they would be unable to grasp either the meaning or significance of this powerful mathematical theorem. Why? Most people have no concrete examples to make clear the meaning of those abstract statements.

Similarly, the glories of Christ and His Church cannot be understood by unbelievers. They can understand sentences about Christ and the Church, but the magnificent glory and implications of that relationship remain beyond their grasp.

Such spiritual glory will be understood only by means of an obvious object lesson. Therefore, God gave the example of Christ and His Church to show a believer how to relate to his wife. As he does this, their marital relationship becomes a visual demonstration to the world regarding the invisible relationship of Christ and the Church.

The husband clearly has a tremendous responsibility, and the wife a most challenging task. Which is easier: to submit to a husband, or to love like Christ loved the Church? For God to be glorified, both partners must do their part. Therefore Paul concludes by reminding each spouse of their God-designed role: "Let each one of you in particular so love his own wife as himself, and let the wife see that she respects her husband" (5:33). Anything less is taking the name of God in vain.

Application

A husband loves his wife by consciously imitating Christ in serving her. He meets her needs physically and spiritually. He is a leader, an example she can follow confidently.

A husband loves his wife by making sure she feels fulfilled in her hidden role. Since she is not in the limelight, most of what she does is rated unimportant and demeaning in the eyes of a world drunken with frivolous glamor. The wise husband eliminates any pressures pushing his wife outside the home to gain fulfillment or additional income. He delights in what she does and honors her for being obedient to God. In loving like Christ loved the Church, he always upholds God's standard.

He treats his wife as a lady, and gives deference to her as the weaker vessel, solemnly realizing anything less will bring hindrance to his own prayer life. He knows his own spiritual growth is circumscribed by his kindness to his wife (1 Pet 3:7).

In deferring to her weakness, he allows for possible emotional swings during monthly hormonal changes, not scorning her as babyish or immature. He understands the burden of postpartum blues, and does what he can to alleviate her feelings at a time when she is completely overwhelmed by her tasks. When she is physically weak due to pregnancy, he intervenes to relieve her of discipline she would normally administer to the children.

He makes sure the children know that any disrespect to their mother is a direct affront to him, and will be disciplined sternly. He takes upon himself the more difficult discipline problems. He realizes her gifts of mercy will sometimes make her too lenient in matters of discipline. He will not berate her as foolishly "letting the children get by with everything," but will instruct her and help her grow in the firmness which is also part of love and lasting mercy.

Sometimes husbands like to recall how Adam should not have listened to Eve (Gen 3:6), and how Abraham should not have taken Sarah's suggestion regarding Hagar (Gen 16:2). Those wives influenced their husbands to do wrong. Unfortunately, few husbands remember how God on another occasion specifically told Abraham to implement Sarah's demand regarding the ejection of Ishmael (Gen 21:12). As the godly husband gives himself to his wife, he does not function as a selfish and autonomous despot. He realizes his wife is a channel of grace and well-being, truly a favor from the Lord (Prov 18:22). He knows God will at times direct his steps by having him heed her words. He has the humility to take her advice when she is right.

It is easy for a husband to be selfish and want his wife to devote herself to him instead of to God. The greatest concern of the husband who loves his wife like Christ loved the Church will be for her personal growth in holiness and sanctification. A devout missionary had this perspective. On his wedding day, he made his wife promise to pray daily: "Lord Jesus, Your love to me is better than Charlie's will ever be." Such a husband will live his belief that his wife's spiritual development is more important than her physical ministries to the family. He will understand that seeking first the Kingdom of God for his wife will result in all other necessary things being added as well.

Christ's love for the Church is expressed by His unceasing intercession on her behalf. He has an unchangeable priesthood, and ever lives to make intercession for the members of His body (Heb 7:24-25). The Comforter Whom Christ sent after ascending to the Father compensates for our troubling weaknesses by making intercession we do not even know we need.

> The Spirit also helps in our weaknesses. For we do not know what we should pray for as we ought, but the Spirit Himself makes

intercession for us with groanings which cannot be uttered. Now He who searches the hearts knows what the mind of the Spirit is, because He makes intercession for the saints according to the will of God (Rom 8:26-27).

Similarly, the husband who loves like Christ loves is an intercessor for his wife. All of us need prayer when our current spiritual experience makes us incapable of making those requests ourselves. This is true for wives just as much as anyone else. When a wife is very discouraged, or tired, or burdened with the cares of the day, the husband can pray for her in ways which her very discouragement prevents her from praying. He can ask God to enlighten her with His Word, to give her joy in His presence, to open doors of opportunity for her in ministry.

This kind of husband will help his wife arrange time for meaningful private devotions. One of the greatest struggles of a busy wife and mother is how to find time for significant communion with God. Little voices clamor for immediate attention. It is hard to find even five consecutive uninterrupted minutes. As soon as she sits down to read her Bible, a little one thinks it is time to sit in her lap. What will the Christian mother say? "Sorry, Sally, I am reading the book of Romans to learn about God. Come back after half an hour!" No indeed!

A busy mother may send her children out to play in the yard, thinking, "Good. Now I can spend some time in prayer." Then in comes a pair of knees needing to be bandaged. What will she say? "Sorry, Johnny. Mother is praying now. Go bleed on the kitchen floor for twenty minutes, and then I'll fix you up." Of course not!

So many tasks demand immediate attention: answers for incessant questions, supper to be fixed, clothes to wash, groceries to buy. If these things are skipped, the whole family will suffer immediately. But no one will notice if communion with God is passed by—at least not right away. Her many duties pressure her to allow important things crowd out eternal things.

The natural constitution of wives is to be short-term in their outlook rather than long-term. Husbands need to help their wives find the time to immerse themselves in the Word and to give themselves to prayer. If a wife is to grow spiritually, she must have time for communion with God. This must be unhurried, or it loses its effectiveness. She needs the refreshment of "God's dew."

> Quietness and absorption bring the dew. At night, when the leaf and blade are still, the vegetable pores are open to receive the refreshing and invigorating bath; so spiritual dew comes from the quiet lingering in the Master's presence. Get still before Him. Haste will prevent your receiving the dew. Wait before God until you feel saturated with His presence. . . . Dew will never gather while there is either heat or wind; so the peace of God does not come forth to rest the soul until the *still* point is reached.[4]

---

[4]Isobel Kuhn, *Ascent to the Tribes: Pioneering in North Thailand* (Chicago: Moody Press, 1956), p. 48.

One father of several toddlers was serious about his wife's spiritual development. He assumed sole responsibility for the children during the first half hour of the day so that his wife could enjoy uninterrupted time with God.

My wife has this testimony: Taking time for communion with God increases efficiency, enabling her to see God's perspective in the interruptions and perplexities of the day. She gets more done, and does it the way God wants it done.

Any woman who is "bored at home with the kids" does not understand the importance and power of spiritual ministry to young children. A husband who loves like Christ loves will help her see the strategic value of her God-given role. He will help his wife grow spiritually by helping her develop a vibrant ministry at home: portraying spiritual truth to her own children and refining their lives into sterling character.

The husband will also help his wife develop spiritual ministries to other women. If she is shy, he will help her take small steps: begin by chatting with some new person after church. One of the great needs of our time is women teaching other women how to be godly (Tit 2:3-5), not merely getting together to do crafts and dine on delicacies. Much contemporary Christian advice to women is merely the disguised fodder of militant feminism. The husband who loves like Christ will help his wife delight in her Biblically defined role. He will help her develop a ministry showing other women how to also experience the abundant fulfillment God intends, not the inane aping after the role God made for men.

Wife: Loving Submission

Recall for a moment the parable of the dream house and the model family. The price for a model family cannot be paid by the husband alone. The wife must also pay her part by being a model wife. She must relate to her husband in the way defined by God in the New Testament.   Obedience to God's requirements for a wife is her fundamental credential for being a co-builder of a model family.

Love Is the Foundation

The Scriptures do not give unnecessary commands. The writers of the epistles never exhort, "Dear brothers and sisters, be sure to remember to breathe!" Such admonition is not needed, and is therefore not included. Whenever the Scriptures give commands, we can be sure those commands are needed. The very presence of a Biblical command implies that the desired action or virtue is not an automatic feature of human experience.

The Scriptures teach a woman to love her husband. Contrary to the popular beliefs promoted by soap operas and romance novels, true love is not automatic. The kind of "love" many people fall into is not love at all, but mere selfishness. Since we are all incredibly selfish, we all need to be taught to love properly.

God assigns the teaching job to the older women. They have weathered the difficulties of life, and know the struggles attendant upon homemaking. They are to teach the younger women "to love their husbands, to love their children, to be discreet, chaste, homemakers, good, obedient to their own husbands, that the word of God may not be blasphemed" (Tit 2:4-5).

Love is at the head of the list of characteristics to be taught, and is to be lavished on husband and children. Lest a wife love her child and neglect her husband, the admonition for loving husbands is placed at the very top of the list.

The wife is not to merely perform acts of love toward her husband and her children. The Greek text portrays her as a "husband-lover" and a "child-lover,"[5] being characterized by devoted affection for them. She is not merely being sweet in order to manipulate her husband into buying her a new coat. She does more than show her children a thin veneer of kindness.

Her love for her husband and children is at the very center of her character. Many wives fail at precisely this point. They are more interested in a personal "career" than in their own husbands. They do not want to be hampered by the demands of children, and therefore cannot be described as ladies who delight in children and love to be with them.

A wife's focal love for husband and children is the basis for the other characteristics which God commands. She is discreet, not flaunting herself. She is chaste, reserving herself totally for the husband she loves. Working at home for her husband and her children is a delight, not a burden. As she lives in this way, true goodness flowers unhindered. This attitude enables her to joyfully submit to her own husband, and thus prevents God's Word from being dishonored.

For many women of today, that final admonition is the ultimate insult. Why should I have to obey him? Why do I have to submit to what he wants? Why can't I be myself? Why can't I express my own creativity? Why can't I be a godly woman in my own right? God knew how difficult submission would be for the wife. Therefore the New Testament exhortations to women devote more attention to submission than to any other topic.

Basis For Submission

Contrary to what the feminist movement would have us believe, the basis for submission is not male chauvinism, but the Word of God. Submission is part of God's plan and is based on principles foundational to human existence: the intrinsic nature of the Triune God, the order of Creation, the implications of humanity's Fall into sin.

---

[5]They are exhorted to be *philandrous* and *philoteknous*.

Biblical submission is not the same as groveling appeasement. Instead, it sacrifices one's own will on the altar of obedience, enabling God to work His purposes in a difficult situation.

Submission is not demeaning. Jesus submitted to the Father in all things, but this did not make him less God, or of a lower intrinsic worth. The authority of the Father over Christ is the analogy by which we are to understand the relationship of a man and his wife: "The head of every man is Christ, the head of woman is man, and the head of Christ is God" (1 Cor 11:3). Both cannot have equal authority, and God has designed the man to be the authority over the woman. For emphasis Paul envelopes the distasteful statement regarding women between the two statements that all can readily accept. Of course, the head of every man is Christ. Of course, the Head of Christ is God. In the center of the envelope: the head of woman is the man.

Paul appeals to the Old Testament to clarify his point. The first reason he gives is rooted in Creation. Adam was created first (1 Cor 11:8,9; 1 Tim 2:13). If God had desired for woman to be the authority, He would have created her first. During Adam's initial hours in Eden it was impossible for the woman to be the authority over him because she was not yet created. Hence, the very sequence of creation shows man to be the authority over woman.

The second reason has to do with the Fall. The woman exercised leadership, and gave to her husband. The Fall was therefore caused not only by disobedience to God's command, but also by violation of the divinely appointed headship order. The woman asserted improper leadership, the man failed to exercise proper leadership, and the result was disaster.[6]

The woman (not the man) was deceived regarding doctrine. The Day of Grace does not nullify the susceptibility of the woman to deception, as is evidenced by Paul's emphatic statement in I Timothy 2:14 that Adam was not deceived, but the woman was completely deceived.[7] In general, women are spiritually more open than men, and therefore more open to error as well as to truth (cf. 2 Cor 11:3). God provides authority to shield the woman from spiritual danger.

What Is Submission?

The root verb used for submission is *hupotasso*. This word occurs many times in the New Testament. A sample of its usage shows submission is often required even if the authority is imperfect.

Jesus was subject to His parents, even though He knew more than they did, even though He was perfect and they were sinful (Lu 2:51). The demons were unwillingly subject to the disciples (Lu 10:17,20). The

---

[6]Homer A. Kent, Jr., *The Pastoral Epistles* (Chicago: Moody Press, 1958), pp. 112-115.

[7]Regarding the deception of Eve, the Greek text adds the preposition *ex* to the verb to increase the intensity.

carnal mind rejects being in subjection to God's Law (Rom 8:7). The creature was made subject to vanity because of man's sin, and groans under it (Rom 8:20). Every person must be subject to the higher powers (Rom 13:1), a subjection not only to avoid retribution, but for conscience sake (Rom 13:5).

The spirits are subject to (under the control of) the prophets (1 Cor 14:32). At the grand consummation of the ages, when all things are subjected, the Son will be subjected to the One who did the subjecting (1 Cor 15:28). The Church is subject to Christ (Eph 5:24), and is an example for wives submitting to their husbands (Eph 5:21,22; Col 3:18). Saints are to submit themselves to God, no exceptions allowed (Jas 4:7).

Christians are to submit themselves to every human ordinance for the Lord's sake (1 Pet 2:13). Servants are to be subject even to unreasonable masters (2:18). Wives are to be in subjection to their own husbands (3:1), following the example of holy women of old (3:5). The younger are to be subject to the older (5:5).

In Ephesians, Paul describes the submission of a wife (Eph 5:22-24,32-33). Her own husband is the object of her submission. "Wives, submit to your own husbands, as to the Lord" (v 22a). She is not to think submission would be feasible if only her husband were wise or intelligent or spiritual like someone else. She is to recognize her own husband as her authority.

The quality of this submission is like the submission given to Christ by the Church (v 22b, 24). The true Church is always obedient, never insists on her own way, always approaches Christ with the attitude of a subordinate and a learner. The same spirit is to pervade the attitude of a wife being properly submissive to her husband.

The reason for such submission is because the husband is the head of the wife, working to benefit her like Christ does the Church (vv 23-24a). She will receive the maximum blessing as she cooperates with his efforts. The Church is to be a model for the wife, who in turn gives a visible demonstration to the world of the Church's relationship to Christ (vv 32-33).

The extent of the required submission is that there are no exceptions. "Just as the church is subject to Christ, so let the wives be to their own husbands *in everything*." (v 24). No provision is made for the wife who has better ideas than her husband, or is wiser than her husband, or is more skilled or gracious than he. The command embraces every circumstance.

Submission also includes the area of sex. This is the final stronghold where many women fight their battles. A woman can exploit the stronger sexual drives of her husband to manipulate him into doing what she wants. Her maneuvers can be so subtle that a husband could be made to feel like he was imagining things if he brought up the subject. Each partner must regard his own body as being under the authority of his spouse, not himself. Without the consent of his spouse, a married person sins if he deprives his partner sexually, even if for so lofty a purpose as prayer and fasting (1 Cor 7:4-5).[8]

If a woman is submissive only in the areas she chooses, she is not really submissive at all. She only obeys her husband when his desires happen to coincide with her own wishes. Ninety-five percent obedience is not obedience at all.

Of course, worldly wisdom rejects such an arrangement. God knew this kind of submission would be very difficult for the woman. Therefore, in His gracious provision, He instructed the Apostle Peter to clarify how submission will work in difficult circumstances.

Why Must a Wife Always Submit?

Peter wrote his first epistle to Christians who were suffering persecution. He exhorts them to submit to the government (1 Pet 2:13-17), and to obey their masters even if they are harsh (2:18-20), following Christ's example in suffering unjustly (2:21-25). In this context of unjust suffering, he then uses the term "likewise" to introduce his command for wives to submit to their husbands (3:1-6).

The command is comprehensive and very emphatic. Wives must submit even to husbands who resist God's Word (3:1). Thus, Peter is dealing with a "worst case" scenario. The wife is required to submit to her husband even if he is one who has heard God's message and rejected its authority. Peter is not merely calling for isolated acts of subjection. The Greek participle *hupotassomenai* literally means "ones who are submissive," suggesting a lifestyle of submission. Since submission is the attitude required *even if the husband is an unbeliever,* submission is required for all wives, even if their husbands are unkind or unreasonable.

The purpose of this submission is to win an unbelieving husband to Christ. He who is disobedient to the Word may possibly be won without the wife saying a word, when he sees her holy conduct coupled with reverence toward him and God. God does not guarantee conversion,[9] but a wife who follows this difficult procedure will be more persuasive than any possible verbal eloquence.

Such a wife will be characterized by holiness. In a debauched age she reserves herself totally for her husband, and lives a life set apart to God. She does not look for "fulfillment" and "a sense of personal worth" outside her marriage. She understands her silent mission of love (3:1-2).

---

[8]Spouses must be considerate of each other. Failure of either spouse opens the door of temptation for the other. A demanding husband causes a wife to resent the sexual relationship and feel used and frustrated, especially if he neglects to help her with several small children. Conversely, a wife who withholds herself places her unfulfilled husband into temptation to look elsewhere.

[9]Neither was Christ's suffering (1 Pet 2:21-25) a guarantee that every sinner would turn from his sins and choose salvation.

She rejects the worldly notion of attracting her husband through outward adornment. The message from the Apostle is in stark contrast to frequent contemporary advice, "A wife should doll herself up for her husband." Peter says instead, "Do not let your beauty be that outward adorning of arranging the hair, of wearing gold, or of putting on fine apparel" (3:3). She will be neat and attractive, but avoids expensive or sensual display. This restriction keeps the focus on the true source of beauty, and avoids sending a set of confusing signals to her unsaved husband.

Adornment has the idea of adding extra details to produce a beautiful effect. A wife who has her focus on external beauty is doomed to failure. Physical attractiveness will inevitably fade, and in twenty years she will easily be outclassed by many younger women. Remember, every plum eventually turns into a prune! A wife who is adorned in the "hidden person of the heart, with the incorruptible ornament of a gentle and quiet spirit" (3:4), will be displaying before her husband a fantastic spiritual attraction uncluttered by the trappings of a trite and frivolous age. Choosing to abstain from adornment of gold, fine clothes, and expensive hair arrangements motivates her to concentrate more devotedly on sterling character that lasts forever, instead of on fading external attraction. She then becomes the channel through which God woos her husband.

Godly adornment is authenticated by saintly history. It characterized holy women of old, who trusted in God, not in their own ability to wheedle and manipulate. A prime example of such a life is Sarah, who obeyed Abraham, calling him lord. The word translated "lord" is *kurios* and means master. The same word is used extensively in the New Testament to refer to the Lord Jesus Christ. The measure of a holy woman is whether she can submit without being afraid of what might happen to her, trusting God to keep her safe (3:5-6).

Because Sarah was precisely this kind of woman, Peter chose her to clinch a point: he is allowing no exceptions for disobedience. Abraham knew his wife was very beautiful, and feared enemies who would kill him in order to have her. Therefore, since she was indeed his half-sister, he directed her to tell everyone she was his sister (Gen 12:11-13; 20:5,12-13). As a result, on two occasions she was accosted into the harem of a nearby king.

God intervened to protect her purity. He plagued Pharaoh (Gen 12:19), and stopped Abimelech in his tracks before he touched her (Gen 20:6), closing up the wombs of his entire household (Gen 20:17-18). God supernaturally protected Sarah when submission to her selfish, faithless husband placed her into extreme danger. The clear lesson is that God will protect a wife who obeys her husband. She does not need to be afraid (1 Pet 3:6b). Women who trust in God are the ones who are really adorning themselves.

This kind of Biblical submission is part of God's plan, and is based on foundational principles of the universe. God explains submission in terms of his own Triune Nature, the order of Creation, and the implications of humanity's Fall into sin.

In contrast, the spirit of our age insists on its own rights, and calls for "tough love" to force a faulty authority to change. It is the antithesis of New Testament commands for saints in difficult situations. It speaks mockingly of a suffering wife being a "doormat for Jesus," while ignoring the plight of Christians who happen to be doormats for oppressive dictators, and must simply remain and suffer in slave labor camps. It disregards the fact that the same theology must work for all nationalities.

The church has slipped a long way with a society that even 100 years ago would have placed a great social stigma upon a woman who abandoned her husband, even if he were nasty. Biblical submission is not a groveling appeasement, but is a relinquishing of one's own will in preference for what God has commanded so that He can work His purposes in the situation.

The New Testament focuses on Christ, the grace He will pour out, and the glory He will produce through suffering. The emphasis is not on *my* needs, *my* hurts, *my* griefs. Instead, the light affliction of this present time is not worthy to be compared with the glory that shall be revealed in us (Rom 8:18). According to Jesus, no matter how excruciating or heart-rending the situation, obedience is better than fulfillment (Matt 5:29). The way of faith never promises escape from suffering (Heb 11).

By tracing through chapters two to four, one can see Peter's instruction to wives in the context of bringing blessings to others through unjust suffering. Right living is to silence the ignorance of fools (2:15). Servants are to submit to unreasonable and harsh masters (2:18). Christ is to be our supreme example of a righteous person suffering unjustly to bring blessing to the wicked (2:21-25). Peter gives the same type of message to wives (3:1-6). Everyone is to be kind, loving, suffering for righteousness' sake, remembering the example of Christ (3:8-22).

By responding kindly to unkindness and by blessing those who revile us, we are consistent with our calling, and place ourselves in a position where God can bless us (3:9). The follower of God refuses to short-circuit God's long-range blessings by succumbing to the temptation to speak evil or by failing to actively pursue peace (3:10-11), knowing that God is paying special attention to the one who suffers and is fully capable of judging those who persist in evil (3:12).

In general, living in this way will decrease the likelihood of further suffering (3:13). But if righteousness causes an increase in suffering, this suffering should be viewed as a special blessing (3:14), because it is an opportunity for growth in sanctification (3:15), and the accompanying false accusations are a platform for testimony (3:16).

Christ is our example. He suffered for sins, "the just for the unjust, that He might bring us to God" (3:18). Jesus brought life to the ones who *killed* Him. Afterwards He was honored and given dominion (3:22). A wife may need to suffer unjustly from an unkind, unfair, uncontrolled husband, so that she may be able to bring him to God. Through it all, the one who suffers in this way is moved to higher levels of holiness (4:1-2).

Peter wants the wife to adorn herself with what is truly glorious. Her faithful obedience will not automatically guarantee the conversion of a wicked husband. However, even if the husband never turns to God, the character of such a wife will flower into the glorious beauty of Christ.

My wife and I once knew a young couple who outwardly may have appeared happy, but were experiencing significant marital problems. The unfaithfulness of the husband was a pressure point in the marriage. Sometimes the woman heeded Biblical counsel given by my wife; sometimes she preferred her own ideas above the clear teaching of Scripture. Then our paths separated for several years when our family moved to another state.

Finally the wife began to call and pour out her troubles. The situation had deteriorated, going from bad to worse. She was disgusted with her husband and was contemplating divorce or suicide. I pointed her to God's message in 1 Peter 3, acknowledging the difficulty of obedience in her circumstances. I emphasized her responsibility as a Christian to obey God, even under excruciating pressure.

Again and again she would call, pouring out her heart. Again and again I pointed her to the same message: obey Peter's direction. Her repeated calls proved she knew deep in her heart God's message was right, and wanted to hear it affirmed in the midst of excruciating circumstances.

Instead of things getting better, they got worse. She miscarried her baby. Her husband's irresponsibility and unfaithfulness caused her to suffer alone at the hospital long before he arrived.

But her character was being transformed. Her friends observed her suffering and exclaimed, "We don't understand it. You just glow!" In spite of her husband's ungodliness, she even began to look at him with affection, visualizing what he could be after God's grace extracted him from the clutches of sin. God brought glory and power into her life because she obeyed.

Difficulties

What if a crisis looms and a wife needs to "take things into her own hands"? Many women have yielded to this impulse, and have engulfed themselves and their families with tragedy. Sarah saw her own barrenness and decided to convince her husband to attempt a fleshly fulfillment of God's promise through Hagar. She tasted the bitter fruit of her folly, and set the stage for centuries of conflict (Gen 16).

Rebecca knew Isaac was more interested in venison than in God's statement about which of his sons would lead the family. She decided to deceive her own husband in order to accomplish God's spiritual purpose. Her meddling purchased great sorrow both for herself and her favorite son (Gen 27).

Apparently Zipporah refused to have her son circumcised, thinking the bloody rite was unnecessary. Not until the Angel of God met her husband Moses on the way to Egypt and wrestled with him in a grip of death was she willing to relent and circumcise the son so Moses could be released (Ex 4:20-26). Her stubbornness nearly caused her husband's death.

A wife will recognize deficiencies in her husband, of course. But she will help him grow by being submissive and fulfilling her responsibilities, not attempting to make decisions for him. Gracious suggestion coupled with prayer is God's format for change.

If her husband insists on his own way against her better judgment, she allows him to experience the results of his indiscretion without berating him for not following her advice. She will allow her husband to be the leader, and will pray fervently for God to strengthen his leadership where it is weak.

What if an ungodly husband requires his wife to do something immoral? Elizabeth Rice Handford has insisted on the validity of the New Testament command for submission, and has counselled many women regarding it. She poses two questions to women who wonder what to do if their husband commands them to do something forbidden in Scripture: "Have you been living in daily obedience to your husband as part of your wholehearted, loving submission to God?" "Has your husband ever actually commanded you to do something wrong?" In hundreds of cases, she cannot remember one woman ever claiming to be submissive in all areas and yet being required by her husband to disobey God.[10]

Women who are not characterized by submission have not fulfilled the prerequisite for God's protection. If a woman does not obey her husband in areas which do not involve moral issues, she cannot expect God to intervene in her husband's life to prevent him from making immoral demands. If we do not obey God in small things, we cannot expect Him to bail us out of large difficulties.

If a husband asks his wife to do wrong, she should examine her own life to make sure she has been obedient in all other areas. She must repent of any disobedience, and ask her husband's forgiveness. She then is in a position to pray for God's intervention in the heart of her husband, so that he may grant her request to do what is right.

God does not expect a Christian wife to be immoral just because her husband demands it. If a life of submissive obedience and gracious appeal does not change the heart of her husband, the wife must gently refuse to do wrong because of her allegiance to Jesus Christ. She will

---

[10]Elizabeth Rice Handford, *Me? Obey Him?* (Murfreesboro, TN: Sword of the Lord Publishers), pp. 37-38.

meekly accept the consequences of her husband's displeasure, trusting in the God who knows everything and controls the universe.

Paul's letter to the Corinthians gives emphatic direction to wives and husbands. The Lord commands, "A wife is not to depart from her husband" (1 Cor 7:10). What should be done on those occasions when a husband may be dangerously abusive to a wife and children? Paul's directives in the very next verse seem to take such situations into account. "But even if she does depart, let her remain unmarried or be reconciled to her husband" (1 Cor 7:11a). Paul recognizes the possibility of a wife departing. He does not condone it as ideal, but assumes it may happen. If it does happen, he insists she has only two choices: remain unmarried or be reconciled.[11]

Conclusion

Many parents desire to have model children, but do not concern themselves with being model spouses. Parents must first deal with their own needs, so they can proceed upon a proper foundation in dealing with their children. A wife who refuses to obey and honor her husband cannot expect her children to honor her. A husband who does not sacrificially love his wife and build her into a more beautiful saint year by year cannot expect to be an effective spiritual leader of his own children.

Sometimes people think they can ignore what God says and still prosper. However, God is not mocked. In the spring of 1992 I visited Martin Weber who had served as prison chaplain for many years at Atmore, Alabama. He said that long ago the warden told him, "Practically all our prisoners have had either a father or mother who did not perform their proper role; and every prisoner that is restless, irritable, and unsatisfiable has had a domineering mother." Martin was surprised at his second point, and began checking for himself. He was not ready to claim an absolute one hundred percent, but confirms that it is a very high percentage.

The foundation of an effective family is commitment to Jesus Christ as Lord of all. This commitment mandates obedience to the principles of Scripture and requires rejection of worldly wisdom. The man and wife who live together according to God's standards for themselves are then situated to have godly children who live according to God's standards for them. The eyes of the Lord are looking throughout the entire earth to show Himself strong for families whose hearts are perfect toward Him. Choose today for your family to be among them.

---

[11]For the best treatment of both church history and the Biblical texts dealing with divorce, see William A. Heth and Gordon J. Wenham, *Jesus and Divorce: The Problem with the Evangelical Consensus* (Nashville, TN: Thomas Nelson Publishers, 1985). Except for the last several pages, this book is a careful analysis of what the Bible says, rather than an "interpretation" trying to accommodate contemporary culture.

"Ahhh! That Ring of Gold!" (cf Prov 11:22)

4

Wisdom For a Happy Family

Sometimes we wish to talk with someone who is truly wise, someone who has decades of *successful* experience in counselling people who have our kind of problems. We would like to sit with them, explain our situation, and then receive answers guaranteed to work.

God affords us an even better opportunity. He has centuries of experience. He understands us better than we understand ourselves. He offers us advice on how to live successfully as a family. His Word provides the wisdom we need for our specific situation. Part of this wisdom is found in the book of Proverbs—a great resource that has guided myriads of families over thousands of years.

It is instructive to investigate the general emphasis of Proverbs as it relates to each component of the family. If we were to name the single predominant theme regarding husbands, what would it be? What theme for wives is repeated more than anything else? What is the focus in Proverbs for parents and for children? This thematic emphasis enlightens our understanding of our own corresponding weaknesses. God gives us emphatic instruction in the precise areas where we are most likely to fail.

Husband: Avoid the Strange Woman

A young man in his thirties had a beautiful wife, two adorable children, and a good job. He enjoyed tackling difficult tasks and applying his skill and energy to turn potential problems into benefits for his company. His work involved long hours and frequent travel. Although this meant time away from home, he felt the ultimate rewards to his family were well worth the immediate sacrifice.

Sometimes he had opportunities at work to share his faith in God. He was especially happy to present Christ to his secretary, who was suffering the trauma of a difficult marriage which had ended in divorce. It was a great joy to see her hungrily respond to the Word of God. As time went on, he had opportunity to help his secretary with other personal problems. Speaking with her began to include time after working hours.

The attitude of his secretary was a contrast to that of his own wife, who seemed less trusting, less open to suggestion, less willing to respond, and more demanding. Eventually he began to enjoy his secretary more than the friendship of his wife. He silenced his conscience by reminding himself how he was helping his secretary spiritually.

His own wife became less and less attractive to him, with his secretary filling each measure of the corresponding void. A sexual experience with her was simply the culmination of a wrong pattern of living. Eventually he left his wife and family so he could continue the new relationship.

Unfortunately, the basic theme of this parable has been repeated in the lives of hundreds of people. Specific contexts change, but the rudimentary principles of disaster remain the same. The dominant message for men in the book of Proverbs is its repeated warnings against immoral relationships with women. The very repetition of this theme indicates men are particularly susceptible to this temptation. Contemporary society is strewn with the wreckage of homes ruined by men who have ignored the warnings and fallen into immorality.

The writer of Proverbs gives counsel as a father to his son. He describes the characteristic tactics of the immoral woman. He graphically portrays the dreadful results of an immoral relationship. He gives clear instruction on how to avoid the snare of the strange woman.

Characteristics of the Strange Woman

The immoral woman appears to be a wonderful person. She seems so gentle, so gracious, so kind. Her lips drip with the sweetness of honey and her words are as smooth as oil, but in the end all relationship with her will prove as bitter as wormwood and as deadly and merciless as a two-edged sword (5:3-4). Her ways are not easily comprehended by one who is young and naive, but those ways lead inevitably to utter destruction (5:5-6). Her beauty is a false attractiveness (6:24-25) which ultimately enables her to parasitically devour her lover (6:26).

Her disreputable activities are done secretively (7:9). She dresses in a way to incite the lust of men, but tempers her boldness with a crafty heart to make an effective snare (7:10).

She gives flattering invitations, and is quick to express her appreciation for those she finds (7:13). While in blatant rebellion against God (cf 2:17), she portrays herself as a spiritual woman, and speaks convincingly of her own devotion and uprightness (7:14). She tells her target she has been searching diligently for a wonderful person and now has finally found him (7:15). "I have been longing for someone who has your talents, your skills, your sensitivity, one who is able to understand me and my needs. Finally I have found you!"

She is a seductress who crouches as a beast of prey in wait for her victim (23:28), and she snares her quarry by flattery (2:16; 6:24; 7:5,21). She gives him a special invitation to join her in the pleasures which she has provided (7:16-18). "I am so concerned about you. I really want you to have the pleasure you deserve. I want you to enjoy a happy relationship."

Although she has a husband of her own, she assures her partner of circumstances guaranteeing they will not get caught (7:19-20). She is like a deep pit or narrow well, which by their very nature prevent the escape of one who has fallen into them (23:27). Her house is the road to hell (7:27). After using another to satisfy her own selfish desires, she excuses herself by claiming she has done no wickedness (30:20).

These warnings are not merely referring to the professional harlot of Forty-Second Street in New York City. The emphasis is on the snare of the adulteress—a woman who already has a husband (6:26,29,32; 7:19). She forgets her covenant with God in the formation of her own marriage, and forsakes her own husband (2:17), rebelliously refusing to stay at home and minister to him. Instead she looks for every opportunity to display herself as an attraction to others (7:11-13).

Such women are lurking everywhere: in the work place, in the market, even in churches and Christian organizations. They have been disappointed in marriage. They are wearied of their present circumstances, and desire to be appreciated and noticed and loved. They crave something new, fresh, and exciting. Instead of living by faith and courageously and sacrificially building their own families, these women are looking outside the home for "fulfillment" and a "personal sense of worth."[1] Men who are not alert are candidates for disaster.

Dreadful Results of Immorality

Depraved men have always thought they could dabble with sin, and yet somehow escape the consequences of transgressing God's moral law. However, their destruction is just as certain as if they had embraced fire, or walked on hot coals (6:27-29).

The immoral man receives an irreparable social blotch on his character. People demand restitution from the thief who stole to obtain bread, but do not despise him in the end (6:30-31). However, he who defiles his neighbor's wife receives wounds, dishonor, and a reproach which will not be wiped away.[2] The defrauded husband will accept no recompense, nor will he be pacified by many gifts (6:32-35).

The man who yields to the temptation of an illicit relationship with a woman opens a door of disaster which is impossible for him to shut. It is a place of no return (7:27). "Her house leads down to death, and her paths to the dead; none who go to her return, nor do they regain the paths of life" (2:18-19).[3] He embraces a floodgate of temptation not experienced by those who walk in purity.

---

[1]Our society has developed many such euphemisms to describe adultery in terms that sound respectable.

[2]God does forgive the penitent sinner, but the blot is not necessarily removed. Neither are the devastating consequences in the family canceled. David was forgiven for his great sin (2 Sam 12:13), but both the blot and the consequences followed him the rest of his life and were even recorded in Scripture.

[3]Possibly his only hope is through intercessory prayer by others (1 John 5:16-17).

The man who chooses the pleasures of sin has selected the way of death. He has taken the bait designed to hasten him to his own destruction. He is merely marching to a spiritual slaughterhouse that has claimed many strong men (7:22-27).

He is given over to dissipation. His vigor is consumed in the satisfaction of his passions, and his years are wasted (5:9). His wealth and his labors are squandered and the only ones who benefit are strangers (5:10). His profligate lifestyle brings him ultimately to utter poverty (6:26). The whole experience is self-destructive (6:32; 5:20-23).

Too late, he finally wakens to the folly of his life, weeping bitterly because even his own body has been consumed (5:11).[4] He deeply regrets his hatred of instruction and scorn of reproof. He could have been spared much sorrow if only he had been obedient to those who taught him (5:12). In the midst of abundant truth, he has chosen disaster and despair (5:13).

Provisions for Safety

Diligent Application of Wisdom

An insatiable desire for wisdom, and the careful application of that wisdom to life is the primary protection against involvement with a strange woman. Many claim to desire wisdom when in fact they only wish for respectable folly: they want to appear distinguished and wise, even while maintaining a lifestyle in opposition to the principles of God. For example, a man may pray eloquently for wisdom in spiritual leadership, even though he is secretly indulging his lust by gazing at sensual pictures. Such a double-minded man will not receive wisdom from the Lord, even if he asks (Jas 1:5-8).

The second chapter of Proverbs presents applied wisdom (2:1-9) as the key for preserving a person from moral disaster (2:10-22). A man who sincerely desires wisdom receives God's words of instruction and regards them as inner treasure (2:1). He is carefully attentive and diligent in application (2:2). Like a hungry baby who will not be pacified with anything other than milk, he is not satisfied with anything less than discernment and understanding (2:3). He regards wisdom as more valuable than wealth, and expends as much effort in obtaining it as does a miner searching for hidden treasures (2:4).

Since he is totally committed in his desire for true wisdom, God grants his request and gives him the capacity to discern proper actions (2:5-9). This discernment becomes the mechanism for preserving him (2:10-11) from evil men (2:12-15) and from the snares of an evil woman (2:16-22).

The same focus on preservation through wisdom is repeated again in chapters 4 and 5. The father exhorts his son to give attention to his

---

[4]Compare the New Testament description of sexual immorality as being against a man's own body (1 Cor 6:18). This can include both disease and a diminishing of physical delight with his own wife.

instruction and keep his heart with all diligence (4:20-27), knowing he has been forewarned of the true character of an adulterous relationship, even though it may initially appear very attractive (5:1-14,21-23). The father admonishes his son to treasure up his words, guarding them as zealously as the pupil of his eye, keeping them in his heart, letting them affect every action, so that these commands may preserve him from the seductress (7:1-5).

Ultimately a man is protected from evil by obedience to God. By choosing to obey rather than to follow the impulses or desires of the moment, he avoids the snares of beauty and flattery (6:20-25). Obedience preserves him when his own emotions and passions would lead him astray. Wherever he goes, such protection effectively guards him against unknown dangers, possibly even including psychological protection during sleep (6:22). Zealous care to keep God's Law as the "apple of the eye" preserves him from the horror of blindness and folly (7:1-5). "The fear of the Lord is a fountain of life, to avoid the snares of death" (14:27).

Joseph is a classic example of such protection at work. By refusing the sensual advances of Potiphar's wife, he did experience trouble (Gen 39), but not the self-destruction which is the inevitable product of immorality. In prison, he worked hard as a servant, even though treated unfairly. This moral determination paved the way for his ultimate exaltation on the throne of Egypt, enabling him to preserve his own family (Gen 45:7).

Careful Guarding of the Heart

Once when I was talking with a friend who had lived in New York City, I asked him what he had found helpful in maintaining pure thoughts. He replied, "In my experience, pure thoughts begin in the muscles of the neck!" On another occasion he told me he usually wore contact lenses, but sometimes walked through the city with them in his pocket instead of on his eyes. He could see well enough to know where he was going, but poorly enough to avoid the sensual sights which so easily generate impure thoughts.

Wisdom is not an entity to be preserved in a vacuum. The first step in applying this wisdom is to carefully guard the heart. Ultimately men fall because of repetitive indulgence in heart adultery. They choose to look when they should turn their eyes away. Those glances affect the heart. "Do not lust after her beauty in your heart, nor let her allure you with her eyelids" (6:25). "Do not let your heart turn aside to her ways" (7:25).

"Keep your heart with all diligence, for out of it spring the issues of life. . . . Let your eyes look straight ahead, and your eyelids look right before you. . . . Do not turn to the right or the left; remove your foot from evil" (Prov 4:23-27), so that you may be preserved from adultery (Prov 5). Jesus amplifies this point in His Sermon on the Mount. The man who even looks at a woman to lust after her has already committed adultery in his heart (Matt 5:27-30).

Avoid Unhealthy Relationships

A woman working outside the home casts herself into special relationships with men other than her own husband. The very role of secretary makes her a sweet servant to her boss. She answers his phone, types his scribbled messages, shields him from unwanted interruptions, fills his coffee cup. All these things are done politely, cheerfully, and efficiently. Her job requires her to do these things and do them well in order to obtain her paycheck.

This kind of interaction begins to affect the heart, especially at points of weakness in the respective marriages. He begins to wish his wife were helpful and gracious like his secretary. She begins to think her husband should appreciate her efficiency and diligence like her boss does.

Many men have fallen because they mistakenly believed they could work closely with an dissatisfied woman and still maintain their integrity. Their fall confirms the need for drastic action: "Remove your way far from her, and do not go near the door of her house" (5:8).

Jesus uses striking metaphors to describe how radical this action must be. Even if it involves the sacrifice of something as important as an eye or as useful as a hand, such loss is far preferable to the snare of immorality (Matt 5:29-30). Get rid of it before you lose your purity. If a woman at work causes you to delight less in your own wife, change jobs.

The simpleton who ignores this advice is finally caught. He chooses a path drawing him closer and closer to her clutches. He passes along the street near her corner (7:8a), and takes the path to her house (7:8b), choosing a time of darkness (7:9). She then catches him and kisses him (7:13), finally enticing him to yield (7:21).

Delight in Your Own Wife

One purpose of marriage is to maintain sexual purity. The strong sexual desires of a man must be satisfied exclusively by his own wife. Both partners are to be affectionate with each other, and are to consider their own bodies under the authority of their spouse (1 Cor 7:1-5). Sometimes men fall into immorality because they have not cultivated a delight in the privileges of their own marriage relationship.

As a woman advances in years, her natural physical attractiveness does diminish. Even so, the highest physical satisfaction is possible only for him who remains faithful to his own wife. No matter how beautiful or enticing the physical endowments of another young woman, they can never compare with the true love and grace of a devoted wife.

> Drink water from your own cistern, and running water from your own well. Should your fountains be dispersed abroad, streams of water in the streets? Let them be only your own, and not for strangers with you. Let your fountain be blessed, and rejoice with the wife of your

youth. As a loving deer and a graceful doe, let her breasts satisfy you at all times; and always be enraptured with her love. For why should you, my son, be enraptured by an immoral woman, and be embraced in the arms of a seductress (5:15-20)?

How foolish to disperse abroad to strangers the seed of manhood, and thus pervert God's blessing into a curse. Cultivate special delight in your own wife, knowing the two of you enjoy a cherished and exclusive relationship not shared by anyone else. The joyous purity of this physical union will be a safeguard against immorality.

Immorality marks a person as a fool. No one desires to be a fool, although many live like fools. Only a fool would forsake exclusive and legitimate enjoyments for those which are promiscuous and illicit. The adulterer lacks understanding and destroys himself (6:32). He is a simpleton (7:6-9). He is the gullible victim of a woman who only wants to use him for her own selfish ends, a fool who is oblivious to his own danger (7:21-23). Such a person is abhorred by the Lord (22:14). Knowledge of how God evaluates the immoral person is a sobering safeguard against immorality.

Application

In our sex-saturated society we must pay more attention to the warnings of Proverbs against involvement with the strange woman. Adultery is so serious that God chose it to illustrate the justice of His judgment on spiritual infidelity (Rev 17-18).

Billboards, advertisements, and commercials employ beautiful and glamorous women to attract attention to their products. A husband must resist the subtle temptation to be dissatisfied with his own wife, thinking she is too much of a "plain Jane" to be any fun.

No one is above temptation. All men must humbly remember to constantly guard against even a lustful look. They must deliberately turn their eyes away from women who display themselves in a way that incites improper thoughts in the male heart. They must avoid feeding lust through books, magazines, or television. Wisdom would even avoid the aisle of sensual magazines in the grocery store.

No wife can ever compete physically with the pinup girls of magazines or television. Whenever a man indulges in a lustful look, he increases his desire for wrong fulfillment and reduces his delight in his own wife. He is destroying his own joy and baiting a trap for himself.

Nothing is more devastating or destructive to the family than to have its integrity shattered by marital infidelity. Wives should guard themselves against sloppiness and obesity, and should live in such a way that will help their husbands delight in them. Many marriages would be greatly strengthened if the wife exhibited to her husband the same kind of attitude and service a good secretary provides for her employer.

Wife: Build Your Family

A young woman in her late twenties had three children who brought her fulfillment as a mother. She enjoyed their childish ways, and loved to watch them grow and develop. She had a handsome husband who earned a good living for the family. He seemed perfect, except for a few minor faults.

She wished he would be a little more gentle with the children. She couldn't agree with his methods of discipline, and often felt the urge to sympathize with her children afterwards. She wished he would be more prompt at fixing things around the house. She couldn't remember the number of times she spoke to him about the cabinet latch before he got around to fixing it. She wished he would remember her birthday and their anniversary without a preliminary sequence of hints.

Basically she knew she had a good husband. She knew not everyone was a self-starter. She wanted to make a good husband better by prodding him to change where she saw need for improvement. If only he would solve these little problems, their marriage would be perfect. What she did not realize was that instead of building her family, she was tearing it down by nagging her husband.

The book of Proverbs pointedly addresses the problem illustrated by the preceding parable. "Every wise woman builds her house, but the foolish pulls it down with her hands" (14:1).[5] A literal house is something built with tremendous effort and expenditure of resources. Any normal woman would carefully treasure her house and do all she could to enhance its beauty and usefulness. No one would foolishly destroy part of her house each day.

A family requires an even greater commitment of effort and resources. A wise woman consciously and continually builds her family, inspiring them with her example, teaching them the principles of life, and sacrificially giving of herself so they may benefit.

A foolish woman destroys her own household. Day by day and bit by bit she is the active instrument to bring about the utter ruin of her family. She tears down her husband with criticism and contention, and can therefore expect her children to respect neither father nor mother. She vandalizes her family with nagging, contention, and anger. The contrast between the wise woman and her foolish neighbor has nothing to do with differences in raw materials. The contrast is in how those materials are used.

Avoid Contentiousness

Down through history, the predominant fault of wives has been contentiousness: an independent spirit setting herself in opposition to

---

[5]The Hebrew word translated "pull down" (*haras*) is a strong word for destruction. It is used to refer to the destruction of the Egyptians at the Red Sea (Ex 15:7), the utter destruction of the Canaanites (Ex 23:24), Gideon's destruction of Baal's altar (Judg 6:25), and the idolatrous destruction of the Lord's altars (1 Kings 19:10,14).

the will of her husband. This opposition can express itself in myriad forms, some overt, and some subtle. A woman may be in harmony with her husband in many areas, and yet on certain issues reserve for herself the "right" to insist on her own views and desires. Such determination is the mark of a contentious woman: one who is willing to engage in strife with her husband in order to have her own way.

Often a wife is more perceptive than her husband regarding the needs of others. When he fails to meet those needs, frequently she begins to offer verbal suggestions for what he should do. It is very easy for this to degenerate into a nagging[6] and contentious spirit which utterly devastates the joy of marriage. The wife soon becomes the self-appointed supervisor of her husband.

Contention also expresses itself in a dissatisfaction with whatever her husband does. When he parks at a shopping mall, he chooses the wrong parking space. When he brings home a specialty from the grocery store, he picked the wrong brand, or should have known she was too busy to fix it. When he tells a story, she corrects him on minor details. When he purchases clothing, he selects the wrong color or style. Worst of all, he never gives her as much money as she needs.

One of the disastrous side effects of women working outside the home has been its effect on their attitude toward the authority of their own husbands. A woman who has authority over other men at work is less inclined to submit to her husband. She who earns a paycheck will be tempted to exercise authority over how it is spent. Every husband should realize that while sending his wife to work may bring in more cash, it will probably make her more contentious.[7] Being happy with less is far better.

Solomon had extensive experience in dealing with women in his own household: seven hundred wives who were princesses, and three hundred concubines. Clearly this could not have been a happy arrangement: a monstrous harem of fiercely competitive women vying with one another for favors from Solomon. Solomon himself formed relationships for political advantage rather than for true love, so it is no wonder he received precious little in return. He experienced the bitterness of being with women who knew how to nag and be contentious, but were woefully deficient in building a loving family relationship. Not one woman among a thousand did he find to really be a delight (Eccl 7:28).

Fortunately, we do not need to marry a thousand women to learn what Solomon learned. We can read what he wrote in the book of Proverbs. Scattered through the book are warnings regarding the

---

[6]"To nag" is "to pester or annoy by constant scolding, complaining, or urging," to "find fault constantly." William Morris, ed., *The American Heritage Dictionary* (New York: Houghton Mifflin Co., 1969), p. 870.

[7]Similar problems arise whenever women get involved in political activism. They come back to their homes and churches wanting to apply the same methods of coercive power maneuvers.

extreme unpleasantness of being married to the wrong kind of woman. No material gratification or joy can compensate for the misery of such a relationship. These repeated warnings suggest strongly that women are particularly susceptible to wrong attitudes and contentiousness in the home. Therefore, they should pay special attention to building their house instead of tearing it down.

The writer of Proverbs places a contentious wife in parallel with the worst calamity possible for a father: to have begotten a fool. "A foolish son is the ruin of his father, and the contentions of a wife are a continual dripping" (19:13). Her willfulness is a continual drip, drip, drip that becomes an unbearable irritation. What is the worst calamity possible for a husband? To be married to a wife who is a drip! Such a woman is a marked contrast to the prudent wife of the next verse (19:14) who is a gift from the Lord, and better than any earthly inheritance.

It is impossible for a husband to stop the continual vexation of a contentious wife. He who attempts to pacify her will find her bossy spirit merely expressing itself with renewed vigor on some new note of dissonance. "A continual dripping on a very rainy day and a contentious woman are alike; whoever restrains her restrains the wind, and grasps oil with his right hand" (27:15-16).

Solomon knew what it was like to live with a contentious woman. His hard experience has been recorded to clarify for us how marriage to a contentious woman is worse than poverty or loneliness. "It is better to dwell in a corner of a housetop, than in a house shared with a contentious woman" (21:9). Evidently even this comparison is not strong enough to express the anguish of such a relationship. A few verses later he becomes even more emphatic: "It is better to dwell in the wilderness, than with a contentious and angry woman" (21:19). Have you ever seen pictures of the Judean wilderness? It is dry, rocky, barren. Even so, such lonely habitat is far preferable to residence with a shrewish woman.

Contentiousness may win a few minor skirmishes, but it clearly loses the war. It is possible for a woman to actually manufacture tidbits of good in her pursuits opposing the will of her husband. But the losses far outweigh the gains. The book of Proverbs portrays a contentious wife as a domestic disaster. If she wants to have a happy, fruitful home, the wife must triumph over this temptation, learn the greatness of servanthood, and taste the joy of building her house.

Cultivate Beautiful Character

The attention of humanity is riveted upon the exterior. Men choose wives because they are beautiful, often ignoring the presence or absence of real beauty as expressed in character. Women vainly spend many hours in front of a mirror trying to improve their outward appearance, often neglecting to devote even a fraction of that effort to the cultivation of genuine beauty.

Proverbs opens our eyes to the realities of life. "Charm is deceitful and beauty is vain, but a woman who fears the Lord, she shall be praised" (31:30). External beauty is of minuscule importance in comparison to the beauty of virtuous character. "As a ring of gold in a swine's snout, so is a lovely woman who lacks discretion" (11:22). The outward beauty corresponds to only a small ring, while the inner person corresponds to a huge, filthy hog. The main characteristic of the indiscreet woman is her similarity to the hog, not her possession of the ring.

God sees the hog. In our blindness we see only the ring, and are so enraptured we essentially say, "I love that ring so much—I think I'll snuggle up to that hog!" God enlightens us: true beauty is measured in character.

A woman has tremendous power over her husband. She can either be an asset or a liability. Her greatest influence is her character. "An excellent wife is the crown of her husband, but she who causes shame is like rottenness in his bones" (12:4). Happy indeed is the man who has a delightful wife. She is truly a crown. The crown speaks of authority, adornment, wealth, respect, and admiration. The virtuous wife brings glory to her husband (cf 1 Cor 11:7b). The contrast is the wife who brings shame, and thus fills her husband with a great inner weariness never relieved, and only intensified by the weight of years.

By definition, a wife is a well-suited helper for her husband. God designed her to be the best possible assistant to the man in the tasks He had given. In the midst of a perfect creation, the solitary male was not good. He was incomplete and insufficient in himself, needing an appropriate helper (Gen 2:18). Therefore, "He who finds a wife [one who is truly a well-suited helper] finds a good thing, and obtains favor from the Lord" (Prov 18:22). Unless a woman effectively assists her husband, she is not a wife in the complete sense God intended. God wants to use her to bestow special blessing on her husband.

A prudent wife is a special gift from God to the man who has her. "Houses and riches are an inheritance from fathers, but a prudent wife is from the Lord" (19:14). The parallelism with rich inheritance shows her vital importance to her husband. The contrast between mere "fathers" and "the Lord" shows how she is of much greater value than any earthly wealth. Wives who wish to be so highly esteemed by their husbands will therefore be zealous in cultivating a prudent and virtuous character.

Be a Virtuous Woman

Every woman should view her unseen ministry to her family as a remarkable opportunity to receive special rewards from God. While many prominent personalities are rewarded by their popularity, every unknown service can only be rewarded by the Father in heaven (Matt 6:1-4; 10:42). Being unrewarded in this life then becomes a potential for greater glory in the next.

The wise woman builds her household rather than foolishly tearing it down with contentious domination (14:1). The book of Proverbs concludes with an extended description of a virtuous woman (31:10-31), which shows how a house is properly built. The life of this woman is the opposite of domestic laziness which so often characterizes contemporary America. She is not selfishly pursuing her own "personal fulfillment." The focal point of all her activities is the bestowal of rich blessings upon her family through the opportunities available in her own home.

The virtuous woman is a rare prize of incomparably greater value than priceless gems (v 10). She is trustworthy in the smallest of details, not squandering any resources (v 11). Her activities are purposed to always bring her husband benefit rather than harm (v 12). She gladly does menial tasks, and expends great effort and organizational skill in the clothing and feeding of her family. Although she operates on a much smaller scale, she is just as careful to make astute purchases as are the merchants of large shipping firms (vv 13-14).

She is no slothful late-riser, but gets up while it is still dark to provide breakfast for her household (v 15). She is discreet and skilled in her use of financial resources (v 16).[8] She does not claim weariness as an excuse for personal indolence (v 17). She makes sure the products made in the home are of good quality, and works diligently in producing them (vv 18-19, 24). She generously shares her bounty with the poor (v 20). She does not fear cold weather because her diligence has provided warm clothing for her household (v 21).

Even her demeanor is one of strength and honor. She has long-term goals, knowing her efforts are investments that will bring joy in the future (v 25). Her words reflect her personal study and application of wisdom, and her high expectations are characterized by kindness (v 26). She is concerned about the ways of her family, and is diligent and consistent in helping them pursue right paths, not just allowing them to "grow up" while hoping for the best (v 27).

Because of her ministry behind the scenes, her husband becomes famous and a leader of others (v 23). She receives the praise and blessing of both her children and her husband (v 28). He recognizes her as the supreme example of an effective wife and mother (v 29), one whose beauty is based on the fear of God (v 30). In the end, she herself becomes well-known because of all she has done (v 31).

Application

A wife must view her role as one of tremendous opportunity. Being at home is not bondage, but is a privilege to function as God intended. Operating according to Divine design brings greater joy than money,

---

[8]Buying a field and planting a vineyard for the family's use does not mean she has a separate career as a real-estate agent. For an excellent analysis of the ideal wife in Proverbs 31, see Mary Pride, *The Way Home: Beyond Feminism, Back to Reality* (Westchester, IL: Crossway Books, 1985), pp. 147-152.

career, or higher standard of living. Families under financial pressure should sell assets or reduce their living standard so they can be free to experience God's reward for obedience.

A wife at home is able to bring multiplied blessings to the intimate circle of those she loves most. She has a flexibility of schedule, a diversity of assignments, and an array of challenges unmatched by any career outside the home: dietitian, chef, clothing designer and manufacturer, horticulturist, speech therapist, secretary, hostess, elementary education instructor, toy repair engineer, detective, prosecuting attorney, jury, judge, interior decorator, nurse, counselor, Bible teacher, social worker, lover.

These skills and deeds of devotion are not to be lavished upon some unknown strangers who would soon forget her kindness, but upon her own family who will rise up and honor her as a special gift from God. Although her toils will be long unnoticed by a world drunken with inane glamor, eventually the success of her own husband and children will be the rich reward of her diligent investments.

Being this kind of woman is to follow the example of Jochebed, the mother of Moses. She invested in her infant son to such an extent that even after a forty-year exposure to the enticements of the Egyptian royal court, he refused the riches of Egypt and chose suffering with the people of God.

Parents: Instruct and Discipline Children

The book of Proverbs does not directly command parents to instruct their children; it simply assumes they *will* instruct them. It is normal, natural, and right for parents to instruct their children. Much of Proverbs takes the form of a father instructing his son. "My son, if you receive my words . . ." (2:1), "My son, do not forget my law . . ." (3:1), "Hear, my children, the instruction of a father . . ." (4:1), "My son, give attention to my words . . ." (4:20), "My son, pay attention to my wisdom . . ." (5:1), "My son, if you become surety for your friend, . . . so do this, my son, and deliver yourself . . ." (6:1-5).

The teaching from the mother is in parallel with the instruction of the father. "My son, keep your father's command, and do not forsake the law of your mother" (6:20; cf 1:8). The mother who fails to instruct her child will be brought to shame (29:15). The same judgment is promised for disobedience to either mother or father (30:17; cf 28:24; 30:11). Clearly both parents are involved as instructors.

However, teaching is not enough. Because of his depravity, the child will sometimes disobey instructions. Appropriate discipline must be administered to help him learn the discomfort of refusing wisdom. Failure to control a child through discipline is a mark of parental hatred. "He who spares his rod hates his son, but he who loves him disciplines him promptly" (13:24). The pain provided by blows from the rod will drive the foolishness from the heart of the child (22:15).

Parents must overcome their own softheartedness and leniency. "Do not withhold correction from a child, for if you beat him with a rod, he will not die. You shall beat him with a rod, and deliver his soul from hell" (23:13-14). The clear command is to discipline your child while there is still hope to steer him in the right path (19:18). The rod coupled with reproof brings wisdom, but a child left to himself brings shame to his parents (29:15). The book of Proverbs sets these issues forth very clearly and sternly, in words shocking to minds long numbed by the false "wisdom" of man's ideas.[9]

Clearly, the instruction and discipline of the child is the moral responsibility of the parents. Proverbs does not even remotely suggest that any other person, organization, or institution has any responsibility for child-rearing. That task is the moral obligation of the parents. By becoming parents they have assumed responsibility for this commitment.

Parents who refuse this obligation, and attempt to pawn it off on the church, the day-care center, the pastor, or the teacher, are disobedient to both the directives and implications of the book of Proverbs. Their parental lifestyle is immoral. Such laissez-faire living must be denounced as sin, and a call issued for repentance. Only when parents diligently fulfill their responsibility as instructors and disciplinarians of their own children can they expect to experience God's blessing on their family.

Children: Obey and Honor Parents

God provides parents for the benefit of the child. The father-author of Proverbs delineates some of those benefits as he appeals to his son for obedience (4:1-27). Parental instruction is to be prized because it is good teaching (v 2), because it includes the wisdom of the grandparents (vv 3-4), because it preserves those who receive it (vv 5-6), and because it ultimately brings honor, grace, and glory (vv 7-9). In general, obedience will bring a long life (v 10), free from unnecessary stumbling and hindrances (vv 11-13). By keeping the parental commands in the heart, the child will be properly guided and protected even in the parents' absence (vv 14-27).

Heeding a father's instruction is the mark of a wise son (13:1), but the rejection of instruction is the mark of a fool (15:5,20). Even though discipline is painful, a wise son will accept reproof (12:1), knowing that poverty and shame will come to the one who disdains correction (13:18), and that such a person actually despises his own soul (15:32).

Parents are due the honor of their children, even in their old age. "Listen to your father who begot you, and do not despise your mother when she is old" (23:22). Those who scorn their parents are worthy only of severe judgment. "The eye that mocks his father, and scorns obedience to his mother, the ravens of the valley will pick it out, and

---

[9]See chapter 12 for a detailed discussion of principles of discipline from Proverbs.

the young eagles will eat it" (30:17). Such children will find themselves besieged by uncertainty and despair when they meet the crises of life. "Whoever curses his father or his mother, his lamp will be put out in deep darkness" (20:20).

In our day, many do not think it is important for children to obey and honor their parents. The legal decisions of the courts remove the obligation to obey parents, even on such issues as teenage abortions or use of contraceptives. The result is a generation of young people filled with immorality, pride, and vicious parasitism.

> There is a generation that curses its father, and does not bless its mother. There is a generation that is pure in its own eyes, yet is not washed from its filthiness. There is a generation—oh, how lofty are their eyes! And their eyelids are lifted up. There is a generation whose teeth are like swords, and whose fangs are like knives, to devour the poor from off the earth, and the needy from among men (30:11-14).

Clearly, the book of Proverbs does not make honoring one's parents an optional matter. Disobedience and disrespect for parents is a heinous sin which merits severe punishment from God. The child who refuses to obey and honor his parents is wicked and immoral. His ultimate need is not better psychology or better motivation. He needs to repent of his sin, and return to the attitude which God demands of children: honor and obey your parents.[10]

Summary

The emphasis of the book of Proverbs suggests strongly that a husband's greatest danger is the temptation of the strange woman. God helps men avoid this danger by defining clearly the characteristics of the strange woman, and showing the horrible results of immorality.

God also helps men take direct steps toward safety. Seeking and applying God's wisdom protects us against passions that would otherwise destroy us. Deliberate guarding of the eyes, and avoiding unhealthy associations with other women, protects us from temptations that have destroyed many strong men.

A great temptation for a wife is to allow her natural sensitivity to degenerate into a contentious spirit that tears down her family. God directs her to be a virtuous woman who is a crown to her husband, one who is continually building up her family. As she does this, the fragrance of her own life helps protect her husband from the temptation of the strange woman.

Failure by either spouse opens a door of temptation for his partner. If a husband neglects to love his wife and devote himself to her, she is likely to become contentious in an attempt to rectify the deficiencies that will inevitably occur. Conversely, if a wife neglects to build her household and approaches her husband with a nagging spirit, he will be increasingly tempted to look toward a woman who is more agreeable.

---

[10]See chapter 7 for further discussion of God's view of parental authority.

Parents are morally obligated to teach their children, and to accompany that teaching with discipline. Children must obey their parents. Contrary to the general feeling pervading our society, parents can be effective in having pleasant, well adjusted children—if they take seriously their responsibility to diligently instruct and discipline them.

The Role of Parents

Dear Lord and Father of mankind,
    Forgive our foolish ways;
Reclothe us in our rightful mind,
    In purer lives Thy service find,
In deeper reverence, praise.

Drop Thy still dews of quietness,
    Till all our strivings cease;
Take from our souls the strain and stress,
    And let our ordered lives confess
The beauty of Thy peace.

—John G. Whittier, 1872

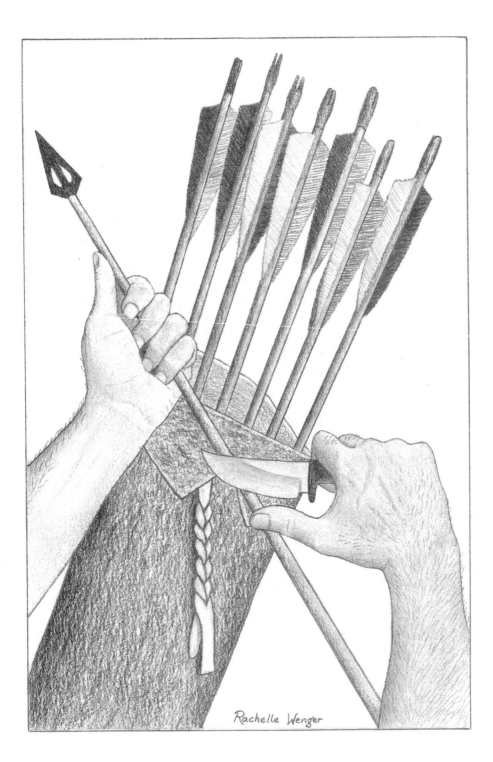

Fashioning Arrows for the Kingdom of God

5

Parents Advancing the Kingdom of God

In an ultimate sense, we all want a task bigger than ourselves. We want to be part of a grand scheme of things, part of something intrinsically valuable, something reaching beyond ourselves to others. God has designed us with this desire, and has assigned such a task to every parent.

Any task larger than ourselves calls for resources greater than those we possess. God has arranged this dilemma for our spiritual benefit. It expands our vision, maximizes our participation, and makes us realize our need for His power in order to get the job done. God intends for the family to be a powerful force in His kingdom. Psalm 127 clarifies how this is to be accomplished.

Futility of Self-Effort

The task of building a vibrant family is impossible by mere human strength. The Psalmist emphasizes this point with a metaphor. "Unless the Lord builds the house, they labor in vain who build it" (v 1a). Physically, a house involves the careful arrangement of diverse materials in order to accomplish a result greater than the sum of its components. A building supply outlet can provide the raw materials for a house: boards, nails, bricks, mortar, shingles, electrical wire, panelling, plaster, pipes. However, although these ingredients are used to *make* a house, they are insufficient in themselves to *be* a house. They need to be arranged by a builder who has in his mind the entire picture of the finished product.

Any workman on a building project can nail boards together. On a small scale he may be doing some things right, and may be working with great skill and craftsmanship. But if he is not working according to the plan of the master designer, his very efforts will mar the final result. No prospective buyer would want a house with a bathroom in the middle of the front foyer, no matter how exquisitely the bathroom was fashioned.

Such anomalies help us see the futility of trying to build a family apart from the Lord. He is the master builder who sees the end from the beginning. The humans who labor see only a small portion of the task. Therefore, they must follow the directions of the One who sees the total picture, so that their portion of the task corresponds to His plan. Otherwise, even their successes pave the way for a ruined result.

67

To reinforce the point, the psalmist speaks of a city subject to attack by enemies. "Unless the Lord guards the city, the watchman stays awake in vain" (v 1b). In ancient times, cities were often built on a hill to make them more difficult to attack. Walls, gates, and watchmen were primary strategies for safety.

The citizens prepared themselves for tough times. They constructed storehouses and filled them with food. They made sure their water supply was adequate and reliable. They reinforced the wall and made their gates strong. They set watchmen to alert the city against approaching enemies. The goal was to be able to remain safely inside the city, secure behind the walls and confident in ample provisions for outlasting a siege of months, or even years.

However, in spite of the most careful plans, every city in history was subject to the same potential disaster: the danger of the unforeseen circumstance. No matter how high the city walls, how strong the city gates, how loyal the guards, or how careful the plans, there was always the threat of a hidden danger impossible to anticipate. A traitor might reveal a secret passageway into the city. A clever enemy might devise a method to destroy the city's water supply. A plague could decimate the inhabitants.

Imagine being the king of a city at the southern end of the Jordan River about 1400 B.C. An enemy army is approaching from the east, so you call your generals together to discuss strategy. You make assignments to insure the adequacy of all standard preparations: food, water supply, weapons, fortifications, manpower, repulsion strategy.

After making sure of all these details you suddenly say, "Men, we must prepare for one more possibility. What if the enemy marches seven times around our city, shouts, blows trumpets, and makes the walls fall down? What will we do then?"

Imagine the reaction of your generals! You would be the laughingstock of the city. No commander in his wildest dreams would imagine such a thing. Yet, this unforeseen circumstance was the key to Jericho's downfall. God was not guarding that city. No matter what the defenders did, the city of Jericho was going to fall.

Every family faces a similar hazard. No matter how detailed the plans, or how diligent the parents, circumstances impossible to anticipate can arise to destroy the family. The sixteen-year-old son is alone on the street when he meets the clever preacher of a cult unheard of by his parents. A teenage daughter suddenly encounters a situation involving overwhelming peer pressure.

It is impossible for parents to solve this problem by their own efforts or wisdom. Only God's wisdom can protect the family from dangers the parents cannot foresee. Zealous diligence will not be sufficient. "It is vain for you to rise up early, to sit up late, to eat the bread of sorrows" (v 2a). Diligence is important, but diligence alone is not enough. It will lead only to frustration and bitter disappointment. Man does not have within himself what is needed to properly guide his steps (Prov 14:12;

16:25). Without God's insight, diligence becomes ignorant zeal hastening destructive processes.

To succeed, parents must be diligent to obey God's direction on how they shall live and how they shall train their children. They must develop their skills as parents on His terms, and be astute observers of cause and effect. They must persevere, sacrifice, and toil.

But even these things are not enough. Parents must also ask God to build their house and guard their city. The promises of God are not automatic benefits given to every individual human being. Those promises must be activated by prayer.

The parent who is serving God recognizes his own insufficiency. He knows he lacks wisdom, and therefore asks God for heavenly wisdom to meet the perplexing problems he faces (Jas 1:1-8). He knows God must intervene in the hearts of children in order to make them receptive to truth. He asks God to arrange circumstances to channel these lives into paths of effective service.

This is not an escape clause to compensate for parental laziness. It is asking God to do what is impossible for us to do ourselves: deal with the hidden, unforeseeable circumstance, woo hearts with His Spirit, open our own lives and the lives of our children to new dimensions of service for Him.

While the parent works externally with the child, he asks God to deal with the child's heart. While the parent teaches the child about sin and grace, he asks the Father to draw that young heart to active and personal faith in Christ. While the parent diligently teaches God's Word, he asks God to protect his children from the snares of Satan.

Parents must get it straight. Human wisdom will fail. Human efforts are not enough. All self-centered efforts will eventually crumble into ashes. Only obedient delight in God's ways, persistent seeking of His wisdom, and humble reception of His grace guarantee a completed house and a safe city. By following God's direction, we are spared the futility of overwork. He gives us rest and peace as we trust in Him and as His principles bear fruit in the home ("for so He gives His beloved sleep", v 2b).

Investing in God's Gift

"Children are a heritage from the Lord, the fruit of the womb is His reward" (v 3). Each child is a special gift from Him Who is the giver of every good and perfect gift, and Who has not even the shadow of imperfection (Jas 1:17). Knowing the Giver assures us of the value of the gift. When a parent realizes the source of this gift and understands this gift to be a special reward from God, he will regard his child as a most precious treasure.

For reasons known only to Himself, God has prevented some couples from having children. Sometimes this is only a delay to prepare the parents for a very special child God wants to give them later (Isaac, Jacob and Esau, Samson, Samuel, John the Baptist). If God has designed for a couple to be barren, it does not mean they are second-class or sub-spiritual. Evidently God has a special ministry for them which can best be performed without children of their own.

Worldly Disdain for Children

Godly regard for a child is a stark contrast to our society's disdain for children. Millions of babies are murdered before they are born. Child abuse runs rampant. Unfortunately, many Christians have believed this lie that children are of no value. They live like the world: A child is a nuisance. A child interferes with *my* career. A child interrupts *my* pleasure. A child obstructs *my* important ministry. A child interferes with what *I* want to do. They therefore agree with the world by despising God's good gift.

A sex-saturated society that disdains the value of children and at the same time demands pleasure without restraint or responsibility has sadly influenced Christian couples to adopt worldly and sinful methods of birth-control. The medical establishment uses frightening statistics to scare couples into opposing God's plans for the family. Usually the total scope of detrimental effects of birth-control is not even mentioned, much less explained.

Self-sterilization is sinful because it deliberately destroys part of one's body—the temple of the Holy Spirit. Even after the operation is finished, the self-destruction continues: after a vasectomy a man's body often begins to produce antibodies against his own sperm, and after a tubal ligation women often develop menstrual and psychological problems. It also presumes on the future: many couples have been overjoyed to have another child when one of their children was taken in a tragic death. Or if one spouse dies, the survivor may wish to remarry and have another child.

Use of the pill is inappropriate because of its many bad side-effects for the wife. Even worse, ovulation is not always suppressed, and like the IUD, the pill interferes with fetus implantation in the womb. Thus, both the pill and the IUD produce automatic spontaneous abortions. All abortions must be denounced as murder.

While physical conception prevention (via the condom, the diaphragm, foam, or coitus interruptus) are not murderous, their usage short-circuits God's design. God's judgment of Onan (Gen 38:8-10) in comparison with the punishment of shame prescribed for merely refusing to take a brother's wife (Deut 25:5-10) raises serious questions about the appropriateness of these methods.[1]

---

[1]The New Testament teaches Christians to be temperate in all things as an expression of the fruit of the Spirit (1 Cor 9:25; Gal 5:23). Although the details of Old Testament Law are not mandatory for Christians, we can certainly learn important principles by examining God's Law. God prohibited married couples from having sexual relations during the first half of a woman's cycle (seven days beyond issue of blood, Lev 12:2; 15:13,24,28), clearly requiring sexual restraint.

After ovulation the human egg lives one day or less, while under conducive conditions sperm can live several days. Therefore sexual relations during the early

Children as Investments

If children didn't cost money, people would have more of them. A hundred years ago, children were an economic advantage, and families were large. This tells us something about contemporary value systems. Jesus said, "After all these *things*, the Gentiles [i.e., pagans] seek" (Matt 6:32). Many people pay more attention to their money than to their children, investing their lives in *things* that will be on the ash heap fifty years later.

The parent who is in tune with God recognizes God's precious gifts as an investment. Anyone who makes investments sacrifices short-term pleasure in order to reap long-term gain. Certainly, a child involves sacrifice and inconvenience for the parent, but the rich dividends are well worth the investment. No one hears old people saying, "I wish I had had fewer children; I wish I hadn't sacrificed for my children; I wish I hadn't spent so much time with my children." As we invest in our children and focus on God's kingdom, we can trust Him to supply our needs.

Arrows As Strategy For Spiritual Conquest

The final two verses of the psalm describe why children are such a worthy investment. A man who has many of them is fortunate indeed because they are a source of effectiveness and power in spiritual conquest that cannot be matched in any other way. "Like arrows in the hand of a warrior, so are the children of one's youth" (v 4).

The warrior of ancient Israel delighted in combat. His life was focused on vanquishing the enemy. Inspired by the example of David, many mighty men did amazing exploits. Adino the Eznite killed eight hundred men at one time (2 Sam 23:8). Benaiah the son of Jehoiada killed two lion-like men of Moab. On a snowy day he went down into a pit and killed a lion. Once with only a staff he wrested a spear from the hand of a seven-and-one-half-foot Egyptian and killed him with his own spear (1 Chr 11:22,23).

When David reigned in Hebron, there was civil war between his kingdom and the declining kingdom of Saul. Abner was leader of Saul's army, and also a mighty warrior. In one battle, he was pursued by Asahel, a man who had the reputation of being as fleet of foot as a deer. Abner knew he would eventually be overtaken, and warned Asahel to chase someone else, but he refused. Suddenly Abner struck his pursuer once with the blunt end of his spear. The blow was so forceful that the spear came out the other side of the body, killing the man instantly (2 Sam 2:23).

---

part of the cycle is more likely to result in pregnancy. Since ovulation ordinarily occurs near day 14, abstinence during the first half of the cycle provides a natural opportunity for the Lord to open and close wombs (cf Gen 29:31), as He controls the exact day when ovulation occurs.

Couples who exercise this period of restraint find a new tenderness developing between them as they experience a season of "courtship" and "honeymoon" each month.

These men were mighty warriors. They knew their weapons, and used them well. They were masters at hand-to-hand combat.

The Value of Arrows

The warrior in this Psalm, however, is not involved in hand-to-hand combat. Instead, he is armed with arrows. The arrow dramatically extends the range of a warrior, enabling him to kill enemies at great distances, even if he cannot be present to strike the enemy with his own hand. Before an alert bowman, an enemy cannot advance unprotected.

In the Old Testament, the phrase "in the hand of" was used to indicate control or power over someone else. God used this expression for His judgment in delivering Israel over to her enemies. "When they forgot the Lord their God, He sold them into the hand of Sisera, commander of the army of Hazor, into the hand of the Philistines, and into the hand of the king of Moab" (1 Sam 12:9).

In Psalm 127, the arrows are *in the hand of* the warrior. This means the arrows are under the control of the warrior, not merely present with him in the house. Many fathers have children, but they are not "in their hand." They are out of control. Such children are useless as arrows. But children who are truly "in the hand of their father" are great arrows. They enable him to conquer at a distance.

As the bowman prepares to use the arrows, he himself is increased in strength. He gives careful attention to his own physique to enable effective shooting of the arrows. He wants to be able to hold the bow at full draw, without wavering. He wants to aim those arrows accurately, and to propel them with force.

The growing strength of the bowman corresponds to spiritual growth in the parent—a growth which qualifies him for broader ministry. As effective shooting of arrows broadens the range of the warrior, so the proper raising of children qualifies the parent for broader ministry in the church.

The reason is because children are easy to mold and lead. They naturally admire their father, thinking he is the best, strongest, and wisest man in the world. Even if he makes mistakes, they quickly and immediately forgive when he repents. Children are a great contrast to adults, who will hold a grudge for years. God has arranged for us to learn how to effectively lead people by making our mistakes on those who love us most, and who forgive us so we can try again.

These facts are relevant to the children who are born while the father is still young ("the children of one's youth"). Such children will mature by the time the father is middle-aged, and still strong and vigorous. They will therefore be able to participate with their father in ministry, with him actively directing and channeling their talents.

This is a stark contrast to conventional wisdom which calls for getting established in ministry first, and then having children later. God has a better idea. Build your family into a powerful unit of spiritual conquerors. Have them participate with you in ministry so that together you can accomplish what would be impossible for you to do alone. Children are not luxuries for parents to indulge in when they have the leisure. Children are invaluable assets for effectiveness in the kingdom of God.

Our daughter at age eleven gave art lessons to a younger girl in the church. At ages nine and eleven, our daughters baked bread as payment for their piano lessons. Our son at age seven mowed lawns for the neighbors. This kind of interaction is a wonderful bridge of contacts into a community. When our family gives seminars on child training, all of the children are involved. Their example in singing, Bible recitation, and general behavior opens hearts for a message like nothing else ever could.

It is instructive to compare the extended range of the bowman with Adam's situation in the Garden of Eden. After God's creative work on days three, four, and five, He evaluated His creation as being good. Suddenly on the sixth day He noted something not good: man being alone. One of the reasons for this was because man was supposed to exercise dominion over the earth. The earth is far too big for one man to exercise dominion over it. The man needed help: other people to assist him in exercising this dominion.

In order to have other people to assist in his God-given task, Adam needed a wife. She would bear children, enabling Adam and Eve to exercise dominion at places where they could not personally be present. The man and the woman were designed to jointly exercise dominion over the earth (Gen 1:26).

Fashioning Arrows

The wise warrior gives careful attention to his arrows. In constructing them he uses only the best materials, and operates with utmost care. He removes each shred of loose bark, and carefully scrapes off each bump that would hinder true and accurate flight. He makes sure the arrow is balanced, feathered with exacting precision, and deadly sharp. He guards his arrows against damage or accidental abuse, and keeps them close at hand for instant action. He knows the crisis of battle forgives no compromise.

The wise parent views his children in the same way. He is preparing instruments to destroy Satan's kingdom. No sacrifice is too great, no attention to detail too meticulous. He demands obedience, commitment, perseverance, loyalty, and integrity to a degree felt unreasonable by most of his colleagues.

The arrow maker is not perturbed when other people call him a persnickety fanatic. He understands the reality of spiritual warfare. Great demands must be made of arrows so they will fly straight and true and with deadly power during the pressures of battle. Once the arrow leaves the bow, the archer has absolutely no control over it. The wise bowman attends to every detail with utmost care, so that when the arrow leaves his hand, it goes precisely where he wants it to go. Parents who neglect their privilege and responsibility to carefully fashion arrows for God's kingdom will discover to their sorrow that their misshapen arrows will veer off course and boomerang back to pierce their own hearts.

In order to fashion straight arrows, the parent must first of all focus on God. He himself must love the Lord his God with all his heart, with all his soul, and with all his might (Deut 6:4). Only then is it possible for him to continually meditate on the things of God (Deut 6:5). This then opens up the possibility to teach his own children the ways of God, a task to which he diligently applies himself (Deut 6:7-9).

Many people have turned away from the Bible as a dusty, dull book. One of the reasons for this distaste is because of the way the Bible has been taught. Some fathers sit down to a table full of deliciously prepared food, open a Bible, and proceed to "have family devotions" while the food gets cold. Such an approach invites failure for two reasons: 1) The children's attention is on the food, and they can hardly wait for their father to finish so they can begin eating. 2) Effective Bible teaching cannot be accomplished by a mere five-minute injection before the meal.

The word translated "teach diligently" is *shanan,* and its root meaning in the Old Testament is "to sharpen."[2] Therefore, the force of the passage could be rendered, "You shall sharpen God's words to your children." The parent who is doing this presents God's message in an insightful and exciting way, because he knows that the power and glory of God's principles transcend anything humanity could devise. He is not content to merely have his children know a few things about the Bible. His presentation makes God's Word like barbs impossible to remove from the mind.

The parent who is teaching diligently does not handle the Word of God carelessly. He is shaping arrows that are straight and true and deadly, because they have been fashioned in terms of insightfully applied Scriptures. Sharpening God's words is a consuming task. It includes formal instruction ("you shall teach them"), informal instruction ("talk of them when you sit in your house"), instruction while traveling ("when you walk by the way"), and making opportunities for instruction by being creative in all activities ("when you lie down and when you rise up").[3]

Such efforts are not a burden. It is a privilege to direct a soul into commitment and effectiveness in the kingdom of God. It is not enough just to have arrows. They must be lethal in their sharpness, and unerring in their flight.

---

[2]Deut 32:41; Psa 45:5; 64:3; 73:21; 120:4; 140:3; Prov 25:18; Isa 5:28.

[3]More detail on how to implement the mandate of Deuteronomy 6 is found in chapter 10.

The parent begins at the child's birth to thoroughly acquaint him with the holy Scriptures (2 Tim 3:15). This knowledge becomes the bulwark of obedience. The child sees the Scriptures as a source of authority even above his parents, and learns to be obedient to the Biblical commands for children.

Proper behavior opens the door for immediate spiritual ministry. "Even a child is known by his deeds, by whether what he does is pure and right" (Prov 20:11). Every parent should be able to say to new converts in the faith (Eph 5:1), "See how my child obeys and honors me? That is how you are to obey and honor God."

A young child can innocently ask questions and make comments that would be awkward for an adult, but can touch someone's heart deeply: "Grandpa, do you love Jesus?" The life and testimony of a young child provide a springboard for parents to share the Source of their wisdom.

Obedience at a young age also prepares the child for future spiritual fruitfulness. David's care of the sheep and Joseph's obedience to his father were important training for later ministry. Even the boy Jesus obeyed his parents instead of staying in the Temple to do "spiritual" work.

A husband and wife who lived during the 1700's illustrate opposite attitudes about their responsibility as parents. The husband wanted to become famous by writing a commentary on the book of Job. The necessary research required expensive books. He purchased those books, even though it meant depriving his family of proper food, and dressing them in rags.

His wife focused her life on the spiritual nurture and training of her children. She wanted them to be consumed with zeal for God so their lives would light a fire sweeping across England and around the world. When her husband was in debtors' prison, she read sermons to her children. She read them so well that soon more people came to hear her read sermons to her own children than came to the church where her husband had preached. After one of her children narrowly escaped death in a house fire, she repeatedly reminded him of God's having saved him for a glorious spiritual purpose.

When two of her sons proposed to go to wild America as missionaries, she gladly encouraged them to go, knowing full well she might never see them again. Her sons John and Charles became such a spiritual force that even secular historians credit their ministry for sparing England from the equivalent of a French Revolution.

The husband's name was Samuel Wesley. He served himself and preached ineffectually in one parish for 39 years. His wife's name was Susanna. She sacrificed her own interests in preference to God's. She shaped arrows that were straight, and true, and deadly sharp. She shot those arrows deep into the hellish dens of Satanic wickedness.

Advantages of Many Arrows

The psalmist continues his statement regarding the warrior and his arrows: "Happy is the man who has his quiver full of them" (Psa 127:5a). This idea directly opposes the philosophy of our world. One of the reasons people are horrified at the thought of having many children is that they have seen one or two untrained rascals already producing such bedlam, that the prospect of having more is unthinkable. Thus, "when sons and daughters are arrows, it is well to have a quiver full of them; but if they are only sticks, knotty and useless, the fewer of them the better."4 Trained children are like arrows. It is better to have many arrows rather than few. It is a blessing and an advantage to have many children. In fact, if parents are willing to diligently apply themselves, a large family is a better environment for raising well-trained children. What are the advantages?

Environment That Mirrors Life

The large family has an advantage because by its very nature it becomes a mirror of life. Its essence is non-homogeneous: different ages, different personality types, different interests, different abilities, different weaknesses. This non-homogeneity prepares the child for life in the broader world beyond the family. He learns the lessons of differences in the context where those lessons are easiest: the loving fellowship and intimacy of his own family.

All these ingredients must be meshed together in harmony in order to have a happy family. The breadth of exposure in a large family conditions the child for dealing with people unlike himself. He learns in simple, natural, easy lessons how to appreciate others who are different, and to view those differences as a delight. What is often termed a "personality clash" is nothing other than the friction between two individuals who never learned to benefit from the differences in God-given personalities.

A large family is a beautiful environment for a child to learn about the foibles of human nature. At age twelve our daughter Rachelle recorded in her journal some thoughts about the interactions she observed in our family. She titled her entry "Some Interesting Observations on Human Nature" and after each incident wrote a short poetic statement about what she learned.

> A few days ago I had made some cookie bars and was cutting them out of the pan to freeze them. I asked Roland [age 8] to get me a container out of a certain cupboard. It was somewhat high, and only half-trying, he quickly gave up.
>
> "I can't do it," he said, and hurried back to the fun thing he had been doing previously.
>
> "Oh, too bad," I said (In cutting out the bars, the cut-outer has the authority to say who gets what crumbs). I continued, "I had been going

---

4C. H. Spurgeon, *The Treasury of David, Vol. 2* (Scripture Truth Book Co., 1984), p. 1127.

to give you a *really* big crumb with a chocolate chip in it, but I guess you can't have it now."

"Oh!" he exclaimed. "Well—of course! I'll *have* to get it. It's hard, but somehow, I'll manage!" And he went and got a chair, and brought me the desired container.

When people see a chance for gains
They'll go to much more trouble, and pains!

Mother was making a pattern for a dress and wanted to use the cut of a certain blouse for the bodice. So she sent Rosalyn [age 6] up to the closet to get it. Rosalyn didn't want to, but of course she had to obey Mother, so she went up to get it. But soon she came down, saying she couldn't find it. Mother sent her up again, and again she returned with the news that she couldn't find it. After this happened several times, Mother sent Rolanda [age 4] up to help Rosalyn, saying, "Well, Rolanda, I know *you* have sharp eyes. You go help Rosalyn find it."

Immediately Rosalyn's manner changed completely. "Oh, no Mother! No! Don't let Rolanda go up with me! Now I think I know where it is! Mother—Mother—!"

But Mother shook her head. "You couldn't find it by yourself, so Rolanda may go along and help you."

The two little girls went racing up the steps. In a twinkling they had returned. "I saw it, Mother! I found it!" cried Rolanda. "Here it is!"

Rosalyn was cross. "I could have found it, Mother," she grumbled. "I didn't need her help!"

Her sudden change of attitude caused some wry chuckles from those who had been listening to the whole affair.

If another is given our job,
We'll then become quite jealous,
And try to keep this former work,
For which before we were un-zealous![5]

A large family helps train the child to have a pleasant attitude. For example, children from small families are generally finicky eaters compared to children from large families. "I don't like these peas!" "I don't want that bread crust!" "I wanted you to put jam on the other side of the toast!" By contrast, if a child from a large family raises a complaint about the food on his plate, he is likely to hear a chorus of several eager voices, "Give it to me; I'll eat it!" This gives him second thoughts. Maybe his food is pretty good after all.

A large family also mirrors life because by the very nature of the situation, the parents are motivated to teach their children responsibility. It is impractical for the parents of a large family to be the humble slaves for each child. The child has to be taught to do things for himself, and to assist the other children, especially the younger ones. In order for the family to function, each member has his part to contribute.

In a large family, Mom and Dad are not running a hotel. They are not the groveling providers of free food (all you can eat), free beds, and free entertainment. It is a great privilege to be a member of a family.

---

[5]Rachelle's Journal, February 10, 1988.

It is an even greater privilege to be a contributing member of that family, since it is better to give than to receive (Acts 20:35). Many parents deprive their children of this higher privilege.

Teaches The Value of People Over Things

The environment of a large family lends itself to teaching true values. It puts a strain on financial resources, so children and parents learn to be content with less materially, and to have a greater joy in people than in things.

The ratio of toys per child is reduced. Imagine having seven children, each with his own tricycle. Children do not expect everything to be brand new when they get it. Of necessity, they learn to share their toys. This pushes them toward more interaction with people, and a lessened infatuation with things. In an environment of brothers and sisters, children learn companionship, rather than isolation in the midst of material abundance. Their upbringing guards their hearts against materialism.

A large family is actually more fun for the child because he does not lack playmates. No parent can spend as much time playing with his child as a sibling can. Together they will spend hours doing things that would be boring to an adult, but delightful to a child.

Once I glanced out the window and saw two of my young children happily using a small stick to poke holes in bare spots they found in the lawn. This would have been tedious for a parent, but was enjoyable for both children.

Sometimes little children will sit together under a piano bench, and with great satisfaction announce, "See us here in our house!" Imagine a doting father trying to play this game with his children. Even if he could get under the piano bench, he would ruin the game: there would not be any space for anyone else.

In a large family, children learn to appreciate the preciousness of a little child. The joy of watching a baby learn to walk, hearing his first words, seeing him grasp a new concept—these joys are not experienced by mere occasional baby-sitting. Families with two children only a couple of years apart are never given this opportunity to naturally develop what is so much needed in our society: love for children. Children from large families love toddlers. They are not as concerned about them "getting my toys" or "messing up my room."

A large family provides a natural classroom for parents to teach their teenagers how to be good parents. They must be taught not to laugh at a toddler's "cute" misbehavior. Older children can learn principles by observing how their parents handle situations with the younger ones. They see how to deal with a toddler when he is sick, or when he is tired, or when he is just plain stubborn.

In a large family, even the youngest child need not miss these kinds of opportunities. By the time he is a teenager, he will likely have one or more older siblings who are married with little ones of their own.

Usually young mothers need help with some of the work. He can be sent to their house to assist, and in the process he can observe your children applying the same principles you have so diligently taught.

Teaches a Servant Heart

Today there is a great lack of servant hearts. All want to be great, but not great in the way defined by Christ (Matt 20:25-28). A large family is an excellent environment for a child to learn a servant's heart. The ordinary events of family interaction teach the joy of servanthood, a joy bestowed on others that boomerangs back to the giver.

Children naturally love to play with other children. Modern society thinks this is best done outside the family with other children of exactly the same age. In a large family, children learn to play together at home. Games include participants having a wide range of ages and skill levels.

In general, the oldest child would be able to win every game. He can run faster and farther and hide better than any of the younger ones. His thinking abilities are more highly developed. But if games are to be any fun, he must gauge his participation according to the ability of the others. In games of tag, he doesn't run as fast as he can, but occasionally lets the little one exuberantly toddle to an escape. In tagging a young child, he does it carefully to avoid knocking him down. He must sometimes allow himself to be caught. The happiness on the face of a three-year-old making a "catch" is greater reward than getting away.

If the game is to be any fun at all, the basic attitude must be cooperation rather than competition. The children learn the joy of cooperation to accomplish what they could not do separately. The fellowship of the game becomes more important than winning the game. Our children enjoy their relationships at home so much that they actually prefer playing among themselves rather than going off to the neighbors to play with other children.

Multi-age group activities facilitate development of eternal values in the group. Even as they play, the children are learning to be servants to the younger ones. They taste the joy Christ intends for us all.

Not only is servanthood taught in play, it is taught in the responsibility which the child is able to handle as his contribution to the family. A nine-year-old child can easily learn to diaper a baby. A seven-year-old can tie the shoes of the smaller ones. A five-year-old can help a three-year-old get dressed. Each has a contribution. Each does what he can. Each learns to be a servant.

The result is corporate consciousness instead of individualism. The family views itself as a unit, an organism, not merely as a small group of individuals who happen to eat and sleep at the same house. The focus is on the group, and on how the individual can be a contribution to that group. This kind of home life sets a mentality conducive to brotherhood and body life in the church. We are indeed members one of another. It is high time to live in our homes what we claim to believe in our churches.

In a small family, children learn that the family serves them. In a large family, children learn to serve the family. Of course, this learning is not automatic. It does take discipline and guidance from the parents. But the environment is conducive toward learning the right lessons, not the wrong ones. Happy is the man who has his quiver full.

Ultimate Reason: More Arrows To Aim At Satan

As important as these reasons may be, they are not the ultimate reason for having a quiver full of arrows. Arrows in the hand of a mighty man have one purpose: to kill the enemy. The ultimate advantage of a large family is to prepare more arrows to aim at the darkest parts of Satan's kingdom.

Individuals steeped in the philosophies of this world do not appreciate the idea of large families. One way to side-step the issue is to slyly ask, "How many arrows are in a quiver?" Most people are surprised by the historical details of warfare in the ancient Near East.

> Since the bow was required to fire numerous arrows during the course of battle, the archer had to have some means of carrying a reasonable complement of arrows in a handy manner which would put them within easy reach and facilitate speedy reloading. In this he was served by the quiver. The quiver had to be capable of holding between *twenty and thirty arrows* and to be made of lightweight material. It was carried either on the back of the bowman or over his shoulder so that both hands were free to fire the bow.
>
> Of the bow, as of the chariot, it can be said that no other weapon in ancient days required so high a technical capacity to produce and such skill to operate. These two qualities in combination were decisive on more than one occasion in determining the course of history [italics mine].[6]

The fundamental idea is a *full* quiver. Any warrior would certainly want more than two or three arrows before going into battle. We are engaged in the spiritual conflict of the ages. Each child is a strategic asset in the battles determining the course of eternal history. Blessed indeed are the parents who have worked hard to fashion arrows that are straight and true and deadly sharp, arrows which they can direct with unerring accuracy to deal catastrophic blows to the forces of evil. Their assistants are their children, whom they have personally trained for twenty years.

Results of Spiritual Investment

The metaphor of the psalmist changes our view of children. It is not enough to play with our children so that twenty years from now we can

---

[6]Yigael Yadin, *The Art of Warfare in Biblical Lands, Vol 1* (New York: McGraw-Hill Book Co., Inc., 1963), p. 9. It is interesting to note that "bronze quivers found in Urartian arsenals contained between 35-40 arrows." Nigel Stillman and Nigel Tallis, *Armies of the Ancient Near East* (Worthing, England: Flexiprint Ltd., 1984), p. 186.

look back with nostalgia, remembering the good times we enjoyed together, the times we sacrificed urgent trivia in order to enjoy the fragrance of those relationships.

Children are arrows, to be prepared for battle. These arrows are not garnered to be displayed on the wall as relics for a comfortable old age. Arrows are to be shot into the hideous hovels of diabolical darkness.

Wherever possible, the father gives the children responsibility for advancing the Kingdom of God. The family continues to work together as a unit to destroy evil. Such a family is a fulfillment of God's intention for man to be His regent in exercising God's dominion on the earth. "They shall not be ashamed, but shall speak with their enemies in the gate" (v 5b).

Parents who have this view of their children will see them emerge as leaders in their own right. These children are not swayed by evil, nor are they intimidated by it. They stand up in the midst of pressure, and withstand the enemy, even if he does have prestige and influence. They have learned their lessons well, and know how to participate in spiritual battles, wrestling against principalities, powers, and wickedness in high places (Eph 6:12).

Conclusion

The technology revolutionizing our world pays incredible attention to the functioning of small things. Microscopic devices are the critical junctures for great discoveries and phenomenal advances. · Ironically, while our world is so attentive to physical detail, it has scorned the personal parental attention needed to maximize the potential of children.

God uses small things to accomplish great victories. What would Shamgar have done without his ox goad? What would David have done without his sling? What would Dorcas have done without her needle? What would Rahab have done without her string? What would Moses have done without his rod, or Mary without her box of ointment? What would Naaman have done without the small servant girl who told him about the prophet who lived in Samaria? An arrow is a small thing, but can be devastatingly effective in disabling an enemy.

The psalmist thus calls all parents to commitment, not to do something in their own strength, not to indulge in their own schemes. The call is to follow God's plan, to participate in His grand scheme. The call is to fashion arrows that are straight and true and deadly in their sharpness. Arrows that will devastate the kingdom of Satan. Blessed indeed is the man who has his quiver full of them.

"My Little Cherub . . . ?"

6

Dealing With Depravity

Understanding ourselves is the first key to effective family living. Fortunately, God plainly informs us about ourselves. His analysis is both clear and very uncomplimentary. In the Garden of Eden, man chose his own way, and thus fell from a state of holiness to a state of sinfulness. Each person receives this depraved nature from his parents. This nature expresses itself as arrogantly proclaimed on a bumper sticker: "Don't lead me into temptation. I'll find it myself!" Left to himself, every human being turns toward evil.

Such a predicament has profound implications for the family, both for parents and children. Children will naturally go toward evil, and parents will make mistakes. Both must have a proper understanding of guilt and forgiveness.

God's picture of humanity is indeed unflattering. But by agreeing with His evaluation, we can access His grace in Christ to rise above the hopeless abyss of depravity. God's prescription deals decisively with sin instead of merely allowing us to grovel aimlessly in insoluble problems.

Proof of Depravity

Every member of the human race is afflicted with a twisted desire for evil. "All we like sheep have gone astray; we have turned, every one, to his own way" (Isa 53:6). Paul insists all are under the dominion of sin, regardless of whether their background has been religious or pagan (Rom 3:9). He proves his point by extended recitation of Scriptures emphatically describing universal human depravity.

> There is *none* righteous, no, *not one;* there is *none* who understands; there is *none* who seeks after God. They have *all* gone out of the way; they have together become unprofitable; there is *none* who does good, no, *not one.* Their throat is an open tomb; with their tongues they have practiced deceit; the poison of asps is under their lips; whose mouth is full of cursing and bitterness. Their feet are swift to shed blood; destruction and misery are in their ways; and the way of peace they have not known. There is *no fear of God* before their eyes (Rom 3:11-18, italics mine).

The Holocaust of World War II, the frightful internal blood baths of communist "liberations," and the moral decay of modern society prove the "enlightened" Twentieth Century is no better than the other ages of history. Unless God intervenes, man greedily pursues evil.

This pursuit is not merely learned from the evil examples of companions or from the lifestyle of parents. It is an innate consequence of the Fall. Children are not innocent little darlings thinking only angelic thoughts. The great Psalmist David confessed, "Behold, I was brought forth in iniquity, and in sin my mother conceived me" (Psa 51:5). He realized, "The wicked are estranged from the womb; they go astray as soon as they are born, speaking lies" (Psa 58:3).

The problem of original sin is so pervasive that it even affects Christians after conversion. The beloved and saintly Apostle John included himself when he wrote, "If we say we have no sin, we deceive ourselves, and the truth is not in us" (1 John 1:8).

Implications For the Family

The fact of human depravity has strong implications for the family. The child is *not* innately good. Instead, he will naturally go toward evil. He will choose a wicked and shameful lifestyle (Prov 29:15).

Parents who wish to be successful must realize that their child (like all other normal children) will intensely desire to satisfy his sinful nature. No parent can be effective as long as he imagines his child to be cherubic and innocent and intrinsically good. A report from the Minnesota Crime Commission correctly evaluates every infant.

> Every baby starts life as a little savage. He is completely selfish and self-centered. He wants what he wants when he wants it—his bottle, his mother's attention, his playmate's toy, his uncle's watch. Deny him these wants, and he seethes with rage and aggressiveness, which would be murderous, were he not so helpless. He is dirty. He has no morals, no knowledge, no skills. This means that all children, not just certain children, are born delinquent. If permitted to continue in the self-centered world of his infancy, given free rein to his impulsive actions to satisfy his wants, every child would grow up a criminal, a thief, a killer, a rapist.[1]

Parents must not be surprised when they experience conflict with their child's depraved will. If parents are upholding what is right, conflict is inevitable. They must then take the necessary steps to produce proper attitudes and behavior in the child. Absence of conflict is strong evidence that the parents are not holding God's standards high enough. At a PTF one parent told me, "I can't understand why you have so much trouble with my son. I never have any trouble with him!" His comment helped me understand why his son was a problem in my high school classroom.

Because parents are also depraved, they tend to neglect their responsibilities. They find it easier to merely "let their children be children" rather than investing the time and effort to diligently train and discipline them. Instructing children is a demanding task, and disciplining them requires determined perseverance. It is so easy to be too tired, too busy, or just simply too lazy to get the job done.

Because of their own sinful nature, parents will make mistakes, and will at times be guilty of improper actions, wrong attitudes, and errors

---

[1]Quoted by Haddon W. Robinson, *Biblical Preaching* (Grand Rapids: Baker Book House, 1980), p. 145.

in judgment. At those times they must repent, ask their children for forgiveness, and walk in the ways of righteousness.

However, these failures do not in themselves disqualify parents as the authority in the home. If perfection were the prerequisite for authority, no earthly authority could exist. Imperfect parents have authority and responsibility from God to train and discipline their children. God knew parents had sinful natures even before He entrusted them with children. He gave commandments to enable parents with sinful natures to properly guide their children. Obedience to these commandments purges imperfections from parental decisions.

Dealing With Guilt

Depraved man sins against a holy God. Because of sin, man experiences guilt. Guilt is the fact of wrongdoing. This fact may or may not be accompanied by remorseful feelings, but remorseful feelings are not what determines guilt or innocence. At a court of justice, guilt is determined by a careful investigation of facts.

Some people feel guilty when in fact they are innocent. They worry about having said something inappropriate to a friend, and force themselves to make an apology even though the friend remembers nothing of the incident. Then they have a new worry—perhaps they slanted their apology, putting themselves in too favorable a light. They feel guilty without being guilty.

Others are guilty without feeling any remorse. When an assassination attempt against Hitler failed, he ordered the culprits to be strangled slowly with piano wire while their slow agony was recorded on film. He stayed up all night "enjoying" the films. Shortly before he died, Hitler commented, "I'm sorry I was so kind!" Hitler was guilty of heinous crimes, but felt no sorrow. Guilt is a fact of wrongdoing, not a feeling about it.

Parents should give their child the opportunity to declare his guilt by asking, "What have you done?" rather than "Why did you do this?" God's dealing with Adam and Eve in the Garden illustrates this approach (Gen 3). He did not ask for motives, but for facts. "Where are you?" When Adam spoke of his nakedness and fear, God asked for more facts: "Who told you that you were naked? Have you eaten from the tree?" When Adam blamed the woman, God asked her for facts: "What is this you have done?"

The parent may need to consider possible underlying causes for the child's wrong behavior. However, it is generally more instructive for the parent to ask himself why the child misbehaves than it is to invite the child to give reasons of his own.

Frequently parents are frustrated by their child's disobedience. They repeatedly ask "why," hoping desperately to impress the child into not repeating his misbehavior. This is inappropriate for several reasons: 1) The most important issue is to establish guilt, 2) asking "why" invites the fabrication of excuses and a plethora of pious-sounding motivations for having done something wrong, and 3) most children are unable at a young age to articulate their motives.

As a beginning parent, I fell into this very trap. When I asked my young daughter, "Why did you do this?" the only answer I would receive was a helpless "I don't know." I began to deliberately ask, "What did you do?" and got much better results.

Reflecting on the situation years later, I began to understand what was happening. Since sin always has an enticing appeal, a young child will at times do what he clearly knows is wrong. But when confronted with the prospect of impending judgment at the hand of a just parent, the pleasure grows wings and flies away. If asked why he misbehaved, the child cannot recall how anything could have been worth risking the punishment he now anticipates. He cannot imagine why in the world he did such a foolish thing. As I explained this process to my daughter (at age ten or eleven), she exclaimed, "That's right! That's exactly how I felt when you used to ask me why I did wrong!"

From the very first day sin entered into the world, man has tried to excuse himself. Instead of facing his own disobedience in eating from the tree, Adam blamed the woman for giving him the fruit, and blamed God for giving him the woman (Gen 3:12). Instead of facing her responsibility, the woman blamed the Serpent (Gen 3:13).

It is never pleasant to face personal responsibility for sin. If parents ask their children for an excuse to explain misbehavior, they will most certainly get it. Many parents fall into the same trap as did Moses when he confronted Aaron regarding the golden calf (Ex 32:21-24).[2]

Moses had gone up to Mount Sinai to receive God's standards for the people. In his long absence, they (like many children) reverted to sinful inclinations which they would have restrained in his presence. They asked Aaron to make a visible god. He told them to bring the gold which God had provided from Egypt, and used the gold to make a calf.

Moses returned from the Mount as the people were engaged in an orgy of sensual idolatry. He did not ask Aaron to confess his guilt, but instead invited him to blame the people: "What did this people do to you that you have brought so great a sin upon them?" Aaron was glad to comply with excuses: "You know the people, that they are set on evil." First Aaron blamed the people. Then he blamed Moses for creating a bad situation by being absent so long: the people didn't know what had become of the one who had led them out of Egypt (32:23). Finally, Aaron tried to get everyone off the hook by blaming the gold itself. "I cast it into the fire, and this calf came out" (32:24)!

Children will be just as ingenious. They will explain that everyone else is doing it, or that Johnny hit me first, or that yesterday Mother let Sally do a similar thing, or that your directions as a parent were

---

[2]The significance of this passage regarding excuses is well described by J. Richard Fugate, *What the Bible Says About . . . Child Training* (Garland, TX: Aletheia Publishers, Inc., 1980), pp. 193-195.

unclear, or that they weren't touching the ball when it went through the window. Each round of excuses contributes to the parent's confusion while adding to the child's repertoire of rationalizations. Parents must confront the child with the fact of his guilt, and teach him to face that guilt. Instead of asking for excuses, parents must require the child to face his sin.

In Leviticus 26, God guaranteed judgment for His people when they disobeyed. But if they confessed their sin, humbled their hearts in the land of their enemies, and accepted their guilt (vv. 40-41), God would remember His covenant. The word translated "accept" is *ratsah* which means "to be pleased with, accept favorably."[3] Cleansing is never complete until a person accepts his own guilt. This acceptance does not mean the chastisement is pleasant (Heb 12:11), but that the offender agrees with God's assessment of his sin.

The child must accept his moral responsibility for his wrong, and accept his parents' authority in setting the standard and judging his wrong behavior. Confession of guilt cleanses his conscience, and enables him to accept his chastisement with the right attitude. Complete acceptance of chastisement enables his conscience to be thoroughly cleansed.[4] Admission of guilt helps prevent the child from resenting his parents for disciplining him, and also helps keep the parent from building up animosity against the child.

Does Forgiveness Cancel Consequences?

Because of sin, we all experience guilt, and need forgiveness. Many parents, however, fail to distinguish properly between forgiveness and chastisement. Forgiveness is the restoration of a relationship marred by sin. Chastisement is administration of consequences which teach the offender to avoid sin in the future. God forgave King David for his great sin (2 Sam 13:13), but this did not cancel the heavy chastisement which the loving heavenly Father promised at the same time (2 Sam 13:10-14). Even at the Judgment Seat of Christ, there are consequences beyond forgiveness. The forgiven Christian will experience "loss" for failures while here on earth (1 Cor 3:15; 2 Cor 5:10).

When parents forgive their children, they restore the broken relationship. The best chastening guides the child into right living, without prolonging the fracture in the relationship. No sensible parent would tell his child, "Because of what you have done, you must go live in a shed for a month."

Sometimes mercy can be extended to the child. But even then, someone must absorb the consequences: the parent must clean up the mess, fix the tricycle, or pay for the broken window. Parents generate a false concept of reality if they insulate their children from the

---

[3]Francis Brown, S. R. Driver, Charles A. Briggs, *The New Brown-Driver-Briggs-Gesenius Hebrew and English Lexicon* (Christian Copyrights, Inc, 1983), p. 953.

[4]Fugate, *Child Training,* pp. 198-202.

consequences of folly. Christ's payment on the Cross is ultimately the only reason we can be pardoned. But His coming in the fullness of time could only be accomplished after thousands of years of bloody sacrificial object lessons: sin is costly and must be paid for. Unless the child is taught the consequences of breaking the Law, he will misconstrue mercy as leniency.

Forgiveness is effective after confession of guilt (1 John 1:9). It must be immediate and unconditional (Isa 43:25; Jer 31:34). It results in full fellowship of parent with child, and is an excellent time to give the child further instruction, since at this moment he is especially receptive to parental authority.[5]

The parent must recognize his own fallibility, and promptly confess any sin against his child. Perhaps he spoke unkindly, or disciplined a child and later discovered the child was innocent. Perhaps he was rude, or guilty of broken promises. Anything meriting an apology to an adult also merits an apology to a child. Do not think he will "just forget it" or overlook it. Humble yourself, confess your sin, and you will actually be exalted in his eyes.

This confession must honestly admit any parental guilt. A woman in her sixties told me with rancor how her father "apologized" for giving her a spanking she didn't deserve: "I'm sorry, but maybe it makes up for the times you should have been spanked, but weren't!" She had continued to resent it for decades.

Supernatural Solution

Depravity has had a devastating effect on the human race. Apart from the grace of God, man's condition is hopeless. When we really see God in His holiness, we see ourselves in our sinfulness.

Job was a great saint of integrity and righteous living. After his excruciating trial, his testimony was: "I have heard of You by the hearing of the ear, but now my eye sees You. Therefore I abhor myself, and repent in dust and ashes" (Job 42:5-6). Isaiah was one of the most eloquent of God's prophets. Yet when he saw God in His glory, he cried out, "Woe is me, for I am undone! Because I am a man of unclean lips, and I dwell in the midst of a people of unclean lips" (Isa 6:5). Daniel lived a life of exemplary righteousness, the Scriptural record of his life not being marred by a single misdeed. Yet when he saw a glorious vision of God's power, all his own splendor was ruined, and he was left powerless (Dan 10:8). The beloved disciple John who experienced a special outpouring of Jesus' love while on earth saw Him in power and glory on Patmos (Rev 1). John's response was to fall at His feet as dead.

These great saints saw God, and therefore saw themselves as needy, sinful, wretched men. We as parents must understand our relationship with our children in this light. Both we and they are bent toward evil. Like Isaiah, we must so desire cleansing that we are willing to receive a

---

[5]Ibid., pp. 203-205.

burning coal from God's altar. Apart from God, our task as parents is hopeless.

Obedience to His grace humbles our own pride, but brings blessing and glory to our homes. As the heavens are higher than the earth, God's thoughts are higher than ours. He has recorded these thoughts in His Word, enabling us to rise above the shackles of depravity. Obedience to God will produce children who are fruitful blessings instead of thorns in our sides. Consider the following passage from Isaiah in terms of what God desires to do for every family.

> Seek the Lord while He may be found, call upon Him while He is near. Let the wicked forsake his way and the unrighteous man his thoughts; let him return to the Lord, and He will have mercy on him; and to our God, for He will abundantly pardon.
>
> For my thoughts are not your thoughts, nor are your ways My ways, says the Lord. For as the heavens are higher than the earth, so are My ways higher than your ways, and My thoughts than your thoughts.
>
> For as the rain comes down, and the snow from heaven, and do not return there, but water the earth, and make it bring forth and bud, that it may give seed to the sower and bread to the eater, so shall My word be that goes forth from My mouth; it shall not return to Me void, but it shall accomplish what I please, and it shall prosper in the thing for which I sent it.
>
> For you shall go out with joy, and be led out with peace; the mountains and the hills shall break forth into singing before you, and all the trees of the field shall clap their hands. Instead of the thorn shall come up the cypress tree, and instead of the brier shall come up the myrtle tree; and it shall be to the Lord for a name, for an everlasting sign that shall not be cut off (Isa 55:6-13).

Summary

Parents who understand depravity are in a position to understand themselves and their children. They realize the child is not an innocent little cherub, but instead will become a monster if left to choose his own way. The first step in effective parenting is to realize that a child left to himself will choose evil.

Parents must help their children understand the basic issues of sin and guilt. Part of this understanding is developed by the way in which parents deal with guilty children. Guilt is a fact of wrong-doing, not merely a feeling about it. Parents should never ask their children for excuses, but should instead require them to admit the wrong they have done. Ask "What have you done?" instead of "Why did you do this?" Confession cleanses the conscience, and helps the child accept chastisement with the right attitude.

Forgiveness does not in itself cancel consequences. Forgiveness restores the relationship. Chastisement may still be necessary. However, after the offense is taken care of, it is not mentioned again.

Seeing God enables us to see ourselves. We then understand our needs, and look to God as the answer to those needs. If we come to Him in repentance and obedience, He will open the windows of heaven to shower blessings upon our families.

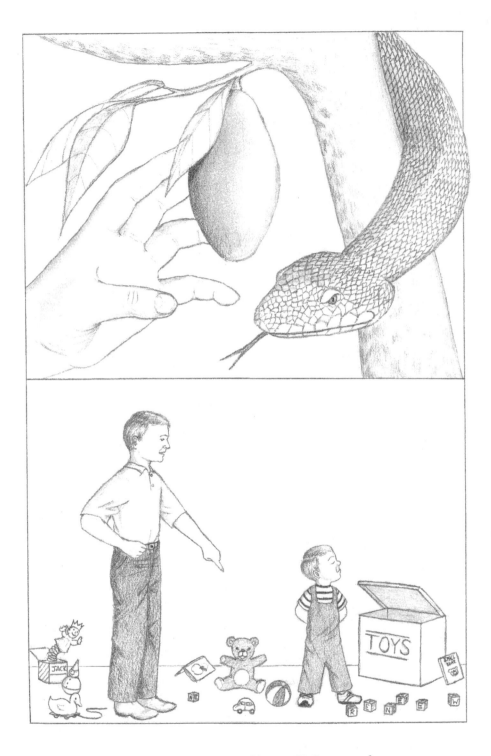

Disobedience to an "Amoral" Command

7

Godly Parenthood

Our society gives parents an inferiority complex. Parents fear they will mishandle their child. They worry about not knowing enough to teach him properly. They are afraid to control him lest they damage his personality. They feel like a pencil with an eraser on both ends: always trying to undo mistakes, never getting anything done. Such a philosophy puts parents into the discomfort of perpetual confusion. They have no clear sense of direction on what to do or how to do it.

Much of this confusion centers around the scope of parental authority. Many parents wonder, "Do I have any authority? If so, what authority do I have? What should I require from my children? How can I get them to obey?"

The answer to this confusion is the Word of God. It gives parents a proper perception of their own authority. It shows them what they should expect from their children. It helps them to effectively train their children, using the circumstances of life as vehicles for teaching truth. Adherence to the Word of God enables parents to develop a proper philosophy of parenthood.

Biblical Perception of Parental Authority

Complete selfish autonomy is a prominent goal of contemporary western society. People actually believe they have the "right" to do whatever they please, even if their actions adversely affect others. This mentality has had a tremendous impact on the family. Many parents view the exercise of authority over their child as synonymous with despotism, and have thus become confused into thinking children should be allowed to do as they please.

Naturally, children move into this authority vacuum as self-appointed despots. They rebel against parental authority in myriads of ways. They refuse to listen to instructions, and respond with back-talk. They consistently "forget" instructions. They belligerently refuse to accept correction. They comply outwardly while harboring internal resentment, an inner seething evidenced by angry facial expressions. They may obey, but in an improper manner. They may even listen politely, but then completely ignore what their parents have said.[1]

All of these actions are manifestations of one basic principle: the child places his own will above the authority of his parents. Left

---

[1]For more discussion on rebellion, see Fugate, *Child Training*, pp. 95-104.

unchecked, the child establishes himself in rebellion and becomes the authority. The parents degenerate into mere groveling advisors, vainly attempting to manipulate the situation toward a livable level of chaos.

The result of an improper perception of parental authority is exasperation and unhappiness for both parent and child. The solution is to return to the Scriptural pattern of parental authority.

Must Parents Earn Their Authority?

God expects the parent to rule the child. The clear commands of Proverbs picture the father and mother instructing their children, and disciplining them when they fail to meet the parental standard. The idea of democracy is totally absent from the Biblical requirements for parent-child relationships.

The parent must never tolerate disrespect to his authority. He has the right to rule because God has given him that right. It is not because he has earned it or because he deserves it. The parent is responsible before God to exercise that authority properly, and may need at times to modify the way that authority is exercised, but he must never allow the authority itself to be compromised. To do so undermines the entire structure of the family, and disseminates chaos.

No parent should allow his child to demand justification for actions which the parent requires. A child does not need to agree with an instruction. He needs merely to understand it. The duty of the child is to obey. Instruction is indeed the responsibility of parents. But parents are the ones who decide when and how this instruction is to be given. Besides, the instruction will be effective only for children who have already learned to obey.

No parent needs to be embarrassed by his role in defining behavior. It is the parent's responsibility to decide when the child is to get up, when he is to go to bed, what he shall or shall not eat and when he shall eat it, what clothes he shall wear, and what chores he shall perform. The parent defines the timetable on which the child shall be expected to do his tasks quickly and well and without being told. The parent has the authority to define which decisions the child may make on his own. As the child grows, he will be given more responsibility to make such decisions. If he responds improperly, the parent has the authority and responsibility to redefine which choices the child is free to make.

God is so concerned about the solidarity of parental authority that He gave stern legislation in the Old Testament against children who disregarded it (Ex 21:15,17). Any child who had the audacity to strike or curse his parents was to be executed. The seriousness of these offenses is emphasized by their inclusion in the text with other capital crimes, and their receiving the death penalty along with kidnapping (v. 16) and premeditated murder (vv. 12-14).

When Israel entered the land, they solemnly declared God's blessings and curses at Gerizim and Ebal (Deut 27:11-26). Great curses were invoked against anyone who would secretly make a graven image, move his neighbor's property boundary, cause a blind person to wander off the road, have sexual relations with a near relative or with an animal, or take a bribe. Near the beginning of the list, a great curse was pronounced against anyone who treated his parents with contempt. God viewed such contempt to be in the same class as these other degraded crimes. The entire nation agreed with this assessment by shouting a resounding "Amen." The child who disregarded his parents was worthy of unrelenting judgment (Prov 30:17).

God also gave parents specific direction for dealing with a rebellious, disobedient son who refused to submit to their authority. They were to bring him to the elders of the city and publicly accuse him of his wickedness. Then all the men of the city were to stone the child to death, purging this great evil from Israel (Deut 21:18-21).

Several points must be noticed regarding this severe command from God: 1) The authority of the parents is unquestioned. 2) There is no evidence of a "trial" in the ordinary sense. The parental accusation is simply accepted at face value. 3) There is no hint of parental failures affecting the outcome. 4) God designed national law to support the authority of the parents in training their children (the exact opposite of current trends). 5) A rebellious child is a cancer in the life of the nation, and must be removed for the benefit of the group (v. 21).

This action stands in stark contrast to current attitudes regarding child rights, which would place the burden of guilt on the parent, and would focus on the history of the domestic conflict to see whether the parent had aggravated the situation. Although we do not live in the Old Testament theocratic kingdom, and would not take such action against children today, these Scriptures show how seriously God views disrespect to parents.

The New Testament emphasizes the seriousness of disobedience to parents by including it in the lists describing wanton sinfulness. Paul gives graphic description of men who deliberately departed from God and abused their privileges. As a result, God gave them up to a debased mind greedily pursuing all kinds of wickedness: sexual immorality, covetousness, maliciousness, envy, murder, strife, deceit, evil-mindedness. Such persons are "backbiters, haters of God, violent, proud, boasters, inventors of evil things, *disobedient to parents,* undiscerning, untrustworthy, unloving, unforgiving, unmerciful" (Rom 1:28-31).

Paul's final letter to Timothy includes a similar passage. Disobedience to parents is placed in the same class as slander, blasphemy, pride, brutality, and self-love (1 Tim 3:1-5). Christian parents must therefore take their cue from God in also viewing it seriously. A parent who tolerates disrespect to his authority is actually undermining the authority of God.

Since God has given authority to the parent, every parent is responsible before God to exercise that authority properly. Christ took time in his busy schedule to gather little children into His arms and announce to His amazed disciples, "Of such is the kingdom of God" (Mark 10:13-16). Parents can therefore be sure that any child abuser will be severely judged by this great Lover of children.

Deep down in his own soul, the child desperately wants his parent to be a leader. His own depravity and immaturity make it impossible for him to go in the right direction on his own. The parents who fulfill their calling and exercise authority over their children are doing them a monumental favor. Only in this kind of environment is it truly possible for "children to be children" in the correct sense.

Children who have not been required to submit to parental authority have automatically and prematurely been forced into a sphere of decision-making intended only for adults. It is impossible for these children to truly be children in freedom and joy. Many become candidates for an authoritarian cult to fill the void and frustration their parents forced upon them.

Maria, the mother who raised the famous Trapp Family Singers, understood how parents frequently force unhappiness on their children:

> The old saying, "Spare the rod and spoil the child" seems like a translation of the Bible: "Who loves his son does not spare the rod." It is to be hoped that the world will soon turn away from its experiment in the realm of progressive education where poor, unhappy children always have to do what they want; the young will is then crippled by its own whims.[2]

Should Children Instruct Their Parents?

In all of Scripture, instruction goes from the parents to the child, not from the child to the parents. The Pentateuch commands parents to diligently instruct their children (Deut 6:6-9). In Proverbs this arrangement is emphasized again and again: the father instructs the son.

The parents are the instructors because God has qualified them through experience and authority. Their knowledge about life enables them to make wiser decisions than even the most intelligent child. God established parental authority to properly channel this wisdom to the child. No parents should ever be intimidated by lack of education or by "average" intelligence. God expects them to control their child, and give him what he really needs.[3]

God judged the wicked Israelites over twenty years of age who left Egypt but continually grumbled and tempted God in the wilderness. He killed those wicked parents gradually in the wilderness in order to retain them as instructors for the next generation of children. God did not suspend His laws requiring honor and obedience to parents. He used wicked parents to teach the next generation, who would fulfill His

---

[2]Maria Augusta Trapp, *The Story of the Trapp Family Singers* (New York: Scholastic Book Services, 1949), p. 235.

[3]Fugate, *Child Training*, p. 86.

purposes in Canaan. This incident illustrates how faulty parents are capable of instructing their own children.

Even more striking is Jesus' example of obedience. Although He was a perfect son, He willingly obeyed imperfect parents (Lu 2:51) who had a faulty understanding of His life purpose (Lu 2:48-50). By the Incarnation, God put an amazing stamp of approval on parental authority.

The child who grows up instructing his parents will develop an unholy arrogance toward any authority. He will always think he has a better idea, or that his feelings should be catered to, or that someone else should do the dirty work. Every authority will be subjected to the court of his own immature judgment. His warped standards will condemn most of these authorities as failures. His resistance to these authorities will hinder his own life and the lives of those around him.

But the ultimate disaster for the deprived child who grows up instructing his parents is his development of the same unholy arrogance toward God. He imagines that God needs to be advised of the newest grand scheme that just popped into his head, and supposes the Divine Arm can be twisted to help put his puny plans into action. A child accustomed to requiring his parents to justify their instructions will make the same kind of demands toward God. He will expect God to justify the operations of Divine sovereignty and providence. Such a child has been programmed by his parents for spiritual disaster.

Samson had the audacity to instruct his parents. He demanded a Philistine wife, directly opposing his parents' desire for him to obey God (Judg 14:1-3). He avoided telling them about his exploit with the lion (v 6), ate unclean honey taken from its carcass, and arrogantly gave some of the honey to his parents without telling them it was unclean (v 9). His participation in a Philistine marriage feast certainly violated Nazirite abstinence from the fruit of the vine.

God used the carnality and wickedness of this son to begin the conquest of the Philistines, but the real victory occurred through David—a man not gifted with supernatural strength, but having a heart that honored his parents and sought after God. David obeyed his father, taking care of the sheep even though he may personally have wanted to go fight against the Philistines. He took provisions to his brothers, although he likely knew he would not be well received (1 Sam 17:14,17,20,28). During his days as a fugitive, David moved his parents to the land of Moab for their safety (1 Sam 22:3-4).

Even though parents are the instructors, they can learn from their children. The alert parent can receive profound insight from the words and actions of a child. But the child is not consciously instructing the parent, and setting himself as authority over the parent. The child is *instructive,* but not an *instructor.*

One of God's greatest tools for teaching parents about the fatherhood of God is their interaction with their own children. I once reached for the hand of my small child as we stepped off the porch onto an uneven walkway: "Here, hold my hand so if you stumble you won't fall." How instructive regarding the care of our Heavenly Father (Psa 37:23-24)!

The Psalmist declared that God has ordained strength in the mouths of infants (Psa 8:2). The simple, trusting requests of the child give the parents a greater understanding of what it means to be a child of the Heavenly Father. For the perceptive parent, the innocent words of a child will often open new realms of profound spiritual understanding.

A child can be under his parents' authority and graciously remind them of failure to implement their own principles (e. g., failure in disciplining a younger child for actions clearly established as wrong behavior). But this is different from a supposedly gracious accusation to the parent: "You are disciplining me in the wrong spirit!" Such a child sets himself up as a judge over his parents.

Parents can have confidence if they follow the clear instructions in the Bible. They can joyfully repudiate the muttering and whispering philosophies of our day which insinuate that parents can never be sure whether they are really doing their job right. The key to their confidence is in exercising their God-given authority to instruct and discipline their children.

Expectations For Children

Many parents are frustrated because they do not know what to expect of their children. They do not want to be too strict, but at the same time are unhappy with the chaos in their homes. Living in a society that has expected so little from its children, these parents have few models to guide their expectations.

Obedience

The single most important issue for children is obedience. All other issues are corollaries. A child cannot even be taught to honor his parents unless he has first been taught to obey. When the issue of obedience is settled, all other good things can follow. Without obedience, nothing is secure.

Many parents actually train their children to disobey. They require obedience only after the fourth, fifth, or tenth repetition of the command, and only if the voice is raised or threats are given. Even then, some parents seldom carry through with their promises, and the child knows he has a good chance of complete freedom in disobedience. Allowing a child to decide when he will obey trains him to make his parents wait for his selfish timing. Permitting a child to argue against obedience or to make excuses is actually training that behavior. It is a sad fact: most parents train their children to be disobedient.[4]

Parents must require obedience to every command—immediately and without back-talk. If the child is old enough to understand a

---

[4]For more discussion on these types of negative training, see Fugate, pp. 57-68.

command, he is old enough to obey. But parents should not make issues of things that don't really matter. Don't insist that your one-year-old let you feed him cheerios instead of his being able to pick them off his tray. If your three-year-old wants to make the faces in his coloring book purple, don't make an issue of it. Never make an issue of something that could threaten your child's health: Do not insist that your toddler say "please" before you give him a drink of water.

If parents are not ready to insist on obedience, they should not give a command. For example, a father may tell his daughter, "Go put on your blue dress." If he does not care whether she wears the blue dress or the pink dress, he should not specify the color. If he really prefers the blue dress, that is enough reason for the command. If the command is given, it should be obeyed.

God's "Amoral" Command to Adam and Eve

Putting away toys or setting the table does not involve an intrinsic moral issue. This is true of many commands parents give to children. Therefore parents are prone to think it is not very important whether or not their children obey. If their child ignores an "amoral command," they assume obedience cannot be insisted upon.

Nothing could be farther from the truth. In the Garden of Eden, God gave a simple command to Adam and Eve, "Do not eat from the tree of the knowledge of good and evil." The freedom to eat from all the other trees proves there was no intrinsic moral issue involved in eating a piece of fruit. Adam and Eve could have analyzed the situation and concluded: "What does eating or not eating a piece of fruit have to do with our relationship to God? Nothing! Physical fruit cannot determine spiritual reality."

Such arguments would not have changed the picture in the least. The issue was authority. Their rejection of God's authority was serious enough to plunge all humanity into depravity. This depravity was so dark and deep that there was absolutely no hope apart from special intervention by God. So serious was the offense that the special intervention to restore fellowship cost the immeasurable sacrifice of God's perfect Son. Even that Sacrifice could not be given immediately, but required thousands of years of preparation before humanity was ready to receive it.

When a child disobeys even a "small amoral command," parents must view his disobedience as a moral similarity to the first sin in the Garden of Eden. They must consider God's action in Eden as an object lesson on how seriously to regard the child's rejection of parental authority.

Must Children Always Obey?

Parents have the authority to expect obedience in every area of the child's life. He must obey when told what to eat, when to go to bed, whom to associate with, what books he may or may not read, what duties he must have in the home, and the kind of attitude to express in the midst of it all. A child may make respectful suggestions, but the authority of the parent is never negotiable.

God's Word is emphatic. "Children, obey your parents in all things, for this is well pleasing to the Lord" (Col 3:20). God does not reserve certain areas where the parent has no authority over the child. Paul admonishes the Ephesians: "Children, obey your parents in the Lord, for this is right" (Eph 6:1). The reason given for this requirement is that it is right for the child to obey.

The expression "in the Lord" can be taken to mean "as long as parental commands do not conflict with God's commands." In making this concession it is important to avoid installing the child as judge over his parents, with the child making the final decision as to whether he should obey. In the Scriptures God has already defined proper behavior, and does not intend for children to "decide" whether their parents are giving appropriate commands. However, He does not require a child to obey when told to do something directly conflicting with the Scriptures.

These commands for children apply to all children, whether they are gifted, normal, or handicapped. God does not cancel His standard of obedience for children with limited ability. I have a friend who has eight children, the oldest being a Down's-Syndrome child. Now in her twenties, she is the nicest such child our family has ever known. I asked my friend for his advice to parents who face this problem. He replied, "We require the same standards, but allow her more time to learn to live by those standards. It takes line upon line, precept upon precept. It takes her longer, but we require the same final result."

Because of society's confusion regarding authority, some parents may feel uneasy or even guilty about demanding obedience from their children. But they must remember this arrangement is God's design, not their own. It is God's authority which commands children to obey their parents. Parents are disobedient and immoral when they fail to implement the authority God requires them to exercise.

Right is Normal

Many parents have unnecessary worries because they have listened to Christians expound philosophies founded in secular psychology. One of these is the concern that if parents enforce strict behavioral norms and high spiritual standards, the child is likely to cast off all restraint as soon as he leaves the authority of the parent.

This will be true for hypocritical demands. It will also be true for the teenager who is suddenly expected to "be spiritual" after his parents have cultivated carnal desires during his childhood.[5] It will not be true if parents live a life of faith demonstrating the supreme

---

[5]Parents who use television to entertain their young children are laying a foundation for teenagers who demand entertainment, and who think Bible study is boring.

superiority of spiritual things. Children will rally to truth lived and articulated with consistency and love.

The child must see that *right is normal.* Right ways of doing things are intrinsically better than the alternatives. It is possible, of course, to drive a car without inflating the tires, but proper inflation will provide much better and safer transportation. When a child becomes properly accustomed to doing right, he doesn't give it a second thought. Since the parent insists on a consistent expression of what is right, the child learns that *right is normal.*

No five-year-old will ever brush his teeth consistently just because his parents have given him ten good reasons for cleaning teeth. He must be required to do what is good for him. Eventually, as this proper habit develops, the child will dislike going to sleep without brushing his teeth because his mouth doesn't feel ready for bed.

Sometimes a great deal of parental perseverance is required to establish *right as normal.* For example, refusal to say "please" is often an expression of childish pride. At age ten, my daughter Rachelle was discussing with my wife, Rhoda, the issue of teaching a young child to say "please." She observed how much easier it had been to teach this to Rolanda (age twenty-one months) than to the other children because "we were too proud to do it." She wondered what made the difference. Rhoda suggested, "Possibly Rolanda has heard it correctly so often she thinks 'please' is part of the thing being requested."

Rhoda's supposition was borne out by subsequent events. Before she was two, Rolanda would request milk by saying, "milk-eeze." After she learned the importance of "please" she said, "Milk-eeze, please." For Rolanda right was normal. The struggle with the earlier children had paid additional dividends for training a younger child.

Most of us have learned to tie our shoes during childhood. From long habit, we can tie them properly without looking or even thinking about it. If our parents were careful how they taught us, they probably gave directions to tie a square knot (even if they didn't know what it was named). Without necessarily knowing all of the reasons for preferring a square knot (resistance to untying, neat appearance), we learned to live this facet of our lives in a way superior to the alternate hodgepodge. If now told as adults to tie our shoes with a granny knot, we would find it awkward and tedious. We have become adults for whom *right is normal.*

Praise can be used effectively to help toddlers establish proper behavior. Too much praise, however, becomes unwieldy froth: he who praises all alike praises none. It is improper to continually reward children for what should simply be normal, expected behavior. Parents should not inundate them with praise and thanks for what should actually be the pattern for every child.

Jesus told a parable to clarify our thinking (Lu 17:7-10). A man does not thank his servant for doing his duty. "So likewise you, when you have done all those things which you are commanded, say, 'We are *unprofitable* servants. We have done what was our duty to do' " (Lu 17:10). The child who goes *beyond* duty is the one who deserves a reward. Reward the child for initiative: seeing work and doing it without being told. Commend him when he sacrifices his own interests in order to make peace with siblings. Reward him for being creative and courageous in pursuing righteousness.

The goal is to have beloved children, who live a pattern of obedience to their parents, choosing those things which their parents approve. The apostle Paul considered this pattern to be normal for children, and used children as an example to new converts: "Therefore be followers of God as dear children" (Eph 5:1). Every parent should ask himself the question: Do my children follow me so diligently that I could use them as an object lesson to new believers on how to follow God? Clearly, this is the kind of home life God expects.

The goal is to have children who tenaciously do what is right even under pressure, children who have learned that right is normal even if others discard it. Children need to be taught, so that in adulthood they exhibit the same kind of fortitude as the Holocaust victim who said,

> I believe in the sun
> Even when it does not shine;
> I believe in love
> Even when it is not shown;
> I believe in God
> Even when He does not speak.

Stages in Child Training

Every parent recognizes different stages in child training. No one expects the same kind of behavior from a six-month old baby and a nineteen-year-old boy. No parent assumes the two cases to be remotely identical.

Observation of contemporary families, however, shows wide disagreement on *exactly how* these situations differ, and exactly what can and should be expected of children at different age levels.[6]

Infant, Child, Youth, Adult

In broad terms, the first twenty years of a person's life can be divided into four major areas: infant, child, youth, adult. The infant is totally dependent on his parents for everything. For all practical purposes, he can do nothing for himself. Even his ability to communicate is limited. In fact, the word "infant" comes from Latin meaning "unable to speak."

Childhood includes infancy and continues until the onset of puberty. During this time the child attempts to assert himself as absolute ruler of his life. He will be naughty just to get attention. He can exhibit amazing self-denial in an attempt to get his own way. He may forfeit a

---

[6]The basic framework on how to handle stages in child training comes from Fugate, pp. 44-48, 71-72, 143.

delicious snack simply to gratify his proud refusal to say "please." It is crucial for parents to utilize this strategic stage when basic patterns of life and outlook are being established. Parental failure during these years sets the stage for a child who does not want to follow his parents, but instead idolizes a movie star, a famous athlete, or a popular singer.

The period from puberty to age twenty can be described as the time of youth. The child matures physically, developing as a man or a woman. He has more privileges and more responsibilities. He makes more decisions for himself. He will seek someone to look up to, someone to follow. His response and attitude toward his parents and their leadership is largely dependent on how they handled him in the childhood stage.

In Biblical history, the child became an adult at twenty, being accountable to God (Num 14:29).[7] The goal of parenthood is to produce offspring who are wise and independent individuals, and who delight in their parents and freely come to them for advice.

Control Before Reason

Imagine approaching a one-day-old baby: "Johnny dear, I am under the strong impression that your diaper needs changing. I will discuss ten reasons why this is in your best interest. I hope you will choose this procedure." Nonsense! No one tries to reason with a newborn baby in order to produce desired behavior. The parents assume complete control, without giving the child any explanations for what is done. Parents bundle their unwilling infant into a warm snowsuit before taking him out into the cold. They even pay a doctor to stick their baby with a sharp needle. They do what is best for the infant whether he likes it or not.

During the childhood stage, the major emphasis of the parental role is in controlling the child. Parents must deal with their child's will. It is unrealistic to expect a child to brush his teeth properly merely because he has heard a detailed lecture on preventing tooth decay. The parent needs to control the child for his benefit in the long run.

This external control establishes proper patterns of living. As the child grows and develops, there is more and more opportunity for the parents to reason with him and to help him understand why some things are good while others are bad. First, the child needs to know *what* is right. Later, he is capable of understanding *why* it is right. Parental failure in this early stage results in a child who does not want to follow his parents.

During the period of youth, control is gradually relaxed as the parents see their child making correct decisions, and as they see his reasoning process in making decisions being molded by the wisdom they have taught.

---

[7]This text may suggest that it is better not to call teenagers "young adults." They are not adults. They are still teenagers. Prematurely calling them adults tends to breed an unhealthy arrogance toward their elders.

By the time the child is twenty, parents direct him through discussion, analysis, and reasoning. External control is no longer necessary, because the child has internalized the control of his earlier years, and has reinforced it with reasons making it his own personal preference.

Many parents reverse this process with disastrous results. Instead of *controlling* their child at the childhood stage, they try to *reason* with him. This approach only makes him more unreasonable and more unteachable. He becomes more stubborn and more out of control. By the time he reaches his teen years, he is totally out of control and the parents have those "difficult teen years" facing them. The parents have created these difficulties by failing to control their child.

The parents then become desperate to salvage something out of the wreckage. Suddenly they try to control the child. Both parents and child are unaccustomed to such an arrangement. The child has always had his own way, and the parents have refused to participate in God's gradual, easy lessons on child control. The result is a domestic firestorm, with both parties despising one another, and looking forward to the day when their paths will separate.

Narrow The Generation Gap

God intended for the teenage years to be the golden age of parental opportunity. The parents should be using these years to guide the youth in discernment and wisdom. Many parents waste these years with conflict because they tried to reason with their offspring at the childhood stage rather than first controlling him. God's golden opportunity has been lost.

The result is what is commonly called the generation gap. The youth has rejected his parents and their authority, and chooses to make his own decisions. Naturally, many of those decisions are foolish because they bypass both divine and parental wisdom. The gap between the generations is simply the portion of parental convictions which have not been instilled in the children.

The teenage years are a grand opportunity to teach discernment, to narrow the generation gap, and to help the youth learn in his teens some of the things his parents learned by hard knocks in their twenties and thirties. The teenage years are a magnificent opportunity for building a mature and wise young adult.

Parents who criticize and nag their adult children are often trying to compensate for their own irresponsible failure to diligently teach them as teenagers.

Release the Reins

As parents, we need to learn how to gradually release our children from control. Ephesians 4:11-16 speaks primarily of interaction within the church. But since each father is to be the spiritual leader of his own family, this passage is also instructive for helping parents bring their children to maturity.

As parents, we need to understand our role before God. Ultimately, the child's loyalty must be focused on God, not on ourselves (vv 12-13). Our role has limitations both in time and in significance. Our job is to focus children into unwavering allegiance to One greater than ourselves, One who is not limited by time, or space, or weakness.

We must watch for clues of maturity, and reward maturity when we see it (vv 14-15). Children appreciate parents who notice their growth and give them appropriate opportunities to demonstrate their faithfulness and ability.

When childishness occurs, we must honestly and lovingly confront it (v 15). We dare not ignore it or treat it with silence. The child needs help to mature properly. The parents hold the key to helping him.

We must help our child discover his own unique abilities and develop them for the glory of God (v 16). Attempting to force a child into a mold we have devised will both frustrate the child and make it difficult for us to properly release control.

My friend who pointed out the relevance of this passage for "releasing the reins" is the father of eight children. He concluded with exhortation to remember two principles: 1) Encourage growth instead of tolerating it, and 2) release continuously instead of suddenly.

Implementation of Child Training

Delight in Your Child

For parents to be effective, they must delight in their children. Contrary to popular contemporary belief, children are an opportunity, not a burden. It is a great privilege to have children, but our understanding of this truth has been fogged by a society that hates its own offspring as it greedily pursues selfish pleasure.

Remember that even small children are persons, companions, and friends. Wise parents enjoy building a delightful relationship with their children. They do not hurry their infants off to a baby-sitter so they can be free to do "more important things," and then ruefully look back when their children are teenagers and regret their neglect of opportunities to delight in the special joys only small children can provide.

Such joys come at unexpected moments. One day five-year-old Rosalyn was drawing a picture of several angels. When she came to the head of one angel, she paused and asked, "Mother, do you think that after all these years, some angels are bald by now?"

Once while I was shaving with an electric razor, two-year-old Raphael asked, "Father, do you have to mow your face?"

My wife's sister once told of how her four-year old son poured special joy into her heart. As he was describing how much he loved her, she could tell his little mind was groping for just the right expression.

Finally he said, "Mama, I love you so much that if I could, I'd get God to come down and give you a kiss."

Parents who prefer not to be bothered with small children are the same parents who wonder why they have no relationship with their teenagers, and who feel neglected and unwanted in their old age. Such parents are merely reaping what they have sown. Their children soon find other interests, and discover other relationships more exciting than their "old man and old woman."

Many parents who would be too polite to speak of a friend's fault in the presence of others think nothing of talking openly about their children: "Our child knows how to manipulate people in order to get his own way." "Our child is just strong-willed." Such statements reinforce wrong behavior by teaching the child that his actions are simply a product of his genetic makeup and that he just as well enjoy it.

Frequently these statements are an excuse for parental failure: "This child is very strong-willed, but his naughty behavior has nothing to do with my parental abilities. It is the inevitable outcome of his stubborn nature." The parents are deluding themselves. There *is* a direct correlation between child behavior and parental diligence.

Parents who delight in their children will be careful not to speak of their children's faults to other people. Of course, there may be times when parents need to get counsel regarding a particular problem. However, this counsel will not be sought in front of the child. The focus of the discussion will be on enabling the parent to correct the deficiencies in the child's character.

Sometimes parents lament: "We can't understand why one of our children went astray, while all of the others turned out right. We treated them all alike." Their final statement may be a partial answer to the problem. The parents treated as alike what God had created as different.

Diversity is a gift from God, expressed in myriad ways throughout the universe. One of these ways is in the family. Each child is unique, a special treasure. He has special aptitudes, special talents. But he also has special weaknesses, special propensities toward evil. A parent who truly delights in what God has given will not expect all of his children to excel equally in every area. He will also realize some children need to be corrected more severely and more frequently than other members of the same family.

This view of diversity is a benefit to the children as a group. They are in a position to notice their differences, and to utilize them as an advantage to all rather than as a point of friction. The family thus becomes an object lesson of how diversity is to be a blessing in the church, rather than a divisive curse.

Our daughter Renee has perfect pitch. When a note is played on the piano she can quickly identify it. She can name the notes which are played together in a chord. Suppose I decided her gift should be the standard for all of our children, and those having difficulty should practice until they could master it. The whole family would become frustrated, rather than rejoicing in her special gift.

One person cannot *excel* in *everything,* but we have missed many blessings by assuming the validity of the phrase, "jack of all trades and master of none." Instead, we should have the philosophy, "jack of all trades and master of *one.*" Parents should be alert to a child's special gift, and make him a master at it. At the same time they should insist on fundamental development in the other areas to ensure knowledge and proficiency in a wide variety of skills.

Frequently one hears the expression: "My wife and I had to get a weekend alone; we had to get away from the kids!" Such a statement is often symptomatic of parents who have been deficient in delighting in their children. Their children are undisciplined, and it is understandable why they would want to get away from them. Their failure to discipline is a demonstration of their lack of love (Prov 13:24), and sets the stage for being unable to delight in their children. Parents who delight in their children enjoy being with them, teaching them, discovering together, taking pleasure in fellowship (Prov 29:17).

Certainly it is not wrong for parents to have time alone together. Many parents would have lots of time alone together every evening if they would teach their children to go to bed promptly without hassle.

Develop Communication

Any task involving teaching requires communication. This communication may be oral or written. It may be example or precept. It may be simply the delicate nuance of a facial expression or the warmth of an embrace. But without communication, no teaching can occur. The number of parents lamenting their inability to communicate with their teenagers is proof that effective communication with older children is not automatic. Parents must build the channels of communication between themselves and their children.

Begin Early

Every infant loves to communicate with his parents. He coos with joy when his mother talks to him, even though he does not understand the meaning of her words. He chortles with delight when she repeats the sounds he makes. A toddler may weary his parents with unending questions. Sometimes he doesn't really care about the answers; he just wants to hear his parents talk. Instead of viewing this as an interruption, parents should view it as a double-edged opportunity: build a pattern of delightful communication with the child, and tell him something worthwhile at the same time.

Parents must maximize this harvest of easy automatic communication in order to build a solid foundation for effective and pleasant communication in later years. By beginning early, the parent develops a pattern of communication with the child. At subsequent crisis points, parents and children do not experience the frustration of being unable to communicate. They understand and appreciate one another's thoughts because they have shared a long history of intimate and personal interchange.

Parents need to develop an atmosphere in which the family enjoys just sitting together and talking, with each person freely sharing his ideas, and all having the goal of coming to a consensus on truth—even if that means jettisoning old opinions and preconceived notions. These discussions can include many different subjects, and may vary depending on the interests of a particular family. A farm family might discuss the relative merits of organic versus chemical fertilizers. I enjoy math and science. The following excerpts from Rachelle's journal describe some meal-time discussions that we thoroughly enjoyed.

> We have been discussing planes and bullets and speeds and relativity and gravity and equations and imaginary numbers and rectangular matrices and decimals and infinity and elevators and trains and throwing balls backwards and forwards and upwards and downwards and light and stars and space and the universe . . . Father is the scientist; I am the skeptic—and very skeptical I am, to be sure: all my comfortable theories and suppositions about my neat and orderly little universe are crashing down about my ears; and it is not easy to change the scope of thought one has used all one's life. To tell the truth, I am beginning to feel like a 16th century Catholic confronted suddenly with a bunch of strange and unconventional ideas to turn the whole world topsy-turvy.

> It all started when Roland announced that American scientists are working on a new plane that will be able to go twice the speed of a bullet!

> "But of course, that plane won't be able to have guns on it," Roland remarked, "because if it would shoot a bullet out the front of the plane, the plane would quickly catch up to the bullet and get shot!"

> "What do you think, you other children?" Father questioned. "Is that how it would work?"

> The answering nods were unhesitating and unanimous. Such a simple matter was easy to see through.

> Father shook his head. "Just think a little bit—how fast is that bullet going *before* it's shot?"

> "It's not moving at all!" declared Roland.

> "Wrong," answered Father. "Anyone else know?"

> "The same speed that the plane's going?" I suggested cautiously. In my head I knew that that must be true, and yet, logical though that conclusion was, it seemed to defy all reason.

> "Right," Father agreed. "Let's call the speed of a bullet x. Then this plane which flies at twice the speed of a bullet travels at what?"

> "$2x$," I responded.

> "Good. So if the bullet is *already* going $2x$ before it's shot, and the bullet travels at x—right?—how fast will the bullet go?"

> "$1x$?"

> "$1\ 1/2x$?"

> "$2x$?"—and other ridiculous mutterings skittered uncertainly back and forth across the table. The way to solve the problem would of course be to add x to $2x$ and get $3x$; however, the very idea of a bullet going three times its normal speed just because it happened to have been shot out of an *airplane* seemed ridiculous. Finally, however, I mentioned $3x$ as the answer and found, to my disgust, dismay, and puzzlement, that I was right. Immediately therefore I began to

contradict myself and argue that the thing was not possible; no, it was possible, and the bewildered contents of my bursting cranium could not sort out a good enough argument to prove the wonder incorrect. But upon some reflection, I realized that the idea was not so mad as it had first appeared, and was soon settling this funny fact into one of the neat piles of the information in my brain about our world.

Then came the shocker.

Father said, "*Now!* what if you are flying at *2x* and fire a bullet out your tailgun! What will happen to the bullet?"

Well . . . nobody knew the answer. . . . Finally everyone gave up. . . . [When he gave the answer] what small remains were left of our ordered, conventional reason evaporated in the heat of the idea.

"The bullet," Father announced calmly, "would follow the plane at *1x*."

Horrified silence and then an explosion of wild protests. . . .[8]

Of course, most of our meal-time discussions are not this technical. We discuss many other topics as well. Sometimes we need to deal with the mundane details faced by every family: "Don't talk with your mouth full." "Don't leave the table without being excused." "Don't interrupt when someone else is talking."

Topics for discussion are as broad as God's universe: animals, gardening, interactions of people as they work, merits of different kinds of machinery or gadgets, politics, ethics. People espouse a variety of opinions on almost every subject. Use this variety to help your children learn how to evaluate reality. Use meal-time to help your children learn to communicate their ideas, evaluate answers, refute inaccurate statements or faulty logic. Enjoyment of these family interactions provides a solid platform for having forthright discussions regarding differing opinions on spiritual realities and how those realities should be applied in life. Life affords many opportunities for developing open communication within your family. Don't let those opportunities slip away unfulfilled.

Parents can also create opportunities for communication by doing something special with each child. My children enjoy having a special time designated for them. For "Roland time," my son can choose what he would like for the two of us to do together. This could mean batting a ball, reading a story, or taking a walk. If he wishes, he may invite the other children to join in the fun, thus creating a time for group interaction where all of the children are involved.

Such activities build the parent-child relationship, and are a natural environment for talking together. For the parent, the focus is not on the activity itself, nor on the pleasant memories it will bring twenty years from now. The activity is the scaffolding which enables the parent to build eternal values.

Communication goes both ways. Receiving from your child is also important. For your own instruction, pay attention to what he says. Good parenthood carefully utilizes the cues children provide as they

---

[8]Rachelle's Journal, January 29, 1989.

communicate with their parents. Be sensitive to the child and his needs. Much of what the child communicates will be in non-verbal form. An alert parent will pay attention when he notices his child is unusually quiet or sad. These cues help the parent wisely lead the child.

Include Sex Education

Sex education is one area of child training which many parents find embarrassing and intimidating, especially if they have not cultivated open and warm communication with their children. Parents who feel uncomfortable teaching their child about sex should view their difficulty as a barometer. It indicates they must work harder to develop the ability to communicate with their children. Parents must shoulder their responsibility to educate their children about sex. They must not relegate it to the church, to the school, or by default leave it for the peers behind the washroom door.

The Bible is very candid regarding all facets of human experience, and the area of sex is no exception. Parents should read to their children from the Old Testament, and encourage them to ask questions about things they do not understand. Questions regarding sex will naturally arise. The Biblical context makes it easy to show how perversion of God's plan brings sorrow, while cooperation with His plan brings joy and blessing.

Use family facts to teach about sex in an ordinary way. Allow the toddler to feel the movements of an anticipated new baby. Look at pictures to show how the baby is growing inside the mother. Tell him about the different stages the baby goes through before birth. Explain how the mother will breast-feed the newborn baby. Utilize natural occasions for instruction and easy communication.

Parents should give clear and frank answers to any questions their child asks about sex. Not only are fraudulent statements sinful, they will be discovered sooner or later, and will severely damage parental credibility. The easy and natural way to begin teaching a child about sex is by answering his questions honestly and simply. He is not asking for a half-hour lecture on the subject, but likely only wants a quick answer to something that has sparked his curiosity. This gradual approach will be particularly helpful in alleviating the awkwardness felt by beginning parents.

A young child should be given only as much information as is necessary to satisfy his immediate question. Don't burden his innocence with more answers than he is asking for, nor cumber his immaturity with more information than he can handle. Many children will at some point ask: Where did I come from? A wise mother once answered: "You are part of me." Eventually that answer needed to be clarified, but it was enough for the child at that stage.

This mother was adept in using discreet language. We live in a promiscuous society, and it is important to teach our children to be discreet in how they say things. Honesty must never be equated with a brazen detail at inappropriate times and places. Discretion is learned by example as well as by instruction. When the child wants to know more about where he came from, avoid giving lots of explicit detail before he asks for it. Simply tell him that the father planted a seed so that the baby could grow inside the mother until it was time to be born. If your child broaches a sensitive question in front of guests, tell him you will discuss it later.

View Difficulties as Opportunities

Sometimes parents get discouraged when they encounter difficulties in the child-rearing process. They view these troubles solely as obstacles to be eliminated as soon as possible. They fail to see these difficulties as opportunities in disguise. They are opportunities for ministry, opportunities for building bonds of love, opportunities for forging strong relationships, and opportunities for instruction.

The Opportunity of Inconvenience

Some parents want only temporary results, not character. They are therefore disturbed when their children behave improperly, but only because those actions cause them personal inconvenience and unpleasantness.

The goal is sterling character, not merely proper results on a given day. For example, some children are careless about closing doors as they rush outside. Many parents take the easy way out, and shut the door for them. If the goal is to merely have all the doors shut, lock them! A much better approach is to take the time and effort to call the child to return to shut the door. The child may need discipline to teach him it is worthwhile to shut the door without your assistance.

The goal is to develop responsible behavior, even when the parent cannot check on the child. The goal is for the child to do things properly from the beginning, without being told. Parents must use inconvenience and interruption as an opportunity for instruction.

The Opportunity of Bad Habits

Even bad habits can be converted to benefit a child. I have a friend whose daughter still sucked her thumb at age five. Her parents had warned her that this could make her teeth crooked, and that other children would likely make fun of her. Her concern about breaking her habit was so great she actually asked her dad for the distasteful medicine sometimes put on thumbs to inhibit sucking. He replied, "No, I want you to break this habit yourself, as you pray to God."

Each night this father prayed with his little girl asking God to help her conquer her habit. Despite her best intentions, she would awake in the morning with her thumb in her mouth. Finally, after five or six months, she suddenly learned not to suck her thumb.

Then the little girl asked, "Dad, why did God take so long to answer my prayer?" He answered, "Maybe God was trying to teach you how difficult it is to break bad habits. You are very young, and God chose to teach you this lesson by something that would not hurt you." Her father saw beyond the need for breaking a habit. He saw an opportunity for teaching an important spiritual lesson.

The Opportunity of Failure

One of the most significant aspects of learning is to have the teaching tested. Tests are the norm in academic experience, and are used to evaluate whether any learning has occurred. The tests of life are much more significant. These tests demonstrate whether the teaching has been internalized, whether the pupil has made the instruction part of his life. Such tests enable the child to see his own need.

Parents must resist the temptation to always physically prevent disobedience. They should not try to put everything out of a toddler's reach. He needs to learn that some things are forbidden. There is no need to mount the stereo high on the wall, or place locks on the kitchen cabinet doors. Such procedures at this stage might make it easier for the parents, but damage the child because they postpone the confrontation of submitting his will to the will of his parents. The result is an even greater struggle later.

> The points of conflict represent the points of change. Parents actually should welcome these confrontations as opportunities to effect the necessary changes. The sooner these confrontations occur and the more intense they are, the sooner a child can be brought under control. From then on, training can be completed in a much more peaceful atmosphere.[9]

This does not mean a parent should set an environment where everything is negative. A mother may choose to have one cupboard where the child can get pans and play being a cook. He will easily learn to distinguish "his cupboard" from the others.

Of course, the child must be protected from actual danger. All poisons should be kept out of reach. No parent would give sharp scissors to a baby as a playpen toy. No child at any age should be subjected to a test "for which the consequence of failure is too severe for the lesson learned."[10]

In making these distinctions, the wise parent is following the example of his own Father in heaven. "God is faithful, who will not allow you to be tempted beyond what you are able, but with the temptation will also make the way of escape, that you may be able to bear it" (1 Cor 10:13).

The Opportunity of Discipline

Parents should not feel frustrated by occasions when their child is disobedient and needs to be disciplined. This very occasion is an

---

[9]Fugate, *Child Training,* p. 92.

[10]Ibid., p. 85.

opportunity for instruction, an opportunity to teach him the seriousness of disobedience, an opportunity to show him how sin does not pay and how sin will find you out, an opportunity to plant more seeds bringing forth the peaceable fruits of righteousness in a great future harvest. After being disciplined properly, the child is ready to receive instruction. Help him to learn reality sooner rather than later when the lessons will be harder. Turn the failure of the child into a blessing, so that he can receive beauty for ashes and the oil of joy for mourning.

The Opportunity of Injury and Sickness

Western culture has produced the image of the macho man who is unmoved by injury and sickness, and for whom compassion and tenderness are marks of weakness. As fathers live out this image, they are especially prone to shortchange their families. But mothers can also fail if they do not use injury and sickness in the family as opportunities to express love, compassion, and tenderness.

We extol missionaries who risk their lives to minister to those in Third World countries suffering from exotic diseases. We know their ultimate goal is not the total eradication of disease, but the opportunity for *spiritual* ministry. Then we fret over our tasks when a family member comes down with the flu. We should remember the missionary goal rather than wishing sickness could be eliminated so life can get back to normal as soon as possible. The goal is to use these occasions as opportunities for the family to minister to the member who is suffering, transforming sickness into an incident of glory.

One precious memory of my grandmother (who lived with our family) was her reading to me by the hour when I was sick with the measles and unable to read for myself. She could have excused herself by saying she was too tired or too old to keep up such a lengthy effort. But instead she used my sickness as an opportunity for ministry, and for building bridges with her grandson.

My wife Rhoda fondly remembers her mother's care when she was sick as a child. When her stomach was upset and she needed to vomit, Rhoda was not left alone. Her mother was by her side with her cool hand on Rhoda's forehead. Her mother's presence and love is the focal point of Rhoda's memory of those occasions.

Once Rhoda had an infection that reached a danger point with a red streak going up her leg. Her father advised her to soak her foot in hot water all night. Her mother could have excused herself and gone to bed, saying she needed strength for her responsibilities with the other six children the next day. Instead, throughout the night she kept getting up, changing the water when it cooled. By morning the danger was over, but the mother had left a fragrant memory of ministry.

When the children were sick, Rhoda's mother did not leave them isolated from the family in a distant upstairs bedroom. Instead she fixed a place in the family room where they could be near the family.

She did the extra work to harness adversity for bonding the family together.

Benefit From Husband-Wife Differences

Sometimes parents sabotage their family by allowing their own differences to be divisive points of contention. Isaac and Rebecca failed on precisely this point. They allowed their personal preferences to divide loyalties in the family. Ultimately Jacob teamed with his mother to deceive Isaac and get the blessing intended for Esau (Gen 25:28; 27:1-46).

In general, men and women think differently, and exhibit different emotional responses. They have a different set of strengths and weaknesses. These differences exhibit themselves in the child-rearing process. The wise parent will capitalize on his spouse's strength to complement his own weakness. Both spouses must act as partners, helping one another.

God has given the husband qualities to assist him in exercising authority. He will be more likely than his wife to refuse to allow compromise and foolishness. But at times this characteristic tends toward harshness. He must learn from his wife how to be tender and gentle.

God has given the wife special gifts of mercy and tenderness which particularly suit her for the extended task of dealing with young children. But these very gifts tend to produce a laxity toward discipline. This deficiency may result in her ignoring disobedience instead of using discipline to take care of the problem. She needs her husband to help her be consistent, not to berate her for being so soft-hearted. She must consciously value her husband's authority as a benefit, rather than rejecting it as too stern.

These differences make it critical for parents to develop and maintain a unity of spirit. They will not always do things exactly alike, but they both must have the same underlying goals. Each must understand the importance of the other's contribution at their own points of weakness. They must support each other, and learn from each other to become better parents.

In working together, the parents therefore avoid public disagreement over the way a child was handled. Even if an occasion of discipline is harsher than necessary, far greater is the damage sustained by the child who realizes he can use his parents' disagreement to play one off against the other.

Negative humor against the other spouse or against the children is destructive and should be avoided. A woman may jokingly say to her husband, "Oh, I noticed you have been decorating the bedroom with your dirty clothes." Or a husband may comment about his wife's cooking, "She loves to serve burnt offerings." Although we chuckle at these statements, we know in our hearts how much they hurt. We know that instead of building bridges, they build little walls that grow with time. These walls prevent the fullness of open communication and love between parents and children.

Instead, spouses should learn a lesson from the Song of Solomon. Although many of the metaphors portrayed there sound strange to Western ears, they do certainly make a major point. Husbands and wives should deliberately think of creative words to describe their affection for one another. They should tell in graphic terms their appreciation for each other as a unique blessing from God. A husband should tell his wife how she "overwhelms him" (Song of Solomon 6:4-10). A wife should tell her husband why he is more impressive than anyone she knows (Song of Solomon 5:9-16).

Summary

Proper philosophy of parenthood is based on a clear understanding of parental authority. This authority is not earned, but is given by God. Every parent must exercise his authority to teach his children the fundamental lesson of obedience. In such an environment the child can learn to honor his parents, and to experience things that are right as being normal.

By controlling the child first, reasoning with him second, and utilizing natural opportunities for communication, a wholesome relationship is formed between parent and child, providing a basis for smooth transition to adulthood.

Many parents desire to have model children, but do not concern themselves with being model parents. Parents who delight in their children, use the difficulties of life as opportunities, and capitalize on their spouse's strengths to assist in overcoming their own weaknesses, will find a new joy both in being parents and in reaping the results in their children.

Following Father's Slippery Footsteps

8

Godly Fatherhood

Since the husband is to be the leader in the family, the first responsibility for proper parenthood falls upon the father. He must lead the family both by instruction and by example. This kind of leadership maximizes the contribution of his wife in her role as mother.

The task of the father is to nurture his children, teaching them to love and obey God. By observing God as our Father, we as human fathers gain deeper insight into godly fatherhood, and understand more clearly how God expects us to relate to our own children.

Nurture Instead of Provocation

Suppose someone gave a quiz with only one question: What is the most serious deficiency of fathers? A clue to the answer is found in the New Testament admonitions to fathers. Every admonition specifically addressing fathers' responsibility to their children speaks to this problem. There are only two such references, and both warn fathers not to provoke their children. This proves provocation to be the major problem for fathers. "Fathers, do not provoke your children, lest they become discouraged" (Col 3:21). Fathers are likely to exasperate their children to the point of discouragement and bitterness.

How does this happen? It happens when fathers require obedience without sufficient explanation or demonstration. It happens when fathers require obedience, but lack love for the child. It happens when fathers abruptly change the rules to fit their own comfort. It happens when fathers publicly humiliate the child. It happens when fathers avoid dirty work by making the child do it. It happens when fathers force children to do more than they are physically or emotionally capable of doing.

Paul's letter to the Ephesians repeats the warning, and gives a clue for the remedy: "Fathers, do not provoke your children to wrath, but bring them up in the training and admonition of the Lord" (Eph 6:4). The key to avoiding the natural tendency to provoke one's children to wrath is to follow the directives in the latter part of the verse.

The Greek word translated "bring them up" is in the present imperative. It suggests continual action, not merely an impulsive act of the moment. The father's task requires diligent and persistent effort (Deut 6:4-9). Effective fatherhood requires continual diligence in the task of rearing children.

The focus of that rearing involves two things. The first is "training," a translation of the Greek word *paideia*. The active use of this word refers to upbringing, training, and instruction chiefly as attained by discipline and correction.[1] Thus, the father is consistently dealing with the will of the child, when it needs to be corrected for disobedience.

The second element of that rearing is "admonition," a translation of the Greek word *nouthesia*. The father instructs the child, dealing with the mind. This instruction internalizes the reasons for the proper behavior already produced by training. Significantly, disciplinary correction comes first, and prepares the child to receive instruction.

This upbringing is not a result of the father's grand imagination or proud theorizing. Its total basis is "of the Lord." Therefore the focus is on the principles of God's Word, and the internalization of His character. This cannot be taught unless the father is having his own soul washed by the Word. As the earthly father continually disciplines and instructs both himself and his children in God's ways, he avoids the trap of provoking his children to wrath.

God's Perfect Fatherhood

Frequently one hears the comment, "A child gains his concept of God by observing his father." Since God is so often portrayed in Scripture as a father, it is no wonder a child builds a mental image of God according to parameters he sees in his earthly father. Such a prospect is sobering to any father.

It is equally important to consider the metaphor from the opposite direction. Since God is the Father of every believer, His actions toward His children are the perfect model of what fatherhood should be. Careful consideration of the fatherhood of God instructs human fathers regarding their own responsibilities and opportunities. God is the perfect model for fatherhood.

Explained by Jesus

Jesus' instructions on prayer illuminate the fatherhood of God. His disciples were impressed with the meaning and power of their Lord's prayer life, and asked Him to teach them to pray. He began His instruction by giving them an outline of prayer, commonly known as "The Lord's Prayer."

This prayer begins by addressing God as "Father," not as "Sovereign Lord" or "Omnipotent Creator." It is then no surprise that the prayer emphasizes issues particularly relevant to a father-child relationship. Since we are to view God as our Father, His relationship to us in this prayer becomes instructive on how to be good fathers ourselves.

---

[1]Walter Bauer, William F. Arndt, F. Wilbur Gingrich, *A Greek-English Lexicon of the New Testament and Other Early Christian Literature*, 2nd ed. revised and augmented by F. Wilbur Gingrich and Frederick W. Danker (Chicago: The University of Chicago Press, 1979), p. 603.

The foundation of the relationship is filial honor and reverence toward the father ("Hallowed be Your Name"). This corresponds to the command that children honor their parents.

The father has total control and gives directions which the child realizes are in his best interests to obey ("Your will be done"). By happy experience, the child soon learns the father's will is better than his own.

The father is responsible to provide for the physical needs of the child ("Give us day by day our daily bread"). The child does not need to worry about his next meal. The father's provision is ample and sure.

The father forgives a repentant child, not holding a grudge against him ("forgive us our sins"). At the same time he expects the children to forgive one another ("as we also forgive everyone"). The father does not tolerate attitudes of squabbling and quarrelling among the children.

The father takes special measures to protect his family from evil influences ("lead us not into temptation, but deliver us from the evil one"). Part of this protection involves the integrity of his own example. It also includes shielding the children from danger which they are unable to handle, such as the evils of television. It may include something as simple as avoiding making unnecessary purchases on Sunday. Such purchases are not wrong in themselves but can confuse the mind of a young child who is beginning to establish patterns of using Sunday for worship and fellowship and spiritual service.

Those who are strong must bear the infirmities of the weak, instead of pleasing themselves (Rom 15:1). It is the responsibility of fathers to act toward their own children in a way consistent with God's example. "God is faithful, who will not allow you to be tempted beyond what you are able, but with the temptation will also make the way of escape, that you may be able to bear it" (1 Cor 10:13).

Jesus emphasizes the perfection of the Heavenly Father in giving gifts to His children (Lu 11:11-13). Even unbelieving fathers would not give a stone to a son who had requested bread, or a scorpion to a son who had asked for an egg. Although human fathers have been affected by depravity, they would not stoop that low.

God, who is also a Father, will not fail to give the Holy Spirit to those who ask. God gives His children the best gift: spiritual power, not merely things. When earthly fathers imitate the fatherhood of God, they do not focus on providing mere material benefits to their children. Unbelievers can do that. Instead, the supreme goal is to lead their children into spiritual communion with God. Adherence to the patterns established by our Heavenly Father enables us to be effective fathers in leading our children into spiritual blessings.

Sterling Example

God is perfect, and can therefore unreservedly instruct His children to be like Himself. Earthly fathers will not attain absolute perfection, but must walk carefully to provide an appropriate example for their children. Eloquent words fall heedless on a heart seeing the opposite modeled in life.

Sometimes fathers think they can maintain their integrity while associating with ungodly men. Believing they can handle it personally, they create a scenario of disaster for their children. In spite of warnings from God, godly king Jehoshaphat repeatedly embarked on projects with Ahab. These projects were politically and economically advantageous to the kingdom of Judah. Jehoshaphat did not realize what was happening to his own priorities, and cemented the alliance by actually marrying his son into the household of Ahab. As a result, his grandson was killed by a scourge of God named Jehu.

The indulgences of a parent tend to go to excess in the lives of his descendants. David had several wives and kept a few war horses. His son Solomon had a thousand wives and thousands of horses, blatant disobedience to God's command for kings (Deut 17:16-17).

The impact of a father's actions goes far beyond his own lifetime. The sins of fathers tend to be magnified in the lives of their children and grandchildren. Abraham told a half-truth about his wife being his sister. His son Isaac told an outright lie about his wife. His grandson Jacob repeatedly lied to his own blind father. His great-grandsons sold their brother into slavery and used the blood of a goat to make their father believe his favorite son was dead.

Some things not sin in themselves are hindrances to spiritual growth and power. Fathers must be willing to lay these aside lest they become sin in the lives of their children (Heb 12:1). As the picture at the beginning of the chapter illustrates, a father sometimes indulges in things which are not especially dangerous for him, but can result in disaster when his child tries to follow in his steps.

As fathers see their own faults mirrored in the lives of their children, they are given a great incentive to repent and to grow in holiness themselves. This growth makes it easier for their children to walk in the ways of righteousness.

The law of entropy naturally results in a reduction of spirituality in each generation. We as fathers must resist this decline by actively stimulating an ascending spiral of spiritual maturity in the generation to follow. We should help our children learn at age ten some of the hard lessons we learned in our twenties. By helping them learn these things sooner than we did, we provide them a platform for building greater spiritual maturity than our own.

Sternness

In a fallen world, God did not begin His revelation of Himself through a loving Son Who came to die for sinners. God began His revelation through the stern demands enacted in Old Testament history. Thousands of years of such regimen were needed before humanity would be capable of properly receiving the greatest Gift of the Ages.

Humanity needed to understand the grace God revealed through Law. Men would never understand their need for a Savior if they did not first understand their own violation of God's holy laws. The Law emphasized strict expectations of righteousness. "The Law was our tutor to bring us to Christ" (Gal 3:24). Children need the same kind of experience. Many children never experience LAW. They grow up thinking God is negotiable (just like their fathers). They think God is a "buddy" whom they can manipulate for their own short-sighted, immature purposes.

Just as God the Father came first to humanity with the sternness of the Law, earthly fathers must deal with their children first in terms of law. Control comes first, and reasoning comes later as the child develops. An absolute standard of behavior is the only context in which a child can learn obedience. By experiencing law, a child learns to rejoice that his father limits him from being wasted by his own immaturity.

Sometimes fathers feel compelled to furnish an explanation for every instruction they give their children. Explanations are for instructional purposes, not as a weak attempt to cajole a child into obedience. Explanations enable older children to internalize the father's standards as their own. Fathers set the stage for trouble if they teach their children to obey only after receiving a convincing explanation.

God demonstrated the proper procedure when He gave the Law to the nation of Israel (Ex 20). He explained some commands, but not all of them. He began by reminding His people how He had delivered them from Egypt (v 1). In this act He had shown His supremacy over all the gods of the Egyptians. This supremacy was strong rationale for the first commandment: "You shall have no other gods before Me" (v 2). God explained why they should not make any graven image (vv 4-6). He explained why they should not take His name in vain (v 7). He explained why they should remember the Sabbath, and why they should honor their parents (vv 8-12). God gave explanations for commands whose benefits were not so obvious.

God gave no explanation for the next five commandments. Any thinking person could figure out for himself why it is good to prohibit murder, adultery, theft, false witness, and covetousness (vv 13-17). God expects His children to utilize their own good sense on why these laws are necessary and beneficial.

Fathers should learn from this example. Some commands should be given with explanation, some without. The goal is greater than obedience. The goal is developing internal wisdom. Simple commands without explanation help the child to develop his own conclusions about the rewards of doing right.

It also protects the child. His quick obedience to unexplained commands preserves him from destruction on occasions when it is impossible to give an explanation.

A visitor was once chatting with a missionary in Brazil. While they sat on the front porch, the missionary's child was playing in the lawn. Suddenly the missionary shouted to his child, "Lie down on the ground." The child obeyed immediately. "Crawl toward me as fast as you can." Obedience was instant. "Now, get up and run toward me as fast as you can." The visitor wondered if he was getting some bizarre exhibition of sadistic child control. But just as the child reached the father's arms, a large poisonous snake dropped down from a tree onto the grass where the child had been playing.

Even more important, obedience without explanation prepares the child to trust in a loving heavenly Father, obeying and loving Him, even when He gives no explanation for the perplexities of life. Job learned this lesson in the midst of affliction. He would never have learned to trust if God had explained the Satanic source of his troubles at the beginning. In fact, God never gave him an explanation. Job finally realized God was trustworthy, and owed him no explanations (Job 42). Some kinds of growth will never occur if the parents explain the details of their dealings with the children. Fathers who refuse to explain every command are helping their children understand God.

God's instructions are often accompanied by promises instead of reasons. Abraham was told to journey to an unknown country. No reasons, but great promises. "To give reasons would excite discussion; but to give a promise shows that the reason, though hidden, is all-sufficient."[2] The implementation of this principle can alleviate friction in the home. Promise your child that persistent piano practice will bring great rewards, rather than trying to answer all his arguments about how he would rather do something else.

God regularly uses delay to teach His children. The delay in giving Abraham the promised son was a crucial instrument in developing his faith to the point where he could offer his beloved Isaac on the altar (Gen 22). The delay in Mordecai's receiving a reward for saving the life of the king was ultimately the key for saving his own life from the vicious grasp of Haman (Esther 6:3-4).

In our materialistic craze for instant gratification, we forget the value of delay. We deny our children the important lessons and soul purgings associated with the anticipation of a promise yet withheld. In following God our Father, there will be times when we make our children wait, knowing delay will maximize the blessing of our gifts.

God's stern giving of the Law shows He will not be trifled with. The very terminology used in speaking of a relationship with Himself is one of fear ("Abraham feared God"). The motley crowd coming out of Egypt was arrogant in their murmuring against the Almighty. Finally, after ten occasions of belligerently testing God, they were doomed to wandering in the wilderness until they dropped dead (Num 14:22-23).

---

[2]F. B. Meyer, *Abraham* (Fort Washington, PA: Christian Literature Crusade, 1978), p. 16.

The entire wilderness experience is a dramatic object lesson for saints (1 Cor 10:1-13): God is not to be trifled with. Earthly fathers must also make it clear to their children that they will not put up with nonsense. Fathers who have God as their model expect to be obeyed with reverence.

Gentleness

However, strict expectations are not incompatible with gentleness. God is approachable. His mercy and tenderness are evident in the pages of the Old Testament. Immediately before giving the Ten Commandments, God described His care in bringing Israel out of Egypt: "You have seen what I did to the Egyptians, and how I bore you on eagles' wings and brought you to Myself" (Ex 19:4). Earthly fathers need to learn from the tenderness of their Heavenly Father.

Before He instituted the Sabbath, God prepared Israel for Sabbath observance. Operating as an example, He deliberately created the universe in six days with a day of rest following. Before formulating the Sabbath as an institutional regulation, He further prepared the way by giving His people manna on six days only, with none being available on the seventh (Ex 16:23). God's action in feeding the people gave them a practice of faithful Sabbath observance even before they received the explicit command (Ex 20:8-11).

Human fathers could ease the acceptance of their own commands if they would take the trouble to gently introduce new requirements. As fathers grow in maturity, they naturally see areas of home life which need revision. They should consciously prepare the way for their children to gladly accept such revisions.

For example, if a father decides television has been a destructive force in his family, he should prepare the way for its removal. Children could be given a special prize for voluntarily avoiding TV for a lengthy period. As they do this, the natural development of other interests would ease the adjustment when the TV is sold.

Fathers need to remember that children are weak and immature. Some jobs easy for an adult are incredibly difficult for a child. Our Heavenly Father has given us the example: "As a father pities his children, so the Lord pities those who fear Him. For He knows our frame; He remembers that we are dust" (Psa 103:13-14).

Special tenderness is appropriate for dealing with young children. When a nine-month-old is learning to eat solids, do not force him to eat a particular kind of food. Infants have very sensitive taste buds (a protective mechanism provided by God) and a child may often refuse food at this stage that he will enjoy a few months later. Or he may lack appetite because he is in a growth slump. Do not fight against a developmental process which God has designed.

God, who continually invites us to come to Him, is an approachable God. One of the most beautiful portrayals of His approachability as Father is found in the New Testament story of the prodigal son (Lu

15:11-32). The wayward son finally came to his senses and decided to return home in repentance. Because the father had been anxiously awaiting his son's return, he saw him when he was a long way off (v 20). The father forgave the son, and received him back.

As earthly fathers model God, they will be approachable. They will not hold grudges against their children for past mistakes. Their lives will openly invite their children to fellowship, mutual delight, and responsible contribution to the family.

Disciplinarian

In a fallen world, instruction must be coupled with discipline. Many fathers shrink back from this responsibility, as did Eli the priest. His strongly worded reprimand to his sons (1 Sam 2:23-25) was regarded by God as failure to rebuke (1 Sam 3:13). God's own example proves "rebuke" is more than mere verbal remonstration, and includes severe action (Ezek 25:17).

God hates sin, and disciplines it severely. Many fathers are poor disciplinarians because they have an inadequate view of the seriousness of sin. A proper view of sin demands stern discipline.

At the same time, one who models God as a father will deal differently with a repentant, responsive child than with one who is resistant and rebellious (Psa 103:15-18).

Sometimes a child needs to be disciplined for irresponsible or careless behavior. It is very easy for a child to think he can commit evil "the first time" and go unpunished. Sometimes he may use legalistic maneuvering to avoid doing what is right. It is not merely a question of whether he knew a certain activity was wrong. It is also a question of whether he had the ability to know truth, but didn't bother to find out. Ignorance of the speed limit does not cancel the traffic violation.

Jesus was very pointed regarding our responsibility before God:

> That servant who knew his master's will, and did not prepare himself or do according to his will, shall be beaten with many stripes. But he who did not know, yet committed things worthy of stripes, shall be beaten with few (Lu 12:47-48).

Children must be held accountable for responsible behavior even if they have been given no explicit commands about a specific detail. No child should get by with doing cartwheels during a funeral just because his parents have never explicitly forbidden it.

One spring evening, we barbecued some chicken. The children filled their plates with food at the table and then went outside to eat. A pea accidentally fell off the three-year-old's plate. The oldest child told her not to eat it because it was now dirty (good advice), but throw it at Roland instead (bad advice).

The five-year-old thought this was a great idea. She knew better than throwing away good food. But if she could make the peas fall off her plate, they would become inedible. Dirty peas would make excellent ammunition. When this legalistic scheme was brought to my attention, I rebuked her irresponsible behavior (she knew better than wasting food). The rebuke included her doing without the dessert which the rest of us enjoyed.

Such chastening rivets a child's attention onto his personal responsibility for knowing the truth and appropriating it in life. It helps him have a proper understanding of a God who holds men responsible for willful ignorance. It becomes a platform for warning him against the error of Balaam (Rev 2:14) who, while not explicitly disobeying God, legalistically maneuvered to get his own way and reaped disaster (Josh 13:22).

God is no sadist who delights in punishment. His heart yearns for the wayward. "How can I give you up, Ephraim? How can I hand you over, Israel? How can I make you like Admah? How can I set you like Zeboiim? My heart churns within Me; My sympathy is stirred" (Hos 11:8). Admah and Zeboiim were companion cities to Sodom and Gomorrah. God knew Israel needed judgment, but it pained His heart to give it. Earthly fathers should have the same kind of feelings: moved by the anguish of discipline, and yet determined to do what is best for their child.

Although God is a consuming fire (Deut 4:24) and promises judgment for disobedience, His judgments are not an end in themselves, but are designed to bring His people in repentance back to fellowship with Him.

> When you are in distress, and all these things come upon you in the latter days, when you turn to the Lord your God and obey His voice (for the Lord your God is a merciful God), He will not forsake you nor destroy you, nor forget the covenant of your fathers which He swore to them (Deut 4:30-31).

Earthly fathers must model God's intent in discipline: bring the erring one back to a full and fruitful relationship. Discipline is for mercy's sake.

God is our example as a disciplinarian. He led His children through the difficult wilderness experience to humble them, and to make them know in their hearts that God was chastening them like a father chastens his son (Deut 8:2-5). The benefits of God's chastening are described in Hebrews 12, and become a model on how earthly fathers should view the disciplinary process. A full discussion of that passage will come later in the chapter on discipline.

Summary

Certainly fatherhood is a demanding task. It is a task requiring continual diligence, effort, and personal soul-searching. It requires persistence in discipline and time for instruction.

The example of God our Father clarifies the dimensions and parameters of the task. From Him we learn how to be stern and yet gentle, how to get children to appreciate being restricted for their own good, and how to utilize the situations of life as opportunities for building character.

Motherhood Accessing Supernatural Power

9

Godly Motherhood

Today the role of motherhood is under attack. The business world beckons with the promise of status and high pay. Many husbands want their wives to work to lighten the burden of providing extravagance rather than necessities. Even the church adds to the pressure, believing "ministry to other people" is ultimately more significant in God's kingdom than "just being a housewife."

These attitudes are the exact opposite of the message presented in God's Word. Motherhood is a noble and highly desirable occupation. Great women of faith preferred motherhood ahead of other ministries. The examples in Biblical history are reinforced by explicit statements in the New Testament: motherhood is a significant and strategic ministry.

Foundation For Motherhood

The foundation text for motherhood is found in the second chapter of Paul's letter to Titus. As is typical in his letters, he gives direction to the various segments of society found in the church: older men, younger men, older women, younger women, servants. As he gives this instruction he naturally addresses those areas where each group is most likely to be deficient. These areas demand extra diligence to meet God's standards of holiness.

Based on Love

The depravity enveloping humanity at the Fall affected every area of life, including the emotions. The Biblical admonitions regarding love prove that proper love is not automatic. It must be taught. Unaided by instruction from God, all humans fail, even in love.

Therefore, Paul directs the older women to give special instruction to younger women regarding love: "Admonish the young women to love their husbands, to love their children, to be discreet, chaste, homemakers, good, obedient to their own husbands, that the word of God may not be blasphemed" (Tit 2:4,5).

Love is the foundation of a mother's role in the home. The construction of the Greek text (*philandrous* and *philoteknous*) proves she is to be a husband-lover and a child-lover. This is not speaking of mere momentary acts of kindness or service. This is speaking of an attitude which is the fountain-head for everything else she does.

She is devoted first of all to her husband. She desires his best at all times. Her loyalty is so steadfast that he can trust her to be an asset in every circumstance (Prov 31:11). A wife who is truly a husband-lover will delight in catering to his wishes, finding it not a burden, but a joy. She does not neglect her husband in preference to her children. Instead, her love for him becomes the foundation for properly loving her children. His strengths will complement her weaknesses so she can love them properly.

Secondly, she is devoted to her children. She views them as a precious treasure, a momentary trust which she can mold for God. She does not view them as a hindrance to a career. *They are her career.* Just as Jesus spent His time on earth molding the lives of a few men, she pours the fragrance of her life into her children, knowing she is investing in eternity. No sacrifice is too great if it enables her to advance God's kingdom by conforming the character of a child into the likeness of Christ.

Being a mother is not "just being home with the kids." It is a glorious opportunity, sanctified by Jesus' coming into the world "made of a woman," not of a man (Gal 4:4). In a sense, every mother can be like Mary. As she welcomes her little child, she is receiving Jesus. Christ makes the point emphatic: "Whoever receives one of these little children in My name receives Me; and whoever receives Me, receives not Me but Him who sent Me" (Mark 9:37; cf Matt 18:5; Luke 9:48). A mother's attitude toward her children is an accurate measure of her attitude toward Christ. She who does not wish to "waste her talents" bringing up children is exhibiting her disdain for Jesus Himself. Jesus counts devoted service to young children as service to Him personally (cf Matt 25:40,45).

Focused on the Home

A godly woman who centers her affection on her husband and children has no desire to go outside the home in order to create a career for herself. Her love helps her to be discreet and chaste (Tit 2:5), doing only those things which would be a crown of glory to her husband and family (Prov 12:4). Her supreme joy is in being a homemaker, fulfilling God's design and command for married women.

In Titus 2:5, the word translated "homemakers" is *oikourgous*. It is translated by the NIV as "busy at home." Literally, the word means "house workers." God commands women to work at home. No appeal to examples from Scripture of women doing outside work will suffice to negate an explicit command of God. Although the Scriptures describe David as a man after God's own heart (1 Sam 13:14; Acts 13:22), no one should appeal to his conduct regarding Bathsheba and Uriah in order to justify adultery and murder. Even righteous men behaved very wickedly at times.

By obeying God's design, it is possible for the wife and mother to be good as defined by God's standards. She then finds pleasure in obeying her husband, and turns a deaf ear to the raucous cries of modern feminists. She has no interest in exchanging her birthright of holy influence in the lives of her children for the self-centered opportunities of "ministry" offered by the world. She demonstrates God's pattern for the Christian mother. She knows her life is not just "her own business," but is intimately related to the reputation of God.

Failure to follow God's pattern has a broad effect in our society which has rejected God's standard for the role of women. A Christian woman who refuses to obey God's direction destroys her opportunity to demonstrate to the world the superiority of God's Word to any philosophy feminists could devise. Her family will never attain the power and glory that would have been possible through obedience. She has squandered a dramatic testimony proving God's ways as best. As a result, society maligns the Scriptures as being old-fashioned and out of date. God's Word is blasphemed on her account (Tit 2:5).

A woman who follows God's commandments for her own life gains opportunities to teach younger women how to excel with her. One of her greatest privileges is in teaching her own daughters. Her example and her words reinforce each other in a powerful demonstration of how to be a good wife and mother.

Marriage Means Motherhood

Popular contemporary philosophy gives the impression that motherhood is an optional matter, left to the personal preferences of a husband and wife. However, Paul's message to the church specifies different terms. Successful motherhood is the first measure of whether a widow has been faithful enough in good works to merit church support in her latter years (1 Tim 5:10).

Paul commands the younger widows to "marry, bear children, manage the house" (1 Tim 5:14). He commands the older women to teach the younger women to be "husband-lovers" and "child-lovers" (Tit 2:4). The decision of whether or not to have children is not an option for the Christian wife. If she does not desire to work at home and have children, then she should not marry.

Children are precious gifts from God. It is a mother's personal responsibility to care for them, bringing them up, diligently performing every good work, managing her household faithfully. The godly woman refuses the temptation to pawn her children off to a baby-sitter so she can squander her efforts in something else.

One of the reasons Paul gives for not allowing women to be teachers in the church assembly is the fact of Eve's deception in the Garden of Eden (1 Tim 2:11-15). Her failure shows that in general, women are more susceptible to deception than men. The conduct of Eve at the dawn of history has left a reproach on women.

However, God has made special provision for women to overcome the stigma of Eve's failure in the Garden: by bearing children. A woman's reproach will be lifted as she bears children, and then properly trains them so they choose a life of steadfast righteousness. "*She* will be saved in child-bearing if *they* [the children] continue in faith, love, and holiness, with self control" (1 Tim 2:15).[1] The pronoun shift to plural in the middle of the verse is the key to understanding an otherwise obscure text. The woman's role as a teacher in the home is God's method for counteracting woman's failure at the Forbidden Tree.

Mothers need to hear an important comment by John Calvin regarding this role in God's program:

> When a woman . . . submits to the condition which God has assigned to her, and does not refuse to endure the pains, or rather the fearful anguish, of parturition, or anxiety about her offspring, or anything else that belongs to her duty, God values this obedience more highly than if, in some other manner, she made a great display of heroic virtues, while she refused to obey the calling of God.[2]

Motherhood Hall of Fame

Abraham's wife Sarah was a woman who heeded her high calling. Her life is a pattern of proper submission to a husband (1 Pet 3:5-6). Although she was a wealthy woman, she worked within the tent, preparing with her own hands the meal for the heavenly guests (Gen 18:5-9).

More than anything else, she desired to participate in God's program by being a mother. When that day finally arrived, she invested her life in her child. She did not allow the availability of servants to prevent her from personally spending her time to train Isaac. She did not use her wealth to have someone else raise him. She was so devoted to this task that when she died, it took Isaac three years to get over the fact of her death.[3]

Sometimes as people survey the evils of our present society, they conclude it is best to avoid bringing children into such a world. They have forgotten the example of Jochebed, a slave woman during some of the darkest days of Israelite history. She lived in Egypt, under the oppressive reign of a Pharaoh who had ordered every Hebrew male baby to be thrown into the Nile.

Jochebed could have decided it was unwise, and even unspiritual to have children in such times. She did no such thing. She and her husband acted in faith, not afraid of the king's commandment (Heb 11:23). By faith, she deliberately placed her infant in a basket in the river at the very spot where she knew the princess would come for

---

[1]This pronoun shift has been obscured by some translations (NASB, NIV) in their attempt to produce a more "readable" version. The KJV and NKJV give a more accurate rendering of this Greek text.

[2]John Calvin, *Commentaries on the First Epistle to Timothy,* trans. Wm. Pringle (Grand Rapids: Baker Book House, 1979), p. 71.

[3]Sarah was ninety years old when Isaac was born (Gen 17:17; 21:5). She died at age 127 (Gen 23:1) when Isaac would have been 37. The Scriptures note specifically that when at age 40 Isaac married Rebecca, he was finally comforted concerning his mother's death (Gen 24:67; 25:20).

religious ceremonial bathing. By faith, she trusted in God to intervene in the heart of that princess (Ex 2:1-10).

She relinquished the formal rights of motherhood to the aristocratic lady of the court, and was willing to be merely the nurse of her own son. In the short time she had with Moses, she so infused his soul with the glory of God that when he became of age he made an astounding decision. After forty years of training in all of Egyptian wisdom and power and glory, he "refused to be called the son of Pharaoh's daughter, *choosing* rather to *suffer affliction* with the people of God than to enjoy the passing pleasures of sin, esteeming the *reproach* of Christ greater riches than the treasures in Egypt" (Heb 11:24-26).

Hannah could have poured her life into other ministries. Her husband already had one wife whom God had blessed with children. She could have presumed God was calling her to assist the poor, or to a more extensive ministry of prayer. Instead, she believed her greatest contribution would be in molding a child for God.

She was so committed to the task of spiritual investment that she vowed to give her son wholly to the work of the Lord. She was not desiring a son for mere selfish purposes, one she could keep at home for the delight of his childish presence. She wanted the opportunity to direct a son into dedicated service for God. When her son was born, she forfeited her usual trip to the Tabernacle in order to care for him as an infant (1 Sam 1:22-23).

Her teaching had to be done early. This teaching was so thorough that it preserved her son even in Eli's house. The old priest had failed in training his own sons. They were immoral and blatant in their defiance of God. Through it all, Samuel became God's channel, the greatest of the Israelite judges.

The writer of the book of Chronicles often specifies the mothers of Judah's kings. These women had great influence. If a son was wicked, he led the nation away from God. If he was good, he destroyed idolatry and turned the people back to Jehovah. In a sense, these women had a greater impact on immediate national life than did the prophets whose message often went unheeded.

These examples must not be belittled as merely the product of a culture having a bizarre focus on the value of children. Instead, they contrast with women of our own culture who lack natural affection, and who look for fulfillment in ways deliberately disobedient to God's commandments.

In the New Testament, the faithfulness of Eunice and her own mother Lois were important ingredients in Timothy's walk of faith (2 Tim 1:5), even though Timothy's father was a Greek (Acts 16:1,3). Eunice's success illustrates how the wife of an unbelieving husband still has a holy influence in the lives of her children (1 Cor 7:14). The teaching Timothy received from the Scriptures as a small child formed the basis for his lifelong ministry in association with the Apostle Paul.

His later years were a continuation of what he learned at his mother's knee.

Paul exhorted him to keep on following the direction begun for him by his mother years earlier. Shortly before his death, Paul sent his final message to Timothy. He did not appeal to the fellowship they had shared, or even to the theological principles Timothy had learned in working with the master missionary. Instead, Paul pointed Timothy back to what his mother had taught. The ministry of his mother in the Word was an even stronger foundation for Timothy than personal exhortation from Paul. This Word would equip Timothy for every good work (2 Tim 3:14-17). Who said mothers do not have an important ministry?

Maximize Early Childhood

The success of Jochebed and Hannah gives dramatic testimony to the strategic value of early childhood. These mothers had only a few short years with their sons. Those sons never forgot what their mothers carefully and diligently taught. That teaching remained more appealing than the enticements of a pagan court or the temptations of a licentious priesthood.

Any mother who "is bored at home with her toddlers" is squandering her opportunities and ignoring her calling. Mothers must clear their minds from the fog that views toddlers as only needing physical care and affectionate companionship. A young child's mind is open and receptive to anything it receives. Only a mother is able to maximize the opportunity of filling this young mind with a love for God. Many mothers despise their spiritual birthright of holy influence in the lives of their children, and sell it for a paltry paycheck. What an unspeakable tragedy! Satan is delighted to fill the vacuum and reap the rewards for himself.

Teach your children God's Word. This can be done from the time of birth. A newborn baby needs his diaper changed ten times per day. Use diaper changing as an opportunity to recite Scripture to him. An infant does not care what his mother says, as long as she says it in a sweet voice. She should take this opportunity to recite Psalm 23. If she cannot recite it, she should type it on a piece of paper and read it while changing the diaper. The child delights in hearing his mother and rivets his attention on her. By the time he begins to talk, he has heard the twenty-third Psalm over and over. His mother can deliberately omit key words as she recites, and she will hear a sweet childish voice fill them in. The child has memorized a passage of Scripture before he can talk.

As he grows in ability to talk, Bible memory can become an enjoyable repetition of familiar phrases. A two-year old can memorize entire chapters. He learns very quickly, but also forgets quickly. Keep reviewing old passages, even while learning new ones.

Small children (before age two) need pictures or visual help in learning Bible stories. Keep the stories short and to the point. Present details in an interesting way. Too often children are taught to despise the Bible because it has been presented in such a dull fashion. In addition to being God's Word, the stories in the Bible are inherently just as interesting as any other story.

When a child is old enough to enjoy a story, begin having a regular personal devotional time with him. Use this time to teach him Bible stories. The goal is two-fold: 1) impart spiritual truth, and 2) establish a pattern of personal Bible study.

Teach your children good music. Developing good taste in music begins long before a child can talk. Make sure all music in the home is of good quality. Christian music should have significant spiritual lyrics, flowing melody, and appropriate harmony. Many parents develop bad musical appetites in their children by having them listen to "Christian" music which is merely new lyrics for music which in itself is fundamentally unwholesome.

Many people are unaware of some of the pitfalls in the contemporary music scene. Frequently even the lyrics themselves are devoid of much spiritual content. There is a vast difference between an often repeated sentimental phrase about "Jesus' love," and the insightful meaning of Christ's love so clearly shown in Isaac Watts' great hymn, "When I Survey the Wondrous Cross."

A second pitfall is the mistaken notion that only the words matter. Music has a power of its own, even without words. David's playing on his harp was so powerful it drove away the evil spirit troubling Saul (1 Sam 16:14-23). When the prophet Elisha needed to hear a word from the Lord in the midst of very disturbing circumstances, he called for a minstrel to play so his spirit could be calmed to receive God's message (2 Kings 3:14-15). These passages clearly show positive effects of good music. Bad music is equally powerful in the wrong direction.

Godly music is an important ingredient in a spiritual home atmosphere. Many times when young children are fussy and discontented, they can be calmed merely by playing a recording of good, solid hymns of the faith. The music calms the soul, and the lyrics guide the heart.

Our children have learned to love great hymns, magnificent choral arrangements, and classical masterpieces. This love is not the result of lecture sessions on the subject, but is based on extensive exposure to high quality music. When they hear shallow vocalizations whining above a heavy rock beat, it sounds cheap and disgusting. Children who have tasted a full-course Thanksgiving dinner are not impressed by moldy beans and soggy crackers.

Sing children's songs to young children. The repetition helps them learn to "carry a tune." Choose lyrics teaching important spiritual content. One of the songbooks we find most useful for our younger children is *Our Hymns of Praise*.[4] It has 150 pages of songs, many of which are great hymns of faith particularly relevant to children. Tasteful art adds to the grace and appeal of the book.

When Rachelle was small, she would page through this songbook while my wife Rhoda was working in the kitchen. Rhoda sang the songs while she prepared supper. This entertained the child and instructed her at the same time. Rachelle enjoyed this so much that our first copy of the book wore out. As a two-year old, she knew which song should be sung on which page—and objected if Rhoda made a substitution.

A mother's prayers constitute an important part of her ministry to her young children. My wife has found it very helpful to keep a prayer notebook.[5] She records the children's strengths, their weaknesses, their fears, their interests. She also records what she plans to do about those things. With eight children, this approach helps her guide what is happening in the family. Daily she prays for all of the children as a group. She prays for one child individually each day. During this time of prayer she experiences special illumination and insight from God on how to deal with that child.

Summary

It is so easy to become confused by the philosophies swirling around us. The solution is to immerse ourselves in the Scriptures, saturating our minds with what God has said, teaching ourselves to think like He thinks.

God shows us motherhood in its true light, both from the examples of godly women of old, and from the Spirit-inspired teaching of the Apostle Paul. The Incarnation of our Lord is God's supreme statement on the value of motherhood.

Love for husband and children is the foundation for godly motherhood, providing the basis for a woman to be a discreet and chaste worker at home, making her lifestyle and ministry an effective demonstration of the power and relevance of God's Word.

God designed marriage to include children. The importance of this ministry is explicitly taught in the New Testament, and is abundantly illustrated in the examples of women in Scripture. Every mother should maximize the early childhood years as an opportunity to mold great saints for God.

---

[4]J. Mark Stauffer, editor, Illus. by Esther Rose Graber, *Our Hymns of Praise* (Scottdale, PA: Herald Press, 1958).

[5]Jean Fleming, *A Mother's Heart* (Colorado Springs: Navpress, 1982), pp. 110-116.

Training Your Child

O fill me with Thy fullness, Lord,
   Until my very heart o'erflow;
In kindling thought and glowing word,
   Thy love to tell, Thy praise to show.

O teach me, Lord, that I may teach
   The precious things Thou dost impart;
And wing my words that they may reach
   The hidden depths of many a heart.

O grant enabling grace to me,
   That I may speak with soothing power
A word in season, as from Thee,
   To weary ones in needful hour.

—Frances Ridley Havergal, 1872

"You Shall Sharpen God's Word to Your Children"

10

Spiritual Training

Someone has said, "If you want your ideas to last for years, write them on paper. If you want them to last for decades, write them on a brick. If you want them to last for centuries, write them in stone. If you want them to last forever, write them on the heart of a child."

Every parent is privileged to mold a life that will live forever. This life will be greatly affected by the kind of teaching received from the parent. God could have commissioned angels to provide perfect instruction and care for children. Instead, He chose fallible human parents, using this arrangement to teach the parents about Himself while they instruct their child.

Effective training must be undergirded by example. This is true for two reasons. First, anyone who fails to live by the truth he is attempting to teach will in the process become less effective in the verbal articulation of that truth. Likely this will gradually degenerate into no teaching at all. God reminded the Israelites of this fact before they entered Canaan:

> Only take heed to yourself, and diligently keep yourself, lest you forget the things your eyes have seen, and lest they depart from your heart all the days of your life. And teach them to your children and your grandchildren (Deut 4:9).

There is a second reason why verbal instruction must be accompanied by example. If there is a discrepancy between the two, the child will ignore the teaching and follow the bad example denying it. The life of the parent hovers over his instructions and thunders so loudly that the child becomes deaf to what his parent is saying.

Parental example undergirds spiritual training, but is not a substitute for it. Example alone is insufficient to get the job done (1 Kings 1:6). Example must be accompanied by diligent instruction.

This instruction is not just five minutes a day to keep the Devil away. It is the consistent and deliberate outpouring of the lives of parents totally dedicated to God. Such parents maximize the natural opportunities to communicate with their children. They continually plant seeds of truth and pray for a great spiritual harvest.

God Is the Center of the Family

The life of the effective spiritual parent is not a dichotomy, with some parts being "spiritual" and other parts being "secular." Every activity is ultimately rooted in allegiance to God and His Word.

Therefore, the total family experience becomes a platform for spiritual instruction, and is superior to anything a church or school could provide.

Deuteronomy 6:4-9 teaches parents how to instruct their children. "Hear, O Israel: The Lord our God, the Lord is one!" This fourth verse introduces the details with a command to heed God's instructions, and includes a reminder of why God is worth listening to.

The pagans had developed a galaxy of gods to handle the uncertainties of life. They had a god of the sea, a god of the dry land, a god of the storm, a god of fire, a god of fertility. Prosperity was possible only by keeping all these gods happy. God is a wonderful contrast to this pantheon of pagan deities. He is holy and good. He is unique, and controls everything. Allegiance to Him is sufficient for success. He is worthy of obedience. We are to "hear" in the sense of "obey."

The commands following the imperative to hear are consequences of that hearing.[1] The shifts in possessive pronouns between verses four and five amplify the point. By truly taking the Lord *our* God to be the Lord *your* God, family life will exhibit the following characteristics.

Godward Affection

This unique, powerful, loving, and holy God is worthy of all affection and allegiance. "You shall love the Lord your God with all your heart" (v 5a). Ask yourself: Is God really the central point of my affection? Do I delight in His presence more than anything else? Would I rather talk to God, or do I prefer to converse with my wife, husband, or friend? Do I love God, or do I love things, reputation, or career? What do my children see as the focal point of my affections?

You shall love the Lord your God . . . with all your soul" (v 5b). Ask yourself: Do the characteristics of my personality show influence of being with God? Are my personality traits becoming more and more Godlike? Do my children and spouse regard me as godly?

"You shall love the Lord your God . . . with all your might" (v 5c). Ask yourself: Am I content with mediocre spirituality, or am I determined to serve God with every ounce of my strength? Can I honestly say that my entire life is an expression of love to God? Have the members of my body truly been made instruments of righteousness?

God is not interested in only Sabbath religion. He is not impressed with people who merely go in and out of church on Sunday. God must be the center of every aspect of life. The rhetorical sequence in this verse emphasizes the comprehensive nature of the love required. Repeated use of the word "all" reinforces the idea of total loyalty. When God is the center of every affection, life conforms to all of Scripture. Undivided love for God is the foundation for building an effective family.

---

[1]The grammarians call these "consequential imperatives." For the grammatical details compare the Hebrew text with Thomas O. Lambdin, *Introduction to Biblical Hebrew* (New York: Charles Scribner's Sons, 1971), p. 119.

Godward Thoughts

It is impossible not to think about what we love the most. Loving God with all our heart, soul, and strength causes our thoughts to be centered on Him and His Word. "And these words which I command you today shall be in your heart" (v 6).

The source of meditation is God's Word ("these words"), not our own philosophy or self-ascribed brilliance, not even what other people say about the Scriptures. The message getting so much attention is not some old outmoded dogma. It is a timeless message from God Himself, and commands immediate attention ("which I am commanding you today"). The Psalmist exclaims in Psalm 119:97, "Oh, how I love Your Law! It is my meditation all the day." He becomes wiser than his enemies, has more insight than his teachers, and gains better understanding than ancient sages because he has internalized and obeyed God's wisdom (Psa 119:98-100).

The action of meditation is personal ("in your heart"). Lip service to the message is not enough. These words must be incorporated into life. Personal study of the Word is important, but is worthless unless obedience follows. Only when the Word is obeyed does it really reside in the heart. The Word of God in the heart permeates the character, and makes it different from what the natural mind would devise. The result: transformation into the likeness of Christ.

Godward Conversation

Many people do not love God with all their heart. They do not love Him with all their soul, and with all their strength. They do not let His Word permeate their character. Therefore they have difficulty teaching their children.

When the Word of God is the focal point of our thoughts, the teaching of God's message to our children becomes the natural outpouring of our thought-life. This teaching is not a casual matter, but is intensive and deliberate. "You shall teach them diligently to your children, and shall talk of them when you sit in your house, when you walk by the way, when you lie down, and when you rise up" (v 7). Verse seven is a unit. There is no time when the parent is "on vacation" from teaching.

Formal Instruction (Family Altar)

"You shall teach them diligently to your children" (v 7). Every family must have regular times of formal instruction for the children, where the Word of God is read, discussed, and applied to life. Illustrate the concepts by describing how you have applied God's principles to situations in your own life. Teach them the Word through the message of the great hymns of the faith. Use music to rivet God's message into the memory. Sing "children's songs"—young children enjoy it even if they are too little to help sing.

In our household, the curriculum for family devotions is the Scriptures. Sometimes I tell a Bible story. More often, we read from the Scriptures, and occasionally we recite Scripture. Sometimes we quote a passage in unison. At other times, each person recites verses of his own choosing and describes why he has found them especially meaningful.

Family devotions is a great opportunity for children to learn how to read the Scriptures with good oral expression. Avoid the fragmentation of both content and expression that comes from having each child read only one verse at a time. When our three oldest children were thirteen, eleven, and nine years old, I divided the chapter into approximate thirds, and gave a section to each of them. I saved a few verses for the six-year old to give her an opportunity without being unduly tedious.

Our children also enjoy dramatic reading. One child reads the narrative, while each of the others is assigned the speeches of one or more characters in the story. This approach adds interest as we read through the chapter.

For one of our young children the book of Job was her favorite book of the Bible. Part of the reason for this was because we had gone through the book in family devotions, helping the children understand the content and meaning of the debates. After all, these debates reveal the central themes and message of the book, while the narrative at the beginning and end provides the setting. Children thoroughly enjoy graphic metaphorical descriptions, and the book of Job is full of them. Our children especially liked Job 10:10, "Did You not pour me out like milk, and curdle me like cheese?"

Our children enjoy devotions most when I give them an assignment ahead of time. I tell them what to study in the next chapter. Sometimes it is a written assignment (limited to those at least eight years old). We all enjoyed their compositions when I told them to write a short story having as its historical context the terrible events predicted in Revelation 9.

Frequently I will ask them to draw a picture of something in the chapter. This requires them to study the chapter, consider its details, and then draw something appropriate. Giving assignments helps them prepare. It gets them involved in the passage. They learn to study the Bible, and to share their insights. They come to family devotions with something to contribute.

For many months, our family devotions centered on the history of Israel. We began reading in Kings. Whenever we came to the time of one of the writing prophets, we interrupted the study of Kings, and read the message of the prophet. For example, according to 2 Kings 14:25, Jonah prophesied during the reign of Jeroboam II. Hosea and Amos also ministered during the same time (Hos 1:1; Amos 1:1). Therefore, we read from these prophetic books, and found out what God thought about a situation outwardly prosperous and wonderful, but inwardly rotten. This provided a significant framework for Biblical chronology, an enhanced understanding of spiritual perspectives, and a deeper awareness of God's sovereignty in history.

Sometimes people think the Old Testament is dull, especially the prophets. In reality, prophetic utterances are fascinating messages to people, and therefore relevant for our instruction. Here is a sample of some of the assignments I have given the children. These assignments are geared toward the older children, but little ones learn amazing things by being exposed to the material (Rhoda also takes time for additional special devotions with the children under seven years old, gearing it more directly to their level).

Amos 8. What were the Israelite merchants like in Amos' time? How severely does God punish sin?

Amos 9. What metaphors in this chapter show it is impossible to escape God's judgments? Find all the places in the chapter showing God's mercy.

Hosea 1. How will God treat the Northern Kingdom compared to the Southern Kingdom? What amazing thing did God have Hosea do?

Hosea 2. What was Israel like in Hosea's time? What acts of judgment and acts of mercy will God perform?

Hosea 3, 4, 5. Look for graphic language.

Hosea 7. Explain all the metaphors about cooking and about birds (Tell what these verbal pictures convey to us).

Hosea 10. Find all the verses about ploughing in this chapter. Also find a place in the Bible where verse 8 is quoted.

Hosea 12. What can you learn about Jacob's life from this chapter?

Isaiah 5. Find the many metaphors and similes in this chapter, and explain them. What in this chapter is difficult for Calvinism?

Isaiah 7. What do you think? Was King Ahaz good or bad?

Isaiah 8. Draw a picture.

Isaiah 14. Is Lucifer Satan or the king of Babylon? Give reasons to support your view.

Isaiah 23,24. God is punishing the nations in these chapters. What do you think is the worst punishment He is giving?

Isaiah 58. What are the characteristics of true worship? of false worship?

Jeremiah 18. What lessons can we learn from the story of the potter and the clay?

Jeremiah 26. Draw a picture.

2 Kings 18. What did Hezekiah destroy? Should he have destroyed it? What arguments could people have used against his destroying it?

Bible study together as a family should not be a dreary spoonful of bad-tasting medicine. It should be a time of fellowship and fun. When Rachelle was twelve years old, she wrote a description of some of our times together in family devotions.

[Recently] family devotions was especially enjoyable. I do not know why, but we were just delighted with the observations made on the text and enjoyed our passage to the full. And then we even had a humorous incident at the end. Part of our assignment had been to find something strange in our next chapter—Isaiah 66. The strange thing is that a woman had a baby before her pain came. Oh yes, and the other part of the assignment was to explain what the strange thing meant.

Get a Bible and turn it to Isaiah 66 and you'll enjoy this story a lot more, I'm pretty sure.

When Roland's turn came to tell the results of what he did on his assignment, he began quite cheerfully, "All right. The strange thing in this chapter was that the woman had a baby before she got pregnant!"

The whole family erupted in laughter, and it was a long time before anyone could stop.

"No!" said Father, even as he laughed. "WHERE did you get THAT idea, Roland?"

But it says so right here," said Roland innocently. "Look! It says that she gave birth before she travailed!"

"Travailed, Roland," said Renee, "means to have labor pains."

"Oh," said Roland. "Anyhow, I'm not done. The other strange thing didn't seem strange to me, but this verse says that it is strange. It says that the lady had a baby boy. And then it says, 'Who has heard of such a thing?' Whoever heard of someone having a baby boy? That seems strange. . ."

He was interrupted by a still greater surge of laughter. "No, no!" exclaimed someone. "The 'who has heard of such a thing' refers back to the statement that before she travailed, she gave birth. The part of her having a baby boy is merely a detail of interest."

"Oh," said Roland again.

Oh, dear! The story doesn't sound one-fourth as funny as it really was! Oh, well. Just try to imagine how the scene must have looked, and try to hear the different voices talking aloud. Take my word for it: We could hardly stop laughing.

The next evening something else happened that was somewhat humorous. We were back in 2 Kings again, where we had left off to trace Isaiah's ministry more closely. So anyhow, we were ready for chapter 21, and the assignment was to draw a picture of something in the chapter.

Roland chose to draw King Amon's death. He made a careful, colorful picture.

Well, on the evenings when the assignment has been to draw a picture of something in the chapter, we all go to Father, from youngest to oldest, show him our pictures, and explain them.

Roland's picture looked somewhat like this [her journal included a sketch]:

"What's that thing that the assassin is standing on?" questioned Father, very much interested.

"Well," replied Roland, "that man couldn't come in front of the king's throne, or the king would see him. So he had to come in back. But he couldn't reach the king with the knife, over the top of the throne. So he got a box and stood on it."

Again everyone laughed heartily.

"Now Roland," said Father, "if a man tried to enter a palace with a knife and box under his belt, do you think the guards would have let him in?"

"But," Roland protested, "it says that his servants conspired against him, so I thought that meant that the guards conspired, too. His guards were his servants, weren't they?"

"Possibly," Father granted.

That picture was funny![2]

All children love stories. Satisfy their interest by telling Bible stories replete with accurate detail. This will make the stories more interesting and will also increase your own insight into the text. Capitalize on your children's delight in hearing the same stories over

---

[2]Rachelle's Journal, February 10, 1988.

and over again. Make your coverage of Biblical history so complete that by the time your children are ten years old they will instantly recognize any Bible story you begin to tell. Make a game by telling stories without revealing the names, and having the children see how soon they can identify the characters.

Before long, this will become too easy for the older ones. Creatively disguise the story while still being faithful to the details. My children loved it when I told a familiar story in this fashion. "Once there was a man in a dark room. He looked in front of him, and saw a pair of eyes staring back. He looked to the left, and saw eyes staring. He looked to the right and saw eyes. He looked behind him and saw eyes. He stayed in that room all night, and all night there were eyes looking at him. The next morning he heard a voice crying out, 'Is your God able to save you from those things with eyes?' "

Bible stories are the verbal equivalent of a picture book. They portray by vivid action how sin fractures relationships with God and with other people. They portray the costliness of sin, and the hopelessness apart from repentance. They portray the fragrance of holiness, and the power of prayer. Use these pictures to create on the walls of those little minds scenes that can never be removed. Explain the principles illustrated by these pictures.

A child's mind is open and ready to absorb whatever the parents place before it. Fill that mind with God's Word. Childhood is prime time for Bible memory. Three- and four-year-olds can memorize entire chapters. The parent benefits by automatically memorizing the passage just from repeating it to the children so often. Extensive internalization of Scripture will safeguard a child against false cults, whose arguments the parents can never completely anticipate.

Begin early to teach your child those admonitions in Scripture which apply specifically to him. Teach him that God in Heaven requires him to obey his parents. He is not free to merely obey in some things, but is required to obey in everything. "Children, obey your parents in all things, for this is well pleasing to the Lord" (Col 3:20). "Children, obey your parents in the Lord, for this is right" (Eph 6:1). The book of Proverbs emphatically teaches children to obey and honor their parents. The child needs to know that God's wisdom on this subject is in direct opposition to the prevailing philosophies of our day, philosophies which have devastated even Christian families.

While a child does have a certain instinctive respect for his parents, this respect does not meet God's standards. The child must be taught to honor his parents. Such an attitude is comprehensive. It includes obedience, but goes much further: a joyful desire to live in the spirit of the parents' instructions. The child needs to know God has designed this arrangement for his own good. "Honor your father and mother, which is the first commandment with promise: that it may be well with you and you may live long on the earth" (Eph 6:2-3; cf Ex 20:12).

Refusal to honor parents leads the child to become a vile person (Prov 30:11-14), and brings severe judgment from God (Prov 20:20; 30:17).

Teach your child to pray by praying aloud with him, and by sharing with him how God has answered your prayers. Help him pray, and help him see how God delights to answer the prayers of his children. You will experience surprise and delight as God chooses to answer the simple requests of a child.

As a present for his seventh birthday, I took my son Roland to a local fishing clinic. While there, he saw a book of maps and fishing tips for all the lakes in the county where we lived, and was disappointed when I did not have enough cash with me to buy the book. But unknown to me, he prayed that we would be able to get one somehow. Toward the end of the session on fishing techniques, the registration numbers of every one in attendance were put into a box. Door prizes were awarded by random selection. I could hardly believe my ears when my number was called to receive as prize the very book Roland prayed for.

Informal Instruction

Teach your children during ordinary household activities. "You shall talk of them [God's words] when you sit in your house" (Deut 6:7b). Let the Word of God be prominent in your informal conversation.

One of the ways to do this is to use common, everyday objects as pointers into the Scriptures. When putting on a child's shoes, ask, "Where in the Bible do we read about shoes? Where do we read about feet?" This opens opportunities to talk about John the Baptist's humble reluctance to untie Jesus' shoes. It allows us to discuss the significance of the Israelites' shoes not wearing out in the wilderness. We can talk about God's Word being a light to our feet, and about having our feet prepared to share the Gospel of Peace.

Mealtime provides one of the greatest opportunities for instructing your children. The evening meal is one of the most important events of the day, and only rare exceptions should permit a child to be absent. Although the food should be tastily prepared and attractively presented, the goal is not primarily the consumption of food. The goal is profitable discussion while the entire family enjoys delicious food in a relaxed and happy atmosphere.

Using this time of fellowship to teach the children in an informal setting will prevent mealtime conversation from degenerating into worthless talk. Prohibit frivolous talk at the table and lead significant discussion. Discuss concepts, insights from Scripture, events of the day. Use the dilemmas which you faced during the day to create a story for the children. Ask them how they would respond, and why.

As a computer consultant doing programming for a large firm, I took a business trip to Salt Lake City to install an inventory package for one of their distributors. After I returned, I told the children a story. I had driven a rental car to Ft. Wayne, Indiana. There I was to catch a plane to Chicago, and a second flight to Salt Lake City.

After getting out of the car, I remembered that I needed to write down the mileage and fuel level for check-in. So I unlocked the car, put the key back into the ignition, and noted the necessary information. As I got out, I heard a gentle "ding-dong," but since I was accustomed to driving older model cars, I was not familiar with cars "ding-donging" at me, and the sound did not register as a warning.

I shut the door and went to the trunk to get my luggage. I reached for the keys, but my pockets were empty. My heart sank when I realized the keys were locked inside the car. What was I to do? The plane would leave in about thirty minutes. The software I was to deliver was in the trunk. If I missed this flight, I would miss my connecting flight.

At this point in the story, I gave the dilemma to my children. What would they do? "Take a rock and break the window!" one of them suggested. I helped them evaluate this response to see why breaking the window would only make the problem worse. The results of such discussion enlighten both parents and children.

In our family I often guide the discussion into Biblical and theological concepts. Once I spoke of the view that Enoch and Elijah were not actually transported to heaven, but died after they got out of sight. Rachelle, who was nine years old at the time, did not like the idea. It just did not seem right to her. I challenged her to find a Scripture disproving that view. She could not think of any, so the subject was dropped.

Months later, our family was enjoying a meal together by candlelight. As we were sitting around the table reciting Hebrews 11, Rachelle suddenly interrupted with, "That's it! Enoch was translated so that he did not see death! That is the answer! Enoch didn't die!" For months she had been rolling the issue around in her mind. Finally, when the mind was fully prepared, the Holy Spirit illuminated the Scriptures to provide the answer.

Teach your children while traveling. You shall talk of God's words "when you walk by the way" (Deut 6:7c). Use travel time as a special opportunity to teach the Word. Do not waste those hours needed to get to the grandparents' house. Your vehicle serves as a little amphitheater. No one will interrupt your wonderful time together.

Recite Scripture, sing together, pray. Have one person read aloud to the family. Read the Scriptures. Discuss the meaning of the chapter just read. Travel time in an automobile is not something to be wishing away in anticipation of the destination, but is a great opportunity for family fellowship and meditation and worship.

Read Christian biography to see how the message of Christ changes those who hear. While traveling in New England we read *In Search of the Source* by Neil Anderson. The well-written narrative transported us into the struggle of learning an unwritten language, and conveyed the drama of finding the proper words to translate the concepts of

Scripture. We saw the decisive power of God's Word as it transformed the hearts of ferocious savages.

Isobel Kuhn has a vivid style and a powerful message. Learn from her while you teach your children. Read *By Searching,* an autobiographical account of how she heeded an agnostic professor and therefore left the lofty ways of God in preference for the misty flats of unbelief. Rejoice to see how God in His tenderness led her back to Himself and prepared her for mission work in China. Read her *In the Arena* and *Green Leaf in Drought Time* to learn what it means to love God in the midst of pressure.

Read *God's Smuggler* by Brother Andrew. Read Bruce Olson's *Bruchko* to learn how a young man single-handedly took the Gospel to a vicious tribe of South American Indians. Read books by Rosalind Goforth, Don Richardson, and Elisabeth Elliot. All children love stories. Read stories that inspire them with the glory of spiritual conquest.

Actively search out opportunities to teach your family the Word of God. You shall talk of God's words "when you lie down, and when you rise up" (Deut 6:7d). Teach your children at every transitional opportunity so often wasted. The next generation cannot be expected to learn truth by mere osmosis (Judg 2:7-10). Parents must creatively seize every opportunity to teach God's ways to their children. Use informal situations to build a strong foundation for dealing with later crises in the lives of your children.

One afternoon as some of us were together in the kitchen, I made a comparison between the human mind and a computer. "Wouldn't it be nice," I reflected, "if the human mind would retain information like a computer? Then whatever was in memory would be there without being smudged by time. And whenever you were finished with certain information, you could just erase that part of memory." My seven-year-old son responded immediately, "Oh, no! That would be bad because some Christians would look at bad pictures, and say, 'Oh well, it doesn't matter because I'll just erase it.'" Such conversation is a natural setting for reinforcing what has already been learned about the importance of pure thoughts.

Godward Activities

Thinking about the Word of God and teaching the Word of God becomes hollow, sterile, and empty unless it bears fruit in a life of obedience. Obedience is illustrated by the metaphors in the next verse.

"You shall bind them as a sign on your hand" (v 8a). The family who is committed to God will renounce activities incompatible with God's instructions. They will refuse to allow their hands to be soiled by disobedience. Parents will administer discipline to help their children live in obedience.

God's words "shall be as frontlets between your eyes" (v 8b). The spiritual family will look only at those things which are in harmony with God's Word. It is impossible to focus on the Word of God at the same time one is looking at evil. Gazing at pornographic pictures will clutter the mind with ungodliness, and seriously interfere with righteous meditation.

Actions have a very definite effect on attitudes. The relationship of the family to the Lord is very definitely affected by the intensity of the family's obedience, and by whether the family's affection for God has been sidetracked by gazing upon unwholesome things. This is reason enough for a family to do without television.

It is vitally important to guard the affections. Wise parents refuse to involve the family in activities that tend to lead the affections in the wrong direction. In our family we choose not take our children to amusement parks. We choose not to have our children playing with snowmobiles and three-wheelers. Although these activities may not be wrong in themselves, they emphasize dissipative pleasure in a world gone mad with self-gratification. Such activities are a negative investment in our attempt to teach our children to love the things which endure beyond the transient course of this age. Desire is a more powerful determinant of destiny than right precepts or philosophies (Prov 4:23). It is nonsense to visualize spiritual ministry for our children while we involve them in activities which cultivate carnal desires.

Godward Atmosphere

Because of our depravity, we need to be reminded to be faithful to God's commands. God says concerning His words, "You shall write them on the doorposts of your house and on your gates" (v 9). Faithfulness to the Word of God is enhanced if we provide for ourselves visible reminders of His Lordship.

The first metaphor suggests private life ("on the doorposts of your house"). Sadly too often our own family relationships demonstrate the least faithfulness—a pathetic exhibition of selfishness, anger, rudeness, and pride. Children understand the meaning of God's Word by having it lived out before them.

Scriptural music is an important ingredient of a wholesome home atmosphere. The majestic spiritual content of the great hymns of the faith provides valuable reminders for righteous living. Mottos on the wall can direct the thoughts toward God, and can stand as a silent rebuke of disobedience. We live in a society pervaded with secularism. The atmosphere of our homes should stimulate us to faithfully obey God.

This faithfulness in private life extends to our guests. How do we treat strangers in the home? Do they really feel welcome? Do we unselfishly give them our best? Can they see a real-life exhibition of what it means to love God?

The second metaphor suggests public life ("on your gates"). In ancient cities, the elders who managed the judicial affairs of the city, sat at the gates. God intended for public affairs to be conducted according to His principles, not according to the whims and philosophies of men. God's Word must permeate every action and monitor every decision.

Teach your children God's principles through the problems they experience with a neighbor child. Remind them that God expects them to love their enemies. He sends the nasty little kid on the block for them to practice on. How would we ever learn to love a persecutor if God did not send some easy lessons first?

Devotion to God as experienced at home should overflow into the community, having an effect beyond the home itself. As parents lead the family into the kind of holiness and obedience God expects, their household will become a city set on a hill that cannot be hidden. It will be a beacon for people to come learn the ways of God.

Godward Perspective

Effective spiritual training reaches beyond the present toward the future. Children must be taught to continue following God, not forgetting Him when they experience prosperity (Deut 6:10-12). Children must be taught how to resist peer pressure (vv 13-15). Children must be taught how to face disappointment, and how to respond to reversals without blaming God (v 16). This perspective is fortified by a solid understanding of history: God has worked in the past by using adversity as a platform for His goodness and grace, and He has provided what we need for life in the present (vv 20-25).

Quantity Time Becomes Quality Time

Determine today to make God the focal point of your affection, to make His message the primary subject of your thoughts. Decide now to make His Word the central theme of family conversation. Require all activities to be in harmony with the Bible. Commit yourself to a lifestyle that both privately and publicly demonstrates love for God.

Doing this will explode the mythological contrast between "quality time" and "quantity time" spent with children. Effective families cannot be expected unless parents and children spend great quantities of time together. According to Deuteronomy 6:4-9, God's definition of "quality time" is not a specialized fragment designed to please the child. Instead, it is a lifestyle of deliberately channeling a great quantity of ordinary experiences to bring the entire family into conformity with God's character. Life is made up of "ordinary experiences." Each of these becomes "quality experience" as it partakes of the fragrance of Christ.

In the long run, ordinary experiences sanctified to God are more significant than the special occasions of trips and parties which we tend to manufacture. Only the parent can provide the continuity and commitment necessary to weld these ordinary experiences into a sculpture of eternal glory.

Transmitting a Spiritual Heritage

Parents who have devoted their lives to bringing up their children in the nurture and admonition of the Lord understand the importance of passing on their spiritual heritage. This notion is foreign to our own culture but received a strong emphasis in the Old Testament.

God wants each generation to build on both the triumphs and mistakes of its predecessors. Therefore parents must be diligent in recounting the history of God's dealings with the family. This rehearsal is to span generations, giving emphasis to truth as the child hears it from parents and grandparents.

> Give ear, O my people, to my law; incline your ears to the words of my mouth. I will open my mouth in a parable; I will utter dark sayings of old, which we have heard and known, and *our fathers have told us. We will not hide them from their children, telling to the generation to come* the praises of the Lord, and His strength and His wonderful works that He has done. For He established a testimony in Jacob, and appointed a law in Israel, which *He commanded our fathers, that they should make them known to their children; that the generation to come might know them, the children who would be born, that they may arise and declare them to their children,* that they may set their hope in God, and not forget the works of God, but keep His commandments; and may not be like their fathers, a stubborn and rebellious generation, a generation that did not set its heart aright, and whose spirit was not faithful to God (Psa 78:1-8) [italics mine].

Although parents are the primary models for their children, they should cultivate friendships with other spiritually-minded families to provide both playmates and additional role models. Utilize the extended family to help you transmit your spiritual heritage. Emphasize both the physical and spiritual heritage embodied in the relationships of grandparents, uncles, and cousins. If your ancestors were believers, tell your children about the sacrifices their grandparents and great-grandparents made in order to be faithful to God. Make family gatherings a time when the older folks come prepared to share those experiences.

Grandparents need to be actively involved in helping their grown children teach and train their children. Too often grandparents view grandchildren as their special sphere of enjoyment, privilege, and boast rather than as an opportunity and responsibility. They love to cuddle the child and spoil him with gifts, but mistakenly believe all disciplinary action can be gladly relegated to the parents. Their attitudes are well expressed in the flippant bumper sticker: "If we had known grandkids would have been this much fun, we would have had them first!" God calls grandparents to not only learn from their own mistakes, but to also help their children be better parents than they were, and to assist them in training and disciplining the grandchildren.

Many families miss great blessings because the grandparents live in a retirement home instead of with their own children. Parents do take extra care when they get old. Now it is the child's turn to pay back a debt he owes. But this is a privilege, not a one-way street.

Grandparents have time to read to the grandchildren, take them for walks, tell them stories. Godly grandparents are a blessing just by being there. Children learn a lot by living with the aged. My grandfather died the same year I was born, so my grandmother lived with our family until she died when I was twenty-six years old. My grandmother was a wonderful blessing to our family.

A spiritual heritage is a valuable possession. Never apologize for not being saved out of the gutter. Help your children rejoice with you in the fabulous advantages accompanying a heritage of righteousness. If you do not come from a believing family, teach your children through the experience of your spiritual family: church history. Much of the free church movement has roots going back to the Anabaptists. Use their example to show your children how faith in God is more valuable than any earthly possession.

The spiritual triumphs God has wrought in your life are part of your children's heritage. One of the purposes for Israel's slavery in Egypt was to help parents teach their children about God. God used Pharaoh's stubbornness as a platform to demonstrate His mighty power, so that parents could teach their descendants about Him.

> Now the Lord said to Moses, "Go in to Pharaoh; for I have hardened his heart and the hearts of his servants, that I may show these signs of Mine before him, and that you may tell in the hearing of your son and your son's son the mighty things I have done in Egypt, and My signs which I have done among them, that you may know that I am the Lord" (Ex 10:1-2).

Similarly, God wants contemporary parents to use the difficulties of life as opportunities for teaching their children of His greatness. Too often we miss the blessing by complaining about our hardships and wanting to eliminate them as quickly as possible. We have failed to consider the greatness of God, the opportunity for Him to reveal Himself, and the privilege of our conveying that revelation to our children.

Object lessons are an important mechanism for transmitting a spiritual heritage. God used this method frequently in the Old Testament. The details of the Passover were designed specifically as an occasion for the father to instruct his son regarding the Lord's deliverance of Israel from Egypt. God deliberately created a situation where the son would be prompted to ask questions about what the father was doing (Ex 13:8-10,14-16). Joshua commemorated the miraculous crossing of Jordan by setting up a memorial of twelve stones. He intended for children to ask their parents what those stones meant (Josh 4:5-7).

Use the events of life to create a vivid reminder for children. A number of years ago I was working at Goddard Space Flight Center as a computer programmer. One day my wife asked me to get a book for her from the local library. I agreed to get it on the way home from work. The library closed at six o'clock, but shortly before six I encountered difficulties with the computer program. I really wanted to stay a little later and solve the problem. I didn't think she would mind if I didn't get the book on that particular day.

But I remembered my agreement, and deliberately left early enough to go to the library. That choice took me along a different road from the one I normally traveled. Looking out of the car window I could hardly believe my eyes when I saw a bald eagle beside the road. I stopped the car for a better look. There was no mistake: the bird was large, and had a magnificent white head and tail. As he flew, he was a spectacular sight. My first sighting of a bald eagle in the wild had occurred at a very unlikely place: within twenty minutes of the Washington Monument. If I had reneged on my "unimportant" agreement with my wife, I would have never seen the eagle.

Sometimes when I wish to remind the children to do what is right, even in things seeming trivial, I tell them: "Remember to look for the eagle!" Do what is right, and you will receive unexpected benefits.

The Church Complements Home Training

Many parents are unhappy with the impact of their church on the life of their children. This is partially due to improper expectations. God never designed the church to be the primary vehicle for spiritual instruction of children. The Scriptures always assign that job to the parents. The church should complement and reinforce the spiritual principles being actively taught by the parents. The church supplements teaching in the home, but does not substitute for it.

Parental Involvement

With this goal clearly in mind, parents should choose a church that teaches the Word of God effectively. There should be clear and dynamic presentation of God's Word, and adherence to theologically orthodox beliefs. These beliefs must evidence themselves in practical living. Too many people pride themselves in attending a "Bible-believing church," even though the church does not make a serious attempt to obey the New Testament. Such an environment teaches the child that Christianity is mere intellectual assent to dogma, not radical living in obedience to Christ. Children and adults need to be part of a "Bible-practicing church."

Integrate church experience into family living. Discuss at the Sunday table the positive benefits and insights gained from the morning service. Have the young children tell what they learned in their Sunday School class. Comment on how the sermon can be applied in daily life.

Lifestyle demonstrates how much parents value the church. Be active in church work. Welcome opportunities to teach, to encourage, or to assist those who do. Where possible, include your children with you in such ministries as taking flowers to invalids, visiting the elderly, distributing Gospel literature, doing door-to-door evangelism.

Avoid a critical attitude toward the church or its leaders. Don't spend Sunday noon criticizing the pastor's preaching style or berating the pianist for her mistakes. Don't discuss church problems in front of your children. However, as your children grow older, frankly answer questions they will ask when they realize that not all church operations are on a high spiritual plane. Don't mask the fact of church problems. Share your own insights on how you relate constructively to these difficulties.

Behavior in Church

Maximize the benefits of the church for your family by checking what is being offered to your children. Far too many "children's services" are crafts and games and entertainment, with very little solid Bible teaching. Watch out for Sunday School classes that permissively tolerate an atmosphere of disrespectful and rowdy behavior. Such classes undermine the teaching of godly parents. It would be much better for the children to accompany their parents to the adult class.

The Biblical model displays children as part of the total assembly. The praise service after the victory of Ai included women and little children (Josh 8:35). The attendance at the national emergency prayer service during the reign of Jehoshaphat included little children (2 Chr 20:13). Evidently children were also present at the all-morning teaching seminar conducted by Ezra and Nehemiah (Neh 8:2-3). The New Testament includes specific teaching directly addressed to children, which assumes they would be in the audience when the epistle was read (Col 3:20; Eph 6:1).

We contribute to spiritual fragmentation in the church by insisting upon chronological segregation in the activities of the church. While children can benefit from specialized classes conducted at their level, they should not be unduly isolated from the congregation. They must be trained to worship with the adult assembly. All ages should have the privilege of lifting their voices together in praise to God.[3]

Prepare your child to pay attention and concentrate on the church service by teaching him to sit still and be quiet during family devotions at home. When your family is at church, require a standard of behavior that cultivates a reverent attitude toward God. Have your children learn from and enjoy "adult" services. Most parents totally underestimate what their children can learn from good preaching.

---

[3]One pastor has actively designed for the church to help parents in this task. His church has a nursery for children up to two years old. At age two they move to what he calls the "training chapel," which has a glassed-in window at the rear of the auditorium. Sound is piped in through speakers, and parents sit with their children and help them learn to pay attention. Visually and orally they participate with the rest of the congregation, without the disturbances that naturally accompany the learning process. This is a temporary arrangement so that parents can then move with their children to the rear seats of the regular auditorium. Bruce A. Ray, *Withhold Not Correction* (Grand Rapids: Baker Book House, 1978), pp. 114-120.

Bring quiet toys and books for infants. When a child moves rapidly in dissatisfaction from one book to another, he is old enough to sit still and listen, without being distracted by books and toys. Playing in church (or in the nursery) contributes to a generation that does not understand reverence, worship, or seeking God. We do not follow spiritual aspirations because they are fun, but because they are right.

Make a practice of asking small children afterward, "What was the sermon about?" One mother sketches pictures of major sermon ideas to help hold the attention of a small child. Help your children grasp insight from the teaching they receive in church.

Sometimes pastors moan, "My family lives in a fishbowl!" They fear for their children because of expectation pressures from the congregation. Actually, higher expectations are appropriate for a leader's children. He should know how to train his family. The Old Testament law had a higher standard for the daughters of a priest than for the general population (Lev 21:9).

Pastors should teach their children to be different because of devotion to the Lord. High privilege brings high responsibility. The often quoted reminder to "do all to the glory of God" (1 Cor 10:31) is especially applicable since the context is dealing with corporate conscience. The issue here is not the parents' reputation, but the reputation of God. Children who bring a spiritual blot upon their family are bearing the Lord's name in vain. They carelessly destroy the ministry God intends to bring to His people through the family.

In fact, if a pastor really does his job as father and husband, most of these "PK" concerns will automatically disappear. The contemporary standards of behavior for children are so low (even in Christian society) that God's standard for a child is regarded as amazing. The godly behavior of properly trained children will prompt parishioners to ask, "How do you get your children to do this?"

Summary

Training children is both a great privilege and an awesome responsibility: a privilege to teach someone else, but awesome in shaping his destiny. Parental example is the foundation for effective instruction, and careful teaching makes the example both comprehensible and appealing.

For this to work, the parent must love God with all his heart, soul, mind, and strength. Only then can God's Word be the focus of his thoughts and of his conversation. Only then can family life receive the outpouring of God's wisdom. Only then can all family activities become "quality time" as they are permeated with the fragrance of Christ.

In this great task of spiritual training, parents do not "go it alone." They utilize the example of others within their spiritual heritage as inspiration to their children, and join hands with a vibrant church family to complement and support what their children are learning at home.

"Of Such Is the Kingdom of Heaven"

11

Leading Children to Faith in Christ

Christian parents desire to teach their children about God. They want their children to be under the influence of a good church to complement their teaching and provide opportunities for fellowship and encouragement. They realize, however, that example, teaching, and fellowship are not enough. While moral principles do pave the way to effective living, they do not earn eternal salvation.

Therefore, Christian parents want to see more than good behavior in their children. They want to see those children personally respond to the claims of Jesus Christ, and accept Him as their Lord and Savior. Christian parents want to lead their children to active faith in Christ.

In order to do this properly, parents must understand what the Bible teaches about children. Important questions beg for answers. Are infants saved? If so, how does God deal with their sinful nature? How are Jesus' statements about children to be interpreted? What should we learn from the examples of children in Scripture? What are the basic theological considerations? What will be our practical conclusion on how to deal with our children?

Obviously, these questions encompass an extensive body of material, some of which touches on soteriological debates that have been raging for centuries. The purpose of this chapter is not to settle the controversy between Calvin and Arminius.[1] Both schools of thought have emphasized important truths. Either school carried to extreme involves serious error. The purpose of this chapter is to carefully consider the spiritual status of children as portrayed in the Scriptures, without a priori assumptions regarding either soteriological system. Understanding the spiritual status of children is the basis for properly leading children to active faith in Christ.

Are Infants Guilty?

A child is a beautiful gift from God (Psa 127:3). Parents naturally love their new baby. He is adorable, precious, special. As the weeks go by, his chubby cheeks, sweet smile, and trusting gaze win him a deeper and deeper spot in the hearts of his parents. It is easy for them to think this precious baby is a cherub, a being who is inherently good.

---

[1]Soteriology is the doctrine of salvation through Christ. Centuries ago, Calvin proposed his understanding of this doctrine, and emphasized God's sovereignty and grace. Arminius felt Calvin's proposal did not give due recognition to human responsibility for receiving salvation.

The Scriptures tell a different story. We are not inherently good, but are by *nature* the children of wrath (Eph 2:3). The wickedness present in every human being does not begin with a sequence of naughty actions. It is an essential characteristic of every person from the very moment of conception: "Behold, I was brought forth in iniquity, and in sin my mother conceived me" (Psa 51:5). A child does not become a sinner by committing certain acts of sin. A child commits acts of sin because he is by nature a sinner.

Although apparently no sins are committed prenatally (Rom 9:11-12), the effects of original sin manifest themselves soon after birth. "The wicked are estranged from the womb; they go astray as soon as they are born, speaking lies" (Psa 58:3). Every parent has seen his infant arch his back and resist parental authority. Obviously, the child is not consciously committing sins against a holy God, but his ignorance does not absolve his guilt (Lu 12:48).

The penalty of sin is death. Even before the Law was given through Moses, all men were guilty of sin, and all experienced the judgment of death (Rom 5:12-14). This infection of sin and its consequence of death includes every person—infants as well as adults. The only hope for humanity is through the shed blood of Jesus Christ. Apart from His sacrificial death, every human being is hopelessly lost and forever doomed to eternal fire.

Are Infants Saved?

What then is the status of an infant who dies? Would God condemn him to hell? How could He be just and condemn one who knew nothing of his responsibility to God? Yet, how could a holy God accept in heaven one tainted by sin? What about a child who is three or four years old? The stakes are the highest imaginable: eternal salvation or damnation. Some church leaders believe the Bible is silent regarding the spiritual status of young children, and that it is impossible to know whether they are saved or lost. As consolation, they exhort us to trust God, because whatever God does is holy and just and right.

Obviously the righteousness of God is unquestionable, even if we do not understand His actions. However, God's righteousness is not very comforting to parents who wonder if their dead infant is in hell. This uncertainty of destiny puts tremendous pressure on parents to "get their child saved" as soon as possible. They desperately want him to receive the benefits of Christ's atonement so that their family circle will be unbroken in eternity. In their concern they often pressure him into an artificial commitment. To be on the safe side, they manipulate him into making a "formal decision for Christ" at a very early age.

One mother told her young child, "My heart is white, because I have accepted Jesus. Your heart is black because you have not accepted Jesus." The child naturally wanted to become good like his mother.

A prospective father once confided to me his plan of naming a son "Christian" but calling him "Sinner" until he accepted the Lord. To his wife's great relief, I was finally able to convince him that his proposal would bring frustration and spiritual danger rather than blessing.

It is easy to make a child feel guilty and in spiritual danger. But only the Holy Spirit can make him realize with an enlightened understanding his intrinsic sinnerhood and his need for the Savior beyond the fact that he believes what his parents have told him. The immaturity of the child and the nature of the parent-child relationship create an ideal scenario for "instant evangelism." Practically any parent can in five minutes persuade his three-year-old child to "become a Christian." A child wants to please his parents, and naturally wants to be like them. No child wants to miss heaven and go to hell. He will gladly recite a flimsy formula and parrot a perfunctory prayer, if that is what it takes to get to heaven.

The result could be aptly described as "Fundamentalist infant baptism." In this case, the "infant" is able to repeat back the phrases which have so much meaning for his parents. The outcome, however, is essentially the same as the infant baptism which we reject in favor of believer's baptism. This procedure can effectively inoculate the child against Christianity. At worst, it makes him spiritually complacent in a decision essentially made by his parents. At best, it sets a devastating precedent for basing spiritual experience on external religious formalism instead of internal reality. Frequently, salvation is based on the "works" of kneeling down and saying a prayer formula.

Jesus' Evaluation of Children

The statements of Jesus are the key for understanding the spiritual status of children. To understand His statements we must know who He means by "children." How old were they? What would they have comprehended about His life and work?

Who Is a Little Child?

The word most commonly used in the New Testament to describe children is *teknon*, which emphasizes filial relationship and makes no distinctions regarding the age of the child. Jesus uses this word to address the paralytic (Matt 9:2). Paul uses it to exhort children to obey their parents (Eph 6:1), as well as to refer to the Christian as being a child of God (Rom 8:16,17). Those who crucified Christ called for His blood to be on them and on their children (Matt 27:25).

Another word is *pais*, which in classical Greek referred to a boy of 7-14 years, to a servant girl or a female slave. It is a general term indicating filial or servant relationship, and is used both ways in the New Testament. The term *paidion* is the classical diminutive of *pais* and referred to a child up to seven years old, or a young male or female slave.[2] The word *paidiskee* (damsel) always occurs in a context

[2]For details regarding Greek usage, see Colin Brown, ed., *The New International Dictionary of New Testament Theology,* Vol 1 (Grand Rapids: Zondervan, 1971), pp. 283-287.

appropriate to older girls, and is even used to describe Hagar (Gal 4:22,23,30).

In the New Testament, *paidion* is by far more common than *pais* or *paidiskee*. It is used to describe newborns (Lu 1:59,66,76), and parallels *brephos* (infant) in Luke 18:15,16,17. It describes the twelve-year-old daughter of Jairus (Mk 5:39,40,41, cf v 42). It is frequently translated "little children" (Matt 18:2,3,4,5; Mk 10:13,14,15), and is the term used to describe the children Jesus took up into his arms (Mk 9:36,37; 10:14-16). The word refers to children who are associated with women (Matt 14:21; 15:38), and children playing in the market place (Lu 7:32).

The focus of the term *paidion* is on young children, not teenagers. Jesus uses this term exclusively when making statements regarding the relationship of children to the Kingdom of Heaven (Matt 18:2-5; 19:13-14; Mk 9:36-37; 10:13-15; Lu 18:16-17).

Children in the Kingdom of Heaven

Our Lord's most extensive discourse regarding children is found in Matthew 18:1-14. Because of its importance, it is quoted here in full.

> At that time the disciples came to Jesus, saying, "Who then is greatest in the kingdom of heaven?" And Jesus called a little child to Him, set him in the midst of them, and said, "Assuredly, I say to you, unless you are converted and become as little children, you will by no means enter the kingdom of heaven. Therefore whoever humbles himself as this little child is the greatest in the kingdom of heaven. And whoever receives one little child like this in My name receives Me.
>
> "But whoever causes one of these little ones who believe in Me to sin, it would be better for him if a millstone were hung around his neck, and he were drowned in the depth of the sea. Woe to the world because of offenses! For offenses must come, but woe to that man by whom the offense comes! And if your hand or foot causes you to sin, cut it off and cast it from you. It is better for you to enter into life lame or maimed, rather than having two hands or two feet, to be cast into the everlasting fire. And if your eye causes you to sin, pluck it out and cast it from you. It is better for you to enter into life with one eye, rather than having two eyes, to be cast into hell fire. Take heed that you do not despise one of these little ones, for I say to you that in heaven their angels always see the face of My Father who is in heaven.
>
> "For the Son of Man has come to save that which was lost. What do you think? If a man has a hundred sheep, and one of them goes astray, does he not leave the ninety-nine and go to the mountains to seek the one that is straying? And if he should find it, assuredly, I say to you, he rejoices more over that sheep than over the ninety-nine that did not go astray. Even so it is not the will of your Father who is in heaven that one of these little ones should perish."

Jesus' disciples had come asking who would be greatest in the Kingdom of Heaven. He called a little child into their midst, and warned His disciples that unless they were converted and became as little children, they would not enter the Kingdom of Heaven (v 3). The attitude of the child embodies true greatness (vv 4-5).

The disciples did not think children were important, but Jesus took special pains to correct this notion. He emphasized the value of the child's spiritual relationship to God. He warned them against the spiritual carelessness of adults which so frequently has a disastrous effect on children. He said it would be better to be drowned in the depth of the sea than to cause a believing child to fall into spiritual destruction. Jesus recommended stringent measures to avoid being a stumbling block for a child: cut off your hand or pluck out your eye (vv 6-9). The severity of Jesus' statements shows He is not talking about a child's temporary lapse into sin. He is warning against being the catalyst causing a child to eternally stray from God.

In verse ten, Jesus continues to emphasize the importance of children. Apparently adults do not automatically have the special relationship with the Father which these little ones enjoy. "Take heed that you do not despise one of these little ones, for I say to you that in heaven their angels always see the face of My Father who is in heaven" (v 10). Angels are ministers for those who inherit salvation (Heb 1:14). Jesus uses their ministry to prove that children have a special, intimate connection with the Father.

Jesus' final statement in this discussion regarding children (Matt 18:14) proves that the intervening verses containing the parable of one hundred sheep refer specifically to the relationship of children to the Heavenly Father. The ninety-nine sheep who did not go astray correspond to children. The shepherd goes to seek the one who goes astray, corresponding to adults who need to be converted (cf v 3).[3]

Understanding the conspicuous context of the parable explains why there is more joy in heaven over the one brought back than the ninety-nine who did not stray. Why would God rejoice more over the return of a derelict than over one who had never strayed? The answer is that here the ninety-nine represent those who have a relationship with God, but have not yet volitionally chosen to follow Him. God is rejoicing over one who has deliberately forsaken a life of wickedness.[4]

Jesus concludes His teaching with a strong assertion: "It is not the will of your Father who is in heaven that one of these little ones should perish" (v 14). Obviously this would be false if God had determined to damn infants who died before being able to comprehend and personally appropriate the plan of salvation by faith.

Those Not Against Us Are With Us

This understanding of Matthew 18 clarifies Jesus' statements to His disciples recorded in Luke 9:46-50 and in Mark 9:33-42. The disciples

---

[3]Even the numbers are interesting. Infant and prenatal mortality suggest that heaven will be heavily populated with people who died before reaching physical adulthood on earth.

[4]Jesus also used the parable of the lost sheep when he spoke to Pharisees who were perturbed about his fellowship with sinners, and it is interesting to notice the difference in wording. There is more joy over the repentant sinner "than over ninety-nine just persons who need no repentance" (Lu 15:1-7). The Pharisees thought they were righteous. They thought they were just and needed no repentance. They had no sense of need, and brought no joy to God.

had been disputing among themselves regarding who would be the greatest. Jesus declared servanthood as the key to greatness. To prove His point, Jesus took a little child, set him in the midst, held him in His arms and said, "Whoever receives one of these little children in My name receives Me; and whoever receives Me, receives not Me but Him who sent Me" (Mark 9:37). Those who are really great treat the most insignificant member of the Kingdom with the same kind of gracious service they would give to Christ. His criteria for judging between sheep and goats (Matthew 25:40,45) proves that true discipleship is measured by how one treats those who belong to Christ, and is ultimately an expression of how one is treating Christ Himself. Our Lord's statement about receiving children being equivalent to receiving Him only makes sense if children are part of His Kingdom.

The Apostle John immediately answers Jesus with something which at first glance seems totally irrelevant: "Teacher, we saw someone who does not follow us casting out demons in Your name, and we forbade him because he does not follow us" (v 38). John did not understand how Jesus could have such a special relationship with children. To him, the idea that children were part of the Kingdom was inconceivable. It was just as inappropriate as the man who was casting out demons but was not part of the special group of Twelve.

The conclusion of Jesus' reply shows the discussion was still focused on children: "Do not forbid him. . . For he who is not against us is on our side. . . And whoever causes one of these little ones who believe in me to stumble, it would be better for him if a millstone were hung around his neck, and he were thrown into the sea" (vv 39-42). Jesus' relationship with adults is the primary focus of Scriptures which speak of the need to actively exercise faith in His atoning work. Here Jesus is asserting that children are also in His fold, but their participation in His kingdom is not predicated by the same circumstances as for adults. Children have not actively set themselves as autonomous authorities in opposition to God. Since they are not against Him, they are on His side.

Therefore, in a certain sense children are in a different "group" than are saved adults. This arrangement in the Kingdom of Heaven naturally prompted John's question about a similar situation which he had recently observed: some other "believer" who was not part of their specific group.

This analysis contrasts properly with a converse statement which Jesus made regarding the Pharisees who had hardened their hearts in opposition to Him. They accused Christ of casting out devils through the power of Beelzebub. Jesus replied, "He who is not with Me is against Me, and he who does not gather with Me scatters abroad" (Matt 12:30). The Pharisees were adults who had rejected Christ. Unless they actively turned, they were already set against Him. Since they were not gathering with Him, they were scattering. Significantly, gathering and scattering would not apply to children, and are omitted in the passages previously cited.

Jesus repeatedly spoke of children and said, "of such is the Kingdom of Heaven" or "of such is the Kingdom of God" (Matt 19:14; Mk 10:14; Lu 18:16). All agree that children have the characteristics associated with salvation: humility, trust, teachableness. Jesus used children as an object lesson to illustrate true Christianity.

However, the actions of Jesus on these occasions make it difficult to limit His statements to a mere object lesson. He would have over-reacted in venting His anger at His disciples for prematurely sending away His illustration. Besides, there would be no reason for Jesus to lay hands on those object lessons and bless them. It is best to realize the value of the object lesson, and also to accept Jesus' statements as literally true of children. His assertion that "of such is the Kingdom of Heaven" corresponds precisely to His other statements regarding the relationship of children to the Heavenly Father. Children are part of the Kingdom of God.

Salvation Without Faith?

The focus of the Scriptures is upon those who are capable of understanding and believing. As adults we are informed, "All we like sheep have gone astray; we have turned, every one to his own way; and the Lord has laid on Him the iniquity of us all" (Isa 53:6).

Active faith and repentance are a key ingredient to salvation. "Without faith it is impossible to please Him" (Heb 11:6). The provision is adequate for the entire world, but not automatically appropriated by the entire world. "God so loved the world that He gave His only begotten Son, that whoever believes in Him should not perish but have everlasting life. . . He who does not believe is condemned already, because he has not believed in the name of the only begotten Son of God" (Jn 3:16,18). "The Lord is not . . . willing that any should perish but that all should come to repentance" (2 Pet 3:9).

In some cases, however, the statements of universality go beyond active faith and are enigmatic unless one understands them to apply to infants or other incompetents unable to exercise saving faith. "We see Jesus, who was made a little lower than the angels, for the suffering of death crowned with glory and honor, that He, by the grace of God, might taste death for everyone" (Heb 2:9). For this provision to be universal, it should certainly include infants who are not yet developed to the point where they could exercise saving faith.

God "desires all men to be saved" (1 Tim 2:4)—a strange wish if He automatically damns infants. The Apostle John described Christ as "the propitiation for our sins, and not for ours only but also for the whole world" (1 Jn 2:2). This unlimited atonement is self-contradictory unless it includes salvation for infants (or others incapable of intelligent belief), because their sin is part of the sin of the whole world.

God's provision of grace is much more abundant than the corruption that entered humanity through Adam. The Apostle Paul makes an emphatic point of this, a point that would be seriously undermined by the automatic damnation of billions of infants:

> For as by one man's disobedience many were made sinners, so also by one Man's obedience many will be made righteous. Moreover the law entered that the offense might abound. But where sin abounded, *grace abounded much more,* so that as sin reigned in death, even so grace might reign through righteousness to eternal life through Jesus Christ our Lord" (Rom 5:19-21, italics mine).

There is a vast difference between the heathen adult and the child. The adult is in full possession of his reasoning powers. God's general revelation makes him without excuse for his choice in setting himself in opposition to God (Rom 1). Therefore, every adult stands guilty before God and under condemnation.

The child, not having made such volitional choice against God, is covered by Christ's sacrifice without the need for active faith. Possibly this is related to Jesus' statements in the Gospels about little children who "believe in Me." What did they believe? Certainly they knew nothing of Jesus' atoning work on the Cross. It hadn't happened yet. The disciples were the sole recipients of that teaching and even they did not understand it. Not having made active choice against the God of general revelation, the child is on Christ's side.

Sometimes people discuss what they call "the age of accountability." This terminology is really a misnomer. There is no one single age at which children begin to exercise active faith. Some genuine conversions occur at a very early age. The accountability does not occur at a specific age, but is rather an awareness of personal responsibility before God.

In the midst of a discussion of soteriology, the Apostle Paul makes a statement illuminating the issue of a child's accountability. He gives his own testimony: "I was alive once without the law, but when the commandment came, sin revived and I died" (Rom 7:9). Paul had careful theological training, even as a young boy. He would have known the law from his youth. He describes himself as first being alive spiritually, and then coming to a point where an awareness of the personal meaning of the law caused him to die (be spiritually separated from God). In the preceding verse he emphasized that sin was not operative apart from the law. Paul's own testimony corresponds precisely with the view that children are part of the Kingdom of Heaven, saved by the blood of Christ.

In all of their work in the Kingdom of God, we have no record of either Jesus or Paul ever inviting little children to repent or come to Christ. If such actions were necessary, it is a glaring omission of a procedure that should have been a critical concern. There is absolutely no hint of the kind of child evangelism pressures so common in our day.

God's Character

For humanity under the condemnation of sin, God provided salvation in Christ. He designed the universe to reveal His eternal character, making all men responsible to Him (Rom 1:20). Responsibility for understanding God's character by observing the universe cannot apply to the infant. God's justice therefore makes it appropriate to provide salvation for infants.

Some reply that our own depravity prevents us from understanding justice as God sees it. But where did we get our sense of justice? Certainly we did not extract it from our own depraved natures. It came from our being made in the image of God and from His revelation regarding justice. God's saints have been given the mind of Christ. Even Abraham could appeal to God regarding his understanding of His justice (Gen 18:25). In all ages of history, highly spiritual men never advance to such supreme levels of spirituality that they rejoice at the idea of infant damnation.

In Ezekiel 18, the Lord speaks extensively about justice and how He would not automatically condemn a son because he had a wicked father. God does not rejoice in the death of the wicked. He emphasizes the responsibility of each person, regardless of parentage. He specifically contrasts His justice with the perverted notions of the Israelites (vv 19,25,29). The whole discussion rings hollow if God automatically damns infants to an eternal hell.

In the Old Testament God guaranteed harsh judgment for those who mistreated the widows and the fatherless. God Himself would avenge the mistreatment of the helpless (Ex 22:22-24). It would be strange indeed if God were so concerned about the physical well-being of orphans, and so utterly callous regarding the eternal destiny of dying infants.

Jesus said that not one sparrow falls unnoticed by the heavenly Father. He reminded His disciples that they were worth more than many sparrows (Matt 10:29-31). If God is so concerned about the fall of one little sparrow, and yet damns infants to hell, His condemnation of the Pharisees for straining gnats and swallowing camels becomes strange indeed.

Salvation is a free gift, not of works lest anyone should boast. But the scenes of God's judgment, whether for good or bad, are focused on works (Rom 2:6-9). Specifically, those actions listed as deserving condemnation are activities of adults, not infants: false religious profession (Matt 7:23), heartless indifference to suffering brethren (Matt 25:41), fornication, idolatry, adultery, homosexuality, sodomy, theft, covetousness, drunkenness, extortion (1 Cor 6:9-10). While there are many statements of Scripture which emphasize God's eternal judgment on wicked men, there are none which ascribe it to infants. This is a significant silence.

Children in the Scriptures

The spiritual status of individual children described in Scripture illustrates both the direct teachings of Christ and the general theological perspective of the New Testament. The experiences of these children clarify the doctrine of infant destiny.

King David's infant son is particularly significant. God's judgment on David's sin included the death of his and Bathsheba's son. David wept and prayed, hoping for God's mercy. Instead, the son died at seven days of age, one day before the covenant sign of circumcision could be performed. To the amazement of his servants, David then stopped fasting and weeping. He explained, "While the child was still alive, I fasted and wept; for I said, 'Who can tell whether the Lord will be gracious to me, that the child may live?' But now he is dead; why should I fast? Can I bring him back again? *I shall go to him,* but he shall not return to me" (2 Sam 12:22-23).

Some have claimed this example gives no clues regarding the spiritual destiny of infants. They think David was not planning to meet his son but was merely anticipating his own death when he said, "I shall go to him." However, David was not going into oblivion. He was planning to go somewhere to meet a person. His case is similar to the grieving Jacob who expected to meet his son Joseph at the grave, even though he thought his favorite son had been torn in pieces and never buried (Gen 37:33-35).

Besides, no grieving parent is ever consoled by his own death (the last enemy to be destroyed). A grieving parent is consoled by the prospect of reunion. Obviously, David was a man of God and his happy eternal destiny is certain. Since David was going to be with his infant son, it is reasonable to conclude that the son was saved also. Significantly, David had no plans to meet the wicked Absalom, but instead was engulfed with inconsolable grief (2 Sam 18:33).

The son of Jeroboam is a fascinating case. God had promised sure judgment on Jeroboam's dynasty and nation because of the false religious system which he had instituted in the Northern Kingdom (2 Kings 14). The occasion of this pronouncement was the sickness of Jeroboam's son, Abijah. Jeroboam had told his wife to disguise herself and question the prophet regarding the recovery of the child.

The old blind prophet was not fooled: In the midst of a scathing judgment, he made this arresting statement to Jeroboam's wife. "Arise therefore, go to your own house. When your feet enter the city, the child shall die. And all Israel shall mourn for him and bury him, for he is the only one of Jeroboam who shall come to the grave, because in him there is found something good toward the Lord God of Israel in the house of Jeroboam" (vv 12-13).

No conclusive statement can be made about the age of the child.[5] However, at least two factors suggest a young age: his strong association with his mother, as well as the sharp contrast to the rest of

---

[5]The Hebrew word *na'ar* is a very broad term. It refers to the infant Moses (Ex 2:6), to Shechem who defiled Jacob's daughter Dinah (Gen 34:19), and to Joshua the servant of Moses (Ex 33:11).

the house of Jeroboam. The goodness of this child corresponds beautifully with Jesus' statement, "He who is not against us is on our side" (Mk 9:40). Apparently God removed the good child before he was corrupted by the rest of his evil family (cf Isa 57:1-2).

Samuel's ministry in the Tabernacle after he had been weaned, and God's revelation through him regarding the judgment of Eli's house shows that active faith can begin very early in a child (1 Sam 2:24,28; 3:1-21). This interaction with God corresponds to Christ's command: "Forbid them not."

Samson was a Nazirite to God "from the womb" (Judg 13:5), indicating a special relationship with God, even as an infant. Probably the most unusual case is John the Baptist. The Scripture describes him as full of the Holy Spirit from his mother's womb (Lu 1:15). Clearly, he was Spirit-filled without active exercise of faith. Although John's experience is not normative for all children, it does show that active faith is not a prerequisite for a proper childhood relationship with God.

Application

The Scriptures strongly indicate that children are saved by the blood of Christ even though they cannot actively exercise faith in Him. This understanding is based primarily on Jesus' explicit teaching in the Gospel accounts, and is corroborated by general theological considerations as well as by the experience of children in Scripture.

Our job as Christian parents is not to create an artificial crisis conversion experience for our children. The child who grows up under the teaching of Christianity is a special case as illustrated by Israelite history. The nation left Egypt, traversed the Wilderness, crossed the Jordan, and entered into the Promised Land. Subsequent generations of Israelites did not need to endure Egyptian slavery or the rigors of the Wilderness in order to have a valid experience of covenant life.

God *intended* for the experience of subsequent generations to be different. He did not want each generation to grow up in bondage. The deliverance through Moses was to provide a redeemed society as an appropriate place for children to grow up, children who from their youth heard God's Law and obeyed Him.

> Gather the people together, men and women and little ones, and the stranger who is within your gates, that they may hear and that they may learn to fear the Lord your God and carefully observe all the words of this law, and that their children, who have not known it, may hear and learn to fear the Lord your God as long as you live in the land which you cross the Jordan to possess (Deut 31:12-13).

The Biblical model for children is not crisis conversion, but nurture (Eph 6:4; Deut 6:4-9; 2 Tim 3:14-15). It is a precious privilege to be nurtured by a family through the Word of God (cf Rom 3:1-2).[6]

---

[6]Some helpful material regarding nurture and conversion can be found in Marlin Jeschke, *Believer's Baptism for Children of the Church* (Scottdale, PA: Herald Press, 1983), pp 66-80.

Our job is to saturate our children with God's Word, the continual kind of exposure pictured in Deuteronomy 6. Children can understand. Children do have an attention span long enough to listen to large sections of Scripture. The example of Ezra and Nehemiah illustrates how important this is. They read the Law "from morning until midday" to an audience of "men and women and those who could understand," undoubtedly a group including children (Neh 8:2-3).

Part of the parent's task is helping his child understand sin and guilt. The natural key to this is for the parent to deal with his child's guilt in the same way God does: require confession and exact a payment of penalty. God used the strict requirements of Old Testament Law to prepare mankind to receive Christ (Gal 3:24). Every disobedience received a just retribution (Heb 2:2).

The child must experience law before he is ready for grace. He will never have a proper understanding of sin, guilt, and his own helplessness against the power of sin unless he first experiences the stringent requirements of law. This experience enlightens his understanding, and prompts him to look beyond himself to the solution of his personal sin problem. Many parents set the stage for a shallow Christian experience by never making consistent and firm demands of young children. Skipping the tutorial grace of the law results in a person who has no depth of earth—one who lacks the commitment to endure adversity (Matt 13:5-6).

Two extremes must be avoided: 1) assuming that young children are under condemnation, and therefore loading them with needless anxiety in order to induce a crisis conversion, or 2) assuming that a decision should be postponed until adulthood.

Instead of pressuring a child to recite a formula for salvation, parents should practice living by faith as illustrated in Hebrews 11. Faith is obeying God even when such obedience contradicts all the wisdom of the natural mind. Faith is living a life whose only goal is the Unseen City built by God. This lifestyle makes faith relevant to the family, and is an object lesson prompting the child to ask why we do what we do (cf Josh 4:6). Let the child express his faith naturally, without trying to have him "make a formal decision for Christ." Beware of the spiritual lethargy generated by mechanical formulas.

Anyone who manipulates his child into conversion has undermined the spiritual experience of his offspring. Our only recourse is to be diligent in teaching the whole counsel of God, trusting His Spirit to work in the child's heart (Jn 1:13). We can be confident that God desires the active faith of our children even more than we do. If we are faithful in teaching, He will faithfully energize His Word to cause our children to personally exercise faith in the shed blood of our Lord Jesus Christ.

As a child realizes his need for a personal relationship with the Savior, do not confuse him with non-Biblical terminology. Rather than speaking about "accepting Christ into his heart," or "giving his heart to

God," emphasize what the Bible teaches: believe on Jesus' shed blood as the only hope for salvation, repent of sin and obey Him as the Ruler of your life.

Summary

Every child is born with a depraved nature. He commits sins because he is a sinner by nature, not because he has learned from someone's bad example. Such a predicament poses two difficult questions. How can a holy God accept a sinful being into His presence? How can God be holy and damn a person who is unable to understand the need for repentance?

The Scriptures do not specifically address the theological details of these questions. However, there are strong indications that infants are saved by Christ's blood, even though they are incapable of exercising active faith.

This conclusion is based primarily on Jesus' explicit teaching in the Gospels. Since children have not actively set themselves against Christ, they are on His side. They are in the Kingdom of Heaven, and have a special relationship with the Father. Anyone who offends one of these little ones merits severest punishment.

A theology of infant salvation is consistent with God's character and His provision for universal salvation. It also corresponds properly to the experience of children in Scripture.

Nowhere in the New Testament is there any evidence for the high-pressure child evangelism tactics so common today. Neither Jesus nor Paul ever asked children to repent. Our job is to diligently teach our children the Scriptures, allow them to express their faith naturally without pressing them for a "formula decision," and pray that the Holy Spirit will energize His Word to call them to active faith. When they hear His call, it is our joy to lead them into personal trust in our Lord Jesus Christ.

"Chasten Your Son While There Is Hope" (Prov 19:18)

12

Principles of Discipline

Probably discipline is the most distasteful aspect of child training, both for the giver and for the receiver. I have never heard of a parent who said, "I certainly enjoyed disciplining my child last night! I can hardly wait until I have a chance to do it again!" Neither have I heard children saying, "My spanking last evening was really neat! I'm looking forward to the next one!"

By its very nature, discipline is distasteful to all parties. However, the chaos in contemporary families is largely due to lack of discipline. Without discipline, teaching ultimately falls on deaf ears. By default, the parents give their children free rein to pursue the demeaning demands of selfishness. The end result is disaster.

Fortunately, this disaster can be prevented. The God of the universe is the infallible authority on the principles of discipline. It is our job to acknowledge Him as wiser than ourselves, and to apply His direction for how to effectively discipline a child.

Why Discipline Is Neglected

In His Word, God has clearly directed parents to discipline their children. However, many parents neglect this responsibility. For some, this neglect is at least partly due to ignorance. They have never studied what God has to say about the subject, and their own parents did not provide good role models for discipline.

The ultimate reason for this neglect is because the intellect, the will, and the emotions have been corrupted by depravity. The result is an improper approach to the training of children, a vain attempt to accomplish good results in another way that is easier and supposedly better.

Fear of Losing the Child's Love

Some parents fail to discipline because they are afraid their children will cease to love them. Parental depravity has blinded them to the fact that the exact opposite is true. "Correct your son, and he will give you rest; yes, he will give delight to your soul" (Prov 29:17).

Parental Disobedience to God's Word

Parents who disobey God's Word experience increased pressure to neglect discipline. Mothers who work outside the home in disobedience to God's command (Tit 2:5; 1 Tim 5:14) are especially susceptible to the fear of losing their child's love. They already feel guilty for spending so little time with their child. The last thing they want is for discipline to mar the few hours they have together. They fear discipline as a further point of alienation between them and the child.

Because such a mother spends so little time with her child, the child may resort to misbehavior to get his mother's attention. Already the mother feels guilty for her neglect of her offspring. To discipline the child at this point makes her feel even worse. The easy way out is to neglect discipline, revel in the little companionship available, and hope for the best.

Concern Over Destroying the Child's Curiosity

The innocent curiosity of a child is truly delightful, and loving parents do not want to damage it. However, it is fallacious to assume that discipline damages curiosity. The personalties of Adam and Eve were not damaged by God's discipline in the Garden of Eden. If God had not driven them out of the Garden, they would have eaten of the Tree of Life and become absolute monsters in irremediable depravity.

Since the Fall, the natural tendency of humanity is toward evil. Therefore, curiosity undirected by the restraint of discipline will eventuate in perversity. "The rod and reproof give wisdom, but a child left to himself brings shame to his mother" (Prov 29:15).

Concern Over Squelching the Child's Creativity

Some parents live by the watchword: "Let the child express himself!" They have forgotten that the natural expression of the child is selfishness and evil. Creativity in doing evil should be squelched.

Besides, neglect of discipline actually hampers positive creativity. The disciplined child knows his boundaries, and is secure in them. He can devote his energy to useful investigation, rather than in trying to figure out if his parents really mean what they say. The undisciplined child's time of interaction with his parents is spent testing moveable boundaries, frustrating everyone.

Desire That "Children Be Allowed to Be Children"

Some parents espouse leniency because they believe "children should be allowed to be children." They recommend few requirements and low expectations, thinking the ideal childhood is composed of blissful indulgence, and that misdemeanors are to be expected and tolerated. This mentality sets the stage for an indulgent adulthood.

Only the disciplined child is free to truly be a child. He does not need to worry with decisions beyond his maturity. The parent who neglects discipline deprives his child of genuine childhood by forcing upon him decisions that should be reserved for later years. He is not ready to choose his friends, or cope with the temptations accompanying the wrong crowd. He is not ready to choose a balanced and nutritious menu for himself. He wants to choose, but will be frustrated with his own choices unless parental discipline helps him choose what is best.

The only way to "allow children to really be children" is to discipline them properly.

Misunderstanding Love

Some parents assert: "I love my child too much to spank him." They have misunderstood true love. True love is self-sacrificing, doing what is best for the other person. Discipline is hard work. It is inconvenient. It takes time. It interferes with important things the parent needs to do. It includes the discomfort of conflict with one's own child. In the presence of family and friends this conflict can be embarrassing.

The parent who neglects discipline is not loving his child. He is merely loving himself. He loves his own convenience and his own indulgent lifestyle. Even though he may "feel affection" for his child he does not love him. The writer of Proverbs is very emphatic on this point: "He who spares his rod hates his son, but he who loves him disciplines him promptly" (Prov 13:24).

The undisciplined child grows up with a false concept of reality. He thinks society owes him something. He is unprepared for the harsh realities of life. By neglecting discipline, the parent actually sets in motion a sequence of events to hasten the child's death. God informs us that these selfish parents actually want their child to die. "Chasten your son while there is hope, and do not set your heart on his destruction" (Prov 19:18).

Concern Over Improper Motives

Other parents neglect discipline because they fear they are not implementing the discipline properly. They see mixed motives in their disciplinary action, and imagine themselves selfish in wanting good behavior from their child.

Sometimes parents feel guilty when they need time to themselves. A pastor may need to be undisturbed while he prepares a sermon. It is not selfishness to expect the child to respect such a need. It is no excuse when the child does something naughty just to get the busy parent's attention. The parent is not *automatically* the selfish cause of the misbehavior. The child follows his own sinful desires (Jas 1:14). Children must learn to respect the needs of others.

When a child is naughty, parents must administer discipline. If the parents have had wrong motives, or if they have been neglecting their children, they need to repent. Parental motives and needed chastisement for the child are two entirely separate issues. Sin in the life of the parent is no excuse for the additional sin of neglecting to discipline one's children.

Guilt Feelings Regarding Anger

Parents often neglect discipline because of their own sense of guilt over being angry. The advice is frequently heard: "You should never discipline your child in anger." Therefore, whenever the naughty deeds of a child arouse the wrath of a parent, he feels guilty and unable to fulfill his responsibility in correcting the child.

In itself, anger is not inherently evil. God repeatedly disciplined His people in anger. Jesus was angry. On occasion, saints have apparently expressed appropriate anger: Saul (1 Sam 11:6), Nehemiah (Neh 5:6), and Moses (Ex 16:20; 32:19).

However, the wrath of man does not produce the righteousness of God (Jas 1:19-20). Human selfishness and pride are often at the core of what people believe is their own "righteous indignation." Repeatedly the Scriptures warn humanity to refrain from the folly of wrath and anger (Eph 4:31; Col 3:8).

It is easy for a parent to become angry when his child misbehaves. God does instruct the saint to "Be angry, and do not sin: do not let the sun go down on your wrath, nor give place to the devil" (Eph 4:26-27). Therefore the parent must be especially careful not to harbor a brooding anger against the child. He must avoid giving place to the Devil by brutality, or by sinning with his mouth.

But these considerations do not obliterate the need for child discipline. In fact, if the parent is frustrated by his own anger and fails to discipline his child, he is likely to develop a smoldering resentment against the child. With a continual lack of discipline, this builds up until the parent's anger suddenly erupts for a minor offense, or possibly overflows onto another child who was basically innocent.

The anger of the parent and the need for child discipline are two separate issues. Whenever a parent sins in anger, he must repent of that sin. He must also in humility fulfill his responsibility before God in disciplining his child.

Punishment Set Too High

Sometimes parents set severe punishments, hoping to scare their children into obedience. The excessive punishment is a vain attempt to make disobedience unthinkable—a kind of disobedience-deterrent theory. A parent who lives several hundred miles from his own parents may threaten, "If you don't obey, you won't be able to go with us to Grandpa's house."

Naturally, the child tests whether his parent's statement is really true. The parent has therefore placed himself into a dilemma where discipline is required, but the promised discipline is either inappropriate or unenforceable. The child could not be left at home by himself. It would be unfair to the family to suddenly cancel the trip. The parent has forced himself into a terrible choice: either be abusive, or else be a liar.

Reliance on Manipulation

Parents naturally shirk the trauma of administering discipline to their children. One of the attempts to eliminate the need for discipline is to use manipulative techniques to get the child to behave properly.

Some parents use scare tactics to control their children. They frighten a naughty child, "The bogeyman will get you!" A mother may threaten her child with "a spanking when Daddy gets home."

Other parents resort to bribery in an attempt to buy obedience. A reward is a positive affirmation for one who goes beyond the call of duty (Lu 17:10), but a bribe is an attempt to buy obedience. "If you behave while we are in the store, I'll buy you a pack of chewing gum." One of the most common forms of bribery is to lavish excessive praise on the child, hoping desperately to bypass the need for discipline by using "positive reinforcement." The use of bribes initiates a degenerative cycle demanding higher and higher prices. The child becomes a terrorist demanding ransom for good behavior.

I have a friend who is a professional photographer. He told me he would never do full-time photography of children. He refuses to stand on his head and do crazy things to get the average child to cooperate.

Once he shot outdoor photographs of an extended family. This group included a family with two children, whose ages he estimated at five and three. The parents had prepared for the occasion by buying toys which they promised to the children for good behavior. The kids were fine for about ten minutes. After that, they refused to pose properly for the photographer. They pouted with long faces, flaunting a controlled tantrum.

In desperation the parents made a second promise: "Just smile nicely for a few more, and you may go to the playground for a half-hour." No avail. The photographer was unable to utilize a beautiful lighting situation because of the children's stubbornness. The shots he had already taken would have to suffice. Grandpa and Grandma would never see the pictures that could have been. Even so, the parents paid the ransom their little terrorists demanded—the new toys, plus a half-hour in the park.

Those parents had actually maneuvered themselves into an extremely difficult situation. What parent would want to be embarrassed by returning a toy because the child had not behaved well enough? What should be done with such a toy if it weren't returned? The playground reward was given even though it was clearly not earned. At an early age those children knew well how to use strategic situations to get things they wanted. They knew how desperately their parents wanted a special picture. They used that desperation to their own short-sighted advantage. By succumbing, their parents propelled them toward long-term ruin.

Other parents believe in the primacy of reason. They think a long litany of reasons will persuade their child to behave properly, and make discipline unnecessary. However, even though parental explanation is an important facet of child training, the parent who uses it as a substitute for discipline is programming his family for disaster.

Sometimes a parent can redirect a child's attention, and thus get him to stop inappropriate behavior. At times this is perfectly legitimate: give the toddler a rubber ball instead of the china cup he just snatched from the coffee table. But redirection of a child's attention will never develop the *internal* standards that are the goal of proper discipline. A parent can never follow a child everywhere, redirecting his attention away from every misdemeanor.

Reliance on Example Alone

Some godly parents believe example alone is sufficient, hoping their children will emulate the godliness they see in their parents. King David, who was a man after God's own heart, had been exemplary in waiting for God's timing to exalt him to the throne. When his own son Adonijah (half brother and boyhood companion of the wicked Absalom) exalted himself, David did not at any time speak a word of rebuke (1 Kings 1:6; 1 Chr 3:2). Similar to his brother, Adonijah became a scheming scoundrel who tried to grab the kingdom for himself in direct opposition to the known will of God (1 Kings 1:9-10; 2:15,22-25). Example alone is not sufficient.

Reliance on Example and Instruction

Other parents hope their example and their instruction will be sufficient to direct the lives of their children, making discipline unnecessary. Eli, the aged priest in the days of the judges, was grieved by his sons' greedy abuse of the sacrificial system and their blatant sexual immorality with the women who came to the Tabernacle (1 Sam 2:12-22). He gave them a very strongly worded reprimand:

> Why do you do such things? For I hear of your evil dealings from all the people. No, my sons! For it is not a good report that I hear. You make the Lord's people transgress. If one man sins against another, God will judge him. But if a man sins against the Lord, who will intercede for him (1 Sam 2:23-25)?

Eli's words lacked moral authority because he himself continued to be intemperate in eating (1 Sam 4:18). No wonder his sons were not interested in moral restraint of their own appetites. Even so, Eli's failure to decisively deal with his sons for their wickedness was counted by the Lord as failure to rebuke them. God regarded this breach so serious that He swore no atonement would be possible to avert the judgment determined upon both Eli and his family (1 Sam 3:12-14).

Guilt From Similar Sins

Sometimes parents fail to discipline their children because they realize their own guilt and personal failure in many areas of life. This problem becomes especially acute when the child follows in similar sins. King David succumbed to the pressure of this dilemma. He had been guilty of adultery, and then murdered one of his loyal men in order to cover his sin (2 Sam 11). God forgave David's sin, but this did not cancel the dreadful flaws his sin introduced into his judgment and into his ability to stand against pressure. He did not perceive the trap his son Amnon was setting for his daughter Tamar. As a result, he agreed to a dangerous situation in which Amnon raped his own sister (2 Sam 13:1-20). Although David as king was supremely responsible for upholding the Law, he did not mete out the required punishment according to the Law: death for incest.[1] He merely became angry and did nothing (2 Sam 13:21). No wonder. The sin of his son was so similar to his own.

His inaction fueled the smoldering hatred of Absalom whose sister had been violated. Finally, after two years Absalom arranged a special party for the king's sons—a party that was really only a cover so his servants could murder Amnon (2 Sam 13:22-29). Again David was faced with a sin similar to his own. While he had not personally murdered Uriah, he had accomplished it through the servants of the king of Ammon. Instead of fulfilling his responsibility as chief executive of the Law and carrying out God's judgment by executing Absalom, David mourned for his fugitive son every day for three years. He became totally confused in mourning for the wicked Absalom and in being comforted regarding Amnon who was dead (2 Sam 13:37-39).

One day a wise woman of Tekoa came and pled with David. She was a widow whose only two sons had quarrelled while in the field. Since no one was there to separate them, one killed the other. If the avengers executed the murderer, the family name would be blotted out. She promised to bear all the guilt if only David would cancel the Law on her behalf. David actually used an oath in God's Name to assure her that he would disregard God's Law (2 Sam 14:9-11).

When David realized this was only a fabricated story to get him to allow Absalom to return, he did not admit his mistake. He deepened it by allowing Absalom to come back to Jerusalem, and salved his conscience by prohibiting any personal meeting. Finally after two more years, David ignored his conscience completely, and accepted the murderer with a kiss (2 Sam 14:21-33).

David's high-handed disregard of the Law meant he was no longer judging the land according to God's absolute standards of righteousness, but according to his own whims and preferences. Inevitably, the king began to make wrong judgments. This made it perfectly natural for Absalom to steal away the hearts of the people by promising justice to everyone who was oppressed. The result was civil war, national disaster, and an attempt by Absalom to murder his own father (2 Sam 15-17). Through God's intervention, the miserable Absalom was finally killed by a disobedient general of David's army (2 Sam 18:14).

This striking example shows clearly that parents must repent of their own sins, and at the same time discipline their children who have followed their own bad example. Such action certainly is embarrassing, but inaction only magnifies the problem. Depravity unchecked

---

[1]Whoever had a sexual relationship with his sister must be "cut off from his people" (Lev 18:9,29), an expression describing execution (Ex 31:14).

multiplies its disaster. Parents refusing to follow God's directives in solving problems become more and more confused, and actually become instruments compounding their own family problems.

Failure to Face Moral Obligation

Finally, many parents neglect to discipline their children because they do not perceive child discipline as their personal moral responsibility. God commands fathers to bring up their children in the nurture and admonition of the Lord (Eph 6:4). He commands mothers to love their children (Tit 2:4). In the book of Proverbs, He shocks us with a very stern statement to parents: "He who spares his rod hates his son, but he who loves him disciplines him promptly" (Prov 13:24).

No matter how much a parent thinks he loves his child, no matter how much he feels affection for him, that parent hates his child if he neglects to discipline him. Our natural impulse is to reject such a statement. However, since God is the Author of this evaluation, we are subdued into accepting it as true. Therefore, failure to discipline one's child is a violation of God's command to love him. God Himself is our perfect Example of One Who expresses love through discipline: "Whom the Lord loves He chastens, and scourges every son whom He receives" (Heb 12:6).

God commands children to obey and honor their parents (Eph 6:1-3). We as parents have the right to rule our children because God has given us that authority, not because we have personally earned it or deserve it. We are accountable to God alone for raising obedient and respectful children. If we do not have disciplined children, we are immoral parents, because we have disobeyed God's specific command.

The aged priest Eli is a striking example of an immoral parent whom God held accountable for not fulfilling his moral obligation to restrain the wickedness of his sons.

> In that day I will perform against Eli all that I have spoken concerning his house, from beginning to end. For I have told him that I will judge his house forever for the iniquity which he knows, because his sons made themselves vile, and he did not restrain them. And therefore I have sworn to the house of Eli that the iniquity of Eli's house shall not be atoned for by sacrifice or offering forever (1 Sam 3:12-14).

When I as a parent realize my personal moral obligation to discipline my child, I become a much better parent. Am I going to be immoral because I'm tired and don't feel like disciplining him? Am I going to be immoral because the situation is personally embarrassing to me? Am I going to be immoral because I'm busy in important ministry? Do I pretend I did not see his misbehavior because I do not wish to invest the time or effort required in discipline? By God's grace, I will choose to be a parent who is an example of righteousness, even when I am embarrassed, tired, or busy.

Philosophy of Effective Discipline

Effectiveness in child discipline is not generated by a long list of detailed procedures and formulas. Success comes from having a philosophy of discipline grounded in the Scriptures. Once parents understand the principles and see some examples, they will be able to creatively apply a Biblical philosophy of discipline to new situations as they arise.

Seek Diligently With Discipline

Discipline is no easy task. Persistent diligence is required. Proverbs 13:24 emphasizes that he who loves his son disciplines him diligently. "He who spares his rod hates his son, but he who loves him disciplines him promptly." According to notes in the margin of The New American Standard translation, this phrase could be literally rendered: "seeks him diligently with discipline."

In applying this verse, the parent will be on the constant lookout for symptoms—little things evidencing big problems. Imagine an emergency-room doctor saying, "This man has a high fever. Quick, let's put ice-packs under his armpits so his temperature registers lower on our thermometer!" Parents are just as foolish when they deal with mere surface symptoms rather than root issues. Some things which people consider cute are actually arrogant expressions of a toddler's rebellion.

Even though the parent may be tired, he will be tireless in his efforts to seek out his child, disciplining him to establish patterns of right living. The loving parent is determined not to give up, not to capitulate to the determined resistance of his child's will. He will transform confrontations into opportunities for molding his child's character into righteousness.

Often the actions of a child seem innocent enough. At times, parents actually enjoy the antics of a two-year old when they should be alarmed and deal sternly with the basic attitude being expressed.

Once some friends visited our house. As they went to leave, the mother said to us, "Watch this." She then told her small daughter to take her hand so they could walk together to the car. The child immediately stuffed her hands into her pockets and pranced off by herself. The mother thought it was really cute.

In reality, however, it was a disaster. The parent boasted about disobedience in front of the child. The child learned legalistic maneuvering to provide a hands-in-pockets excuse for not obeying. By laughing at the disobedience, the parent rewarded the child for expressing her foolish determination to run her own affairs independently of parental authority.

Proverb: Now or at Age Thirteen?

When I taught Christian school at the secondary level, I was astounded at the number of students in high school who hadn't learned the basic lessons of life—lessons they should have learned at age three.

They had not learned to apply themselves diligently to the task assigned. They had not learned to respect authority. They had not learned to obey.

Seeing these things was very sobering to me as a beginning parent. As I saw in my own children "small things" exhibiting wrong attitudes, I wanted to deal quickly and decisively with the root issues they represented.

For example, refusal to eat vegetables at age two is the moral equivalent of refusing to come in by ten o'clock at age sixteen. Both actions are expressions of the exact same problem: determination to manage life without interference from parents. Unless stern measures are taken, the ugly embryo of stubbornness in the two-year-old will develop into the hideous belligerence of a teenager.

Repeatedly I said to my wife, "Well, do you want to deal with this now, or wait until age thirteen?" This became a proverb in our home. We were committed to solving root problems before our children became teenagers.

Many people thought we were too strict. They thought "children should be allowed to be children." They thought some wrong behavior should be winked at and ignored. They thought we expected too much. Now that our children are older, no one tells us we are too strict. Instead, we hear expressions of amazement at the results in our family. We are simply experiencing the blessing described in the Bible: "Correct your son, and he will give you rest; yes, he will give delight to your soul" (Prov 29:17).

Transform the Terrible Twos

Many parents have lamented with exasperation, "My child is going through the Terrible Twos." They suppose Christian longsuffering calls them to somehow slog through the turmoil, bear with the chaos, and put up with the mess until the child grows out of this awful stage.

Nothing could be farther from the truth. The "Terrible Twos" is probably the single greatest strategic opportunity parents will ever have in training their child. At this age he really comes into awareness of his selfhood and independence as an individual person. He realizes that his desires conflict with what other people want. He asserts himself to get his own way.

The basic roots of every evil problem are present at this stage. But because the child is small he can express these wrong attitudes only in ways relatively harmless to himself, his family, and society. At worst, his overt actions are only inconvenient, messy, embarrassing, or rude. Parents make a colossal mistake when they "put up with" these expressions, thinking they are exercising forbearance. Actually, they are training the child to continue his course of foolishness.

The "Terrible Twos" should be renamed. They should be called the "Opportunity Twos." This young age is the perfect time for parents to deal decisively with the root attitude of independent autonomy.

Solving problems early is much easier than waiting until the child has grown into a teenager. The small child respects and loves his parents. He thinks they are the greatest. He forgives their mistakes. Utilize these advantages while you have them, and your child will love you as a teenager.

God has even designed human development in a way to help parents train their children. Very few children can remember anything before age three. This is God's mechanism for having the child learn the basic lessons of life without remembering the specific disciplinary events required. Teenagers, however, are in an entirely different category. They can remember (with grudges) for years.

The parents of every toddler should lift their eyes to heaven in thanksgiving for the "Opportunity Twos." God designed this stage of development to enable parents to root out evil in the life of their offspring while it is relatively easy. Use this gift for your child's spiritual advantage.

Of course, parents need to make allowance for the child's immaturity and weakness (Psa 103:13-14). The goal is to discern basic attitudes. A child may need to feed himself just because he must learn not to be lazy. However, the wise parent will give gentle assistance when the child needs help because he is too tired, or because he has a genuine difficulty eating a particular kind of food.

How Early to Begin
Beginning early in discipline is a crucial point. Many parents say their child understood discipline when only a few weeks old. By beginning early the parent avoids a host of subsequent problems. The old proverb, "A stitch in time saves nine," is eminently true in the area of child discipline. Right patterns are established early, automatically bypassing many kinds of wrong behavior.

A beautiful garden is the result of hard work and diligent attention to detail. A wise gardener would never say, "I just let gardens be gardens! I'm waiting until my garden grows out of this weed-infested stage!" The gardener who destroys weeds when they are little saves himself lots of work. Waiting until later makes it more difficult to destroy the weeds, and also allows the weeds to choke out good plants. In fact, early and persistent cultivation actually destroys weeds before they can be seen—just after they have begun to germinate under the ground.

In teaching a child to say "please" and "thank you," we can begin as soon as he is able to talk, or we can wait until he is two or three years old. By waiting, he becomes accustomed to getting what he wants without all this "please and thank you stuff." The job is harder. It is like pulling a big weed—a weed that has already stunted the formation of a grateful spirit.

By beginning early, the parent maximizes his own opportunity to grow in disciplinary wisdom and skill while the child is still young and easy to handle. He also maximizes the potential for training his child to be wise. "Chasten your son while there is hope, and do not set your heart on his destruction" (Prov 19:18). Parents must capitalize on a young child's strong sense of right and wrong. Careful training produces older children whose example and understanding of principle assist parents in establishing patterns of goodness in the younger ones.

A child needs to experience control as soon as he exhibits defiant resistance to his parents' will. This is usually evident long before his first birthday. An infant commonly expresses defiance by arching his back and holding himself rigid. Respond by firmly bending the child into a normal position, and holding him tightly so he cannot move. Eventually the child will cease to struggle, and will accept you as the one in charge.

Sometimes an infant refuses to cooperate when his diaper is being changed. He is in a very exposed position right then. Give him a sharp slap on his bare thigh. He will learn that it is more fun to hold still and cooperate.

As the child grows older and understands the meaning of words (even before he talks himself), discipline will need to increase in intensity. Before a child can talk, he can be taught to understand the meaning of "No," "Stop," and "Come." His obedience can protect him from danger, and save him unnecessary pain. It is cruel to expect your child to learn by hard experience that the stove is hot and produces severe burns on the hands. Detailed explanations will not work. Obedience to your words spares him from trouble.

Be alert to the onset of a child's capacity to make connections between dissimilar things, such as how a comb is applied to the hair. Such insight indicates an ability to make cause and effect connections, an ability to understand how misbehavior brings pain. It will be obvious to the parent if at some point the child does not understand why he is being disciplined.

Use a Physical Rod
Any discussion of child discipline eventually encounters the question of technique. What method of discipline should be used? Should children be spanked, or is this a brutal hangover from barbaric ancestors of earlier generations? What kind of parent would have the gall to deliberately strike his own child?

Contemporary thought rejects the notion of spanking a child for misbehavior. Supposedly we have outgrown such primitive techniques, and our sophisticated understanding of human personality gives us better methods for molding proper behavior.

God's Proposal
However, a serious reading of the book of Proverbs gives a very different kind of impression. A physical rod is presented as the natural, normal, and effective method for child discipline. The emphasis on

"*beating* with a rod" (Prov 23:13-14) makes it clear that the "rod" is not merely a figure of speech referring to whatever kind of discipline one would choose.

God presents the physical rod as an effective method, not as a last resort to use when all else fails. "Foolishness is bound up in the heart of a child, but the rod of correction will drive it far from him" (Prov 22:15).

The fundamental problem plaguing all of humanity is foolishness: believing we can live an effective life by having self as the ultimate authority. This was Adam's problem in the Garden of Eden. He chose himself as the ultimate authority, rather than acting on what God had said. He would find out for himself whether the fruit of the forbidden tree was really good.

For fallen man to set himself as authority insures moral corruption. The New International Version notes regarding Prov 1:7, "The Hebrew words rendered *fool* in Proverbs, and often elsewhere in the Old Testament, denote one who is morally deficient." This foolishness is not a superficial problem, but is deeply ingrained in the nature of the child. Early and persistently he asserts his determination to manage his own life independently of any authority.

The text speaks of foolishness as being "bound up" in the child's heart. This is a translation of the Hebrew *qashar*. Its basic meaning is to bind together,[2] and is used in contexts where the binding is not expected to come loose. The midwife who attended Tamar bound a scarlet thread on the hand of Zerah so they could be sure which twin was firstborn (Gen 38:28). God commanded His people to bind His words as a sign on their hand (Deut 6:8). Rahab bound a scarlet cord in the window so that her family would be spared in the annihilation of Jericho (Josh 2:18,21).

The word is also used to refer to a powerful bond between people. Judah pleaded for Benjamin on behalf of his father because of how Jacob's life was "bound up" with the life of his youngest son (Gen 44:30). The hearts of David and Jonathan were bound together in love (1 Sam 18:1). Many times the word is used to describe political conspiracies overthrowing a king (see 1 Kings 15:27; 16:16; 2 Kings 15:10,25,30).

The word *qashar* therefore portrays foolishness as a severe cancer tightly entwined about the heart of the child. It is not going to go away, or disappear when the child finally finishes "going through a stage."

Fortunately, we have not been left to ourselves to figure out what to do about this problem. God has told us that the rod of correction will drive foolishness far from the child (Prov 22:15). Awareness that his parents will use the rod when necessary changes the child's attitude

---

[2]R. Laird Harris, Gleason L. Archer, Jr., Bruce K. Waltke, editors, *Theological Wordbook of the Old Testament,* Vol 2 (Chicago: Moody Press, 1980), p. 818.

toward authority. It makes him willing to accept someone else as the ruler of his life. The rod is not a last resort, but the primary tool for molding a child's character in the way of righteousness. The use of a physical rod is the gibraltar of effective discipline.

In chemistry, many reactions cannot occur in the absence of a catalyst. Even though the catalyst is not used up in the reaction, it enables other elements to work together in ways which would otherwise be impossible. The diligent use of the rod acts as a catalyst to energize reproof so that wisdom can result. The rod alone is not enough. Reproof alone is not enough. But together, they bring wisdom. The use of the rod makes the child realize that wrong choices bring unpleasant experiences. The use of the rod gets the child's attention. He is ready to listen to instruction and apply it to life, lest he experience a repeated incident of pain. The rod makes the reproof effective in producing wisdom. "The rod *and* reproof give wisdom" (Prov 29:15).

Why the Rod is Effective

Naturally, God's solution for child discipline is effective. There are a number of factors which contribute to the effectiveness of a physical rod as an instrument of chastisement.

First of all, the rod is a powerful and effective symbol of parental authority because it is used exclusively for discipline. Therefore, it is far superior to wooden spoons, hair brushes, or other improvised utensils. Such instruments are absolutely worthless as symbols of authority, and they are physically poor tools for spanking—they were specifically designed to do something else.

A wooden spoon was made for stirring things up. Using it on your child is more likely to stir him up than calm him down. Use a rod instead. A 3/8-inch dowel rod has strength and some flexibility and is available in four-foot lengths at hardware stores. Cut one in half: one for upstairs, one for downstairs.

Small children understand the pain of the rod better than any other type of discipline. The basic framework for childhood obedience is established during the first six years. It is common sense to use the type of discipline most easily understood at this strategic age.

Equally important, children hate to have the rod used on them. They prefer other methods: missing dessert, denial of privileges, going to their room. By definition chastisement must be something painful, something significantly unpleasant.

My children have often lamented, "But I don't like to have a spanking!" I remind them, "Spanking is supposed to hurt. You should think about the pain before you do what is wrong. If you choose to do wrong, you also choose to suffer the consequences, but you cannot choose what those consequences will be."

The rod is superior because it is quick and simple for parents to use. It places the burden of discipline on the child, and does not encumber the parents with a long and complicated disciplinary regimen which must be carefully monitored. They can effectively administer the discipline, and then get on with their other work. It is also quick and simple for the child. It is soon finished, and does not burden him with a prolonged sense of isolation or rejection.

Punishing a child by having him stand with his face in the corner for thirty minutes dooms the parents to monitoring him the whole time. What if he turns around after twenty-eight minutes? The parents have a new disobedience to deal with. Both parents and child become more and more exasperated.

The rod is also superior because its usage does not require physical strength. The severity of the spanking arises in the leverage that comes from vigorously flexing the wrist. Therefore the mother can spank just as effectively as the father. A husband who doesn't believe it should bend over the bed and have his wife practice by giving him three good whacks.

How to Use the Rod

Failure to correct the child is actually depriving him. It is withholding something good, something he needs. Correction is more than verbal remonstrance. It includes the administration of pain to communicate reality.

God knew parents would be timid about using the rod to chasten their children. He therefore gave specific direction to counteract this unwholesome timidity. "Do not withhold correction from a child, for if you beat him with a rod, he will not die. You shall beat him with a rod, and deliver his soul from hell" (Prov 23:13-14). The proper use of the rod is not damaging to the child. The purpose of spanking is not to express parental exasperation, but is to benefit the child by delivering his soul from hell. The temporary pain of the rod guides him away from the evil patterns leading to eternal pains.

The child, of course, does not have such long-range goals in view. His primary desire is to escape pain in the present. Therefore he will likely cry as if he is dying (v 13b). The parent must be undaunted by such tactics, and proceed to administer proper correction.

The word translated "beat" is the Hebrew *nakah*, and is used in the Old Testament to refer to very severe action. Hundreds of times it is used of action fatal to the recipient. David killed the lion and bear which came after his flock (1 Sam 17:35,36), and vanquished Goliath in a duel (1 Sam 17:9,46). The word is very prominent for designating the destruction of an enemy in battle or conspiracy (Deut 20:13; Judg 15:16; 1 Kings 15:29; 20:21). It is also used to describe God's plagues on Egypt (Ex 3:20; 9:15), the killing of the firstborn (Psa 135:8), and the action of the destroying angel after David's sin in numbering the people (2 Sam 24:17). It refers to God's great judgments in the future against a wicked world (Isa 11:4).

Much less frequently it refers to non-fatal action, but in the context of severity. Balaam struck his donkey for turning aside from the angel

(Num 22:23,25,27). According to the Law, a wicked person was to be publicly beaten with no more than forty blows (Deut 25:2,3). When Elijah and Elisha struck the Jordan with a mantle, it parted for their crossing (2 Kings 2:8,14). A severe sun beat upon the head of Jonah as he waited to see the destruction of Nineveh (Jonah 4:8).

Related words indicate disablement of normal function. Jonathan had a son named Mephibosheth who was smitten *(nakeh)* in the feet, and therefore a cripple (2 Sam 4:4; 9:3). The same word refers to the contrite spirit that God regards so highly, because such a person no longer asserts his own will but trembles at God's word (Isa 66:2). The noun form *makka* means "blow, wound, plague, slaughter, defeat."[3] The one being struck is disabled, defeated, rendered powerless. The idea of defeat is very significant in disciplining a child. We want the will of the child to be defeated in its belligerence, channeled for good by submitting to an authority better than self.

The conclusion of this study in terminology is that Biblical discipline mandates severe action. Of course, THIS SEVERITY MUST NEVER INVOLVE BRUTAL TREATMENT OR FATAL BLOWS. But it is more than a mere angry slap from an exasperated parent. It is an *event*. The child is taken aside, and the rod is applied diligently and forcefully so that he will urgently desire to avoid a repeat performance.

The severity of the disciplinary event is a key factor in its effectiveness. This corresponds precisely with Proverbs 20:30. "Blows that hurt cleanse away evil, as do stripes the depths of the heart." Then the parent must take time to comfort the child and reassure him that all of this is part of true love (Heb 12:6).

When parents take the time and effort to make discipline worthwhile, they will find it needed less often. After presenting some of this material at a church, one brother wrote me this note:

> I see my "love of Absalom" as a humanistic deterrent to effective beatings. A review of those verses in Proverbs and your Biblical definition of "beat" convicted me that my discipline should decline in frequency and increase in intensity.

Severe Enough to Be Worthwhile

Discipline must be severe enough to motivate the child to not repeat the offense. If a child must be disciplined repeatedly for the same wrong behavior, the discipline is not stern enough. The pleasure of sin is simply greater than the pain of chastisement. When my wife and I encounter this type of situation, we say to one another, "We must put more teeth into it." The discipline must have a more severe bite. It must be stringent enough to motivate the child to avoid wrong behavior and attitudes.

The child must learn that "the way of transgressors is *hard"* (Prov 13:15, KJV, italics mine). Eventually our sin will find us out. The

[3]Ibid., p. 578.

eternal perspectives of heaven and hell demonstrate how sin exacts a penalty far in excess of its pleasure. Parents must teach their child the costliness of sin. Appropriate severity in discipline is an important part of this training.

Years ago we lived in a house having a tall steel antenna structure at one end. Part way up the side of the house, a blue jay had built a nest in the structure. One day the other children informed me that my five-year-old son had disturbed the nest. Upon investigation, I found my son guilty on several counts: 1) disturbing the nest, even though he knew without being told that he should not have done it; 2) disobedience to his mother who had explicitly told him not to disturb it; 3) dishonesty when questioned about what he had done.

I realized my son had not found it worthwhile to do what was right. We had been spanking him when he did wrong, but something had to be added, something to make a stronger impression. Therefore I increased the intensity of chastisement. I told him I would give him a spanking for each offense, but spread them out over the next three days. Each day I reminded him of what the present spanking was for, as well as reviewing the purpose of the previous ones. In addition, we required him to sit alone in his room whenever the other children went out to play. This would be especially trying for an active boy on a beautiful day. It made a definite impression. We noticed a marked improvement in general behavior. He had learned something about the ways of transgressors being hard.

Our Heavenly Father designs tests for the purpose of teaching us something, not merely to find out what we know. We should be doing the same thing with our children.

Larry Burkette tells how he dealt with his financially irresponsible son—a spendthrift who frequently asked his dad for money. One day when the son came begging for money, the father decided to give him an emphatic lesson. He told his son, "I will loan you the money ($30), but it will need to be repaid at $10 per week, with an exorbitant interest rate. You will also need something for collateral."

"What is collateral?"

"Collateral is goods of value which the lender may claim if there is a default in payment."

So the son agreed to provide his skateboard (worth $80) and his stereo (also worth $80) as collateral. The first payment was made on time, but he missed the second one. The father promptly took the skateboard and sold it for $10. The son was furious, but was reminded that according to the terms of the agreement the skateboard actually belonged to the father. The next week the son defaulted again. The father took the stereo, sold it, and paid off the loan. Years later the son thanked his father for teaching him financial responsibility.

Taking this kind of action is obviously a distasteful procedure for the parent. It hurts to deliberately engineer a painful lesson, knowing full well your child will likely fail. It hurts even more to carry that lesson to completion. But the parent must not give in. To do so is worse than no teaching at all: the child is bailed out of difficulty, and thus rewarded for wrong behavior. The key to learning is for the erring child to feel the burden of disastrous consequences.

In learning that the way of the transgressor is hard, the child must pay for the inconvenience of his wrong behavior. The Old Testament Law had stern demands for thieves. "If a man steals an ox or a sheep, and slaughters it or sells it, he shall restore five oxen for an ox and four sheep for a sheep" (Ex 22:1). It is not enough to merely return the equivalent of what was stolen, muttering a feeble apology. Theft brought inconvenience and loss to the owner, especially if his ox was gone at plowing time. These losses were not to be borne by the owner, but by the thief. If the thief had nothing for restitution, he was to be sold as a slave (Ex 22:3). The Mosaic Law required full restitution even for accidental losses. Mere apology was not sufficient (Ex 22:6-15).

Proper discipline places the burden of payment squarely on the offender. Therefore, parents should deliberately choose disciplines that will be difficult and painful for the child, but convenient for the parent to administer. Children should pay for the inconvenience and loss arising from their wrong behavior, not the parent. Children must experience reality. Sin is costly. Accidents are costly. Irresponsibility is costly.

Once one of our children attempted to hold her baby sister and at the same time carry a younger sibling on her back. As a result, she accidently dropped the baby. When the baby hit the floor, it received a severe blow to the head, and suddenly became lethargic, suggesting the possibility of severe injury. Fortunately, a visit to the doctor indicated nothing serious. The older child felt terrible and was in tears because of the accident. We reassured her of our love and forgiveness, but at the same time needed to give her an unforgettable lesson on the costliness of irresponsibility. We spanked her and required her to pay the twenty-two dollar fee for the doctor visit.

Parents should choose penalties appropriate for the offense.[4] If a child carelessly or intentionally damages property, he should have to pay for it. This should include clothing or toys his parents have provided. The child who has broken something should be required to clean up the mess. The child who injures others needs to be chastised. This includes potential danger, such as an older child goading a younger one into bare-handedly catching a bumblebee. Older children must learn to protect younger ones from harm. Rudeness and unkindness may need to go beyond apology to isolation so that the child learns not to disturb others.

Sometimes disciplinary measures can work in a multiple purpose fashion to accomplish several goals at once. One autumn day Rhoda and I were in the kitchen, and I became aware of a squabble in the

---

[4]Fugate, *Child Training*, pp. 157-159.

living room between Rosalyn (age four) and Rolanda (age two). My attempts to ascertain the cause were not too fruitful. Apparently Rosalyn had grabbed Rolanda's arm, because Rolanda had pretended to withhold some of Rosalyn's play money. As usual in this type of problem, the symptoms were extremely muddied, but the problem was clear: instead of enjoying the privilege of each other's presence, they were antagonizing one another.

Therefore, I delivered the following directives: Each child could choose one book, and then each must sit on a separate spot on the floor of the living room, their only pastime being to look at that book. Since they did not choose to benefit from one another's company, they would now see the weariness of isolation. They could be excused only if their mother needed them to do chores.

I left them to themselves, and went back to my work. Rosalyn did get a break when the baby needed to be entertained. Later, when Rosalyn was again at her post, I heard her childish voice wafting into the kitchen: "Mother, do you please have some work for me to do?" Following this example, Rolanda said the same thing: "Mother, do you have something for me to do?"

This incident illustrates several principles: 1) This type of discipline cannot be applied unless you already have a strong relationship with your child, and unless they already know the importance of obedience. Otherwise, the parent has to spend too much time directly monitoring the situation and also dealing with secondary disobedience (refusing to stay in the spot). 2) The children personally experience the costs of quarrelling, and are given an incentive to take the initiative in having fun together. 3) Even work is more fun than the costly results of wrong-doing. This last point was a serendipity benefit—the Lord granted me to see how it worked after I had initiated the discipline. When parents are serious about fulfilling their responsibilities in discipline, the Lord Himself will provide you with unanticipated wisdom.

Naturally, the child hates discipline, and will try to escape it whenever possible. He may go whining to his room. He may drag his feet and refuse to cooperate. He may refuse to submit while being disciplined. The parent needs to view these things as added offenses meriting additional punishment.

Sometimes children will attempt filibuster in order to avoid punishment. If the child truly has something significant to say, he will be able to present it promptly without a barrage of irrelevant verbiage. The parent who is faced with filibuster but is sure the child is guilty should spank first and have the discussion afterwards. Once my three-year old tried this tactic. "Wait! Wait! Wait! I need to tell you something!" After giving her the spanking I said, "Now you can tell me what you wanted to discuss." "No," she replied, "that would take too long!" The spanking eliminates the desire for a dishonest discussion. It prepares the child to receive instruction. Children must learn that rationalization is a lie, a potent instrument for self-deception.

Not Too Severe

Discipline must match the offense in terms of dealing with root issues of depravity. It must match the offense in terms of giving the child incentive to avoid offense in the future. However, discipline must not be too severe. The severity of discipline must not go beyond the seriousness of the offense.

In all cases parents must be sure the child is guilty. By disciplining their child for something he did not do, they build a massive barrier between themselves and their offspring. The child has a strong sense of fairness, and knows he has been unjustly treated and is without any hope of justice. The parental wrong fastens itself deep in his heart.

It is much better for a child to escape needed discipline than to be punished for a crime never committed. If he truly did do wrong, he will think he is clever and try it again. Parents have now been sensitized to the problem, and can carefully watch for the next offense of the same type. Then discipline can be carried out with appropriate sternness.

Punishment must not go beyond the child's ability to pay. Suppose a four-year old throws a ball through a therma-pane bay window. The cost of repair could easily amount to hundreds of dollars. In this circumstance, parents should follow the example of the Heavenly Father Who in Christ paid a debt we could never pay. However, a teenager who broke the same window could handle the expense, and should be required to pay it.

Parents dare not go beyond appropriate discipline by gloating over the punishment or by forcing the child to give them unfair advantage. The Lord used men and nations to punish His people for their wickedness. He then became very angry with those who went too far, gloating in the destruction. Jehu was God's instrument against the house of Ahab. However, God judged his dynasty for his excesses in Jezreel (Hos 1:4). God judged the Ammonites for gloating and rejoicing in the destruction that God had ordained against Judah (Ezek 25:3,6). He set Himself against Tyre for desiring personal advantage in Jerusalem's destruction (Ezek 26:2). God's judgment on nations that abused their role as instruments of His chastisement (Obad 12; Zeph 2:8,10; Zech 1:15) is a stern warning against improper parental severity in the discipline of children.

The Mosaic Law gave careful direction on how a wicked person was to be beaten. God did not want the offender to be unnecessarily humiliated. The maximum penalty was forty blows, lest he be beaten far beyond this, and "your brother be humiliated in your sight" (Deut 25:1-3). The Law was not written merely to instruct the ancient Israelites about the treatment of criminals. It was written for our benefit as well (cf 1 Cor 9:9-10). Parents should discipline their children in a way not involving excessive humiliation.

Since infants and toddlers are small and tender and bruise easily, parents must be cautious about excessive discipline. Sometimes a child will refuse to obey even after being spanked. For example, suppose parents spank their child for refusing to put away his toys. Possibly they tell him again, and then need to spank again for a second refusal. If two or three spankings do not result in obedience, it is best to drop the incident. Give his posterior a little time to recuperate. Proverbs 23:13 is not a guarantee that parents could not kill an infant with excessive spankings. Remember that each spanking satisfactorily concludes the *previous* disobedience. To demonstrate his need to obey, parents can take his hands and physically force him to put the toys where they belong. If a child has not learned his lesson, he will be disobedient again on a later day, and can be spanked then.

Parental delight in children safeguards against excessive discipline. Develop a relationship with your young child as a person. Enjoy the specialities only a child can give: the softness of a pudgy little hand, the patter of tiny feet, the sweetness of a baby voice learning to speak, the innocent amazement at simple discoveries in the everyday world. Remember, discipline is only a tool to direct your child into the ways of righteousness.

Appropriate Time and Place

Whenever disciplining a child, choose an appropriate time and place. Never slap a child in the middle of a church service. Take him out where the discipline can be done properly and without disturbing others.

In public places parents should avoid making a scene. Our world does not understand the difference between proper discipline and child abuse. Promptly inform an older child that his behavior is unacceptable and that he will be disciplined after he gets home. The anticipation of the coming chastisement can be part of the punishment and also amazing therapy in producing an immediate change of behavior.

For very young children, the discipline needs to be immediate. Otherwise they will not remember what it is for, and will not understand what is happening. Only frustration, bitterness, and fear can result. If you are in a public place, skip the discipline on that particular occasion. Concentrate instead on the incidents within the privacy of your own home. As he learns to obey at home, his general behavior in public will also improve.

Prayer For God's Intervention

Discipline is a difficult task. Sometimes it is exasperating and frustrating, and parents feel at their wits' end. Although prayer is never a substitute for obedience (cf Josh 7:10), it is a crucial ingredient in the spiritual warfare waged by every parent. Christian parents will utilize their own skills, and also call upon God for His intervention, asking Him for wisdom and creativity in dealing with difficult situations. For example, one of our children who cried easily when confronted with wrong was actually less contrite than Rhoda first thought. The child was crying because she had gotten caught and because her pride had been wounded. Parents need God's wisdom to differentiate between situations that are fundamentally different even though they outwardly appear similar.

It is especially important to ask God to work in the heart of the child, for Him to deal with the child's will internally while we as parents deal with him externally. Parents should pray *together* for God's intervention in persistent discipline problems.

The disciplinary occasion can also be an opportunity for prayer with the child: prayer for God's forgiveness (1 John 1:9), and for God's fortification against similar temptations in the future.

God's Example As Disciplinarian

Jesus frequently referred to God as His Father, and in His model prayer invited His followers to address God in the same fashion. Since God is a Father, He disciplines His children when they do wrong. The twelfth chapter of Hebrews explains His purposes and techniques in chastisement. His approach is our perfect example for proper disciplinary methods.

Love Does Not Give Up

Hebrews 12:5-6 includes an exact quote from the Septuagint text of Proverbs. The NASB translation is presented here in proper poetic form to highlight the parallel structures:

> My son, do not regard lightly the discipline of the Lord,
> Nor faint when you are reproved by Him;
> For those whom the Lord loves He disciplines,
> And He scourges every son whom He receives.

The particular words used indicate a parallelism between lines one and three, and between lines two and four. "Discipline" in line one and "disciplines" in line three are translations representing the same basic Greek root, *paideuo*.

It is easy to have a wrong response to discipline. The first wrong response is to "regard it lightly." The recipient pays no attention to the discipline. He stoically ignores it, and continues living as if it had never happened. He has despised discipline as irrelevant and worthless.

The second wrong response is to faint or become weary *(ekluo)*. The same root word describes the tendency to be discouraged in the face of adversity (Heb 12:3). It is also used to refer to the hungry crowds in the desert (Matt 15:32; Mk 8:3), and to the fact that believers will certainly reap if they do not grow weary (Gal 6:9).[5] Those who faint in the

---

[5]Colin Brown, ed., *The New International Dictionary of New Testament Theology*, Vol 3, p. 189.

wilderness never make it home. Believers who faint because of hardship fail to reap. Those who faint under the Lord's discipline do not profit from it because they give up in bitterness, and become like Cain who said, "My punishment is too great for me to bear." He bitterly accused the Lord of punishing him too severely, and departed from God's presence to found a line of ungodly men (Gen 4:13-17).

The term used in the text for discipline *(paideuo)* has two basic meanings. It can mean "to teach" or "to instruct." Moses was educated in all the wisdom of Egypt (Acts 7:22), and Paul was instructed by Gamaliel (Acts 22:3). It can also mean "to whip." Pilate offered to whip Jesus and release Him (Lu 23:16,22). Significantly, this word does not make an intrinsic distinction between instruction and chastisement. In the Biblical view, proper instruction includes chastisement.

The Lord instructs His children and chastises them when necessary. Probably the chastisement being referred to is a relatively mild form compared to the scourging spoken of later. But if this initial discipline is regarded lightly, the Lord continues to love with a more severe form of discipline.

The word translated "scourge" is *mastigoo,* and was applied to the brutal Roman punishment of scourging.[6] Pieces of bone or metal were tied to leather thongs, and these pieces cut into the back of the person being flogged, sometimes laying the flesh bare to the bone. No wonder Paul appealed to his Roman citizenship to avoid unnecessary scourging.

Scourging is therefore a very severe form of discipline, much more stringent than ordinary chastisement. It is tougher medicine, something breaking through the stoicism which ignores milder discipline. It is the ultimate discipline. There is no hope for the person who refuses to respond under it.

If we take discipline lightly we set ourselves up for the scourging. If scourging causes us to give up in bitterness, we become candidates for irremediable disaster. "Harsh correction is for him who forsakes the way, and he who hates reproof will die" (Prov 15:10). "He who is often reproved, and hardens his neck, will suddenly be destroyed, and that without remedy" (Prov 29:1).

Our job as parents is to handle our children the way God does. God does not give up when His children ignore His teaching and gentle discipline. His love demands stronger medicine to bring repentance.

Parental love dictates the same thing: Take stronger methods, using tougher discipline to cause the child to turn to righteousness. All the while the parent assists the child in avoiding the peril of wrong responses: stoicism under chastisement, or giving up under stronger discipline.

---

[6]This is a stronger word than *rapizo* which was used in classical Greek literature to denote the beating of a slave or a child with a rod for minor offenses. This milder root is also used to describe how the soldiers struck Christ with their hands (Matt 26:67; Mk 14:65; Jn 19:3). Colin Brown, ed., *New International Dictionary*, Vol 1, p. 162.

Guidelines for Parents

The next four verses refer to human parenting in a way which indicates God's view of normal disciplinary action. The text assumes the presence of certain factors in the parent-child relationship.

Every true son experiences discipline. "What son is there whom a father does not chasten? But if you are without chastening, of which all have become partakers, then you are illegitimate and not sons" (vv 7-8). Therefore, a father who fails to discipline his child is not treating him like a son. He is neglecting him in the same way an immoral man ignores the offspring of his illegitimate union. Consequently, an undisciplined child does not have a father in the true sense.

Parents must insist on a respectful response to disciplinary action. The author of Hebrews assumes this as normal procedure. "We have had human fathers who corrected us, and we paid them respect" (v 9a). Whenever a child is disrespectful toward parental discipline, he needs additional chastisement. He is still in rebellion against the authority God has given. The parent must administer additional discipline until the child respects him in it.

Appropriate child training helps him see the long-term benefits from the pains of correction (v 9b). Parents can increase their child's respect by helping him understand how discipline is best for him in the long run. Sometimes parents can instruct their child in right living, and then stand back and let the consequences of disobedience catch him. This is a great opportunity for the child to see that his parents' directions are not arbitrary, but are for his good.

One of our friends was putting her three-year-old son to bed when she noticed he had a chapstick. "Where did you get it?" she asked. "At the store," he replied. "It wasn't where it was supposed to be, so I just picked it up." She explained how something being out of place did not justify his stealing it. She emphasized that stealing brings all kinds of bad results, and that thieves go to jail. He wanted to know what a jail was like, so she described it to him. She had him confess his sin to God, and assured him of God's forgiveness.

The next morning he needed to face the consequences of his deed. He must go to the manager of the store and pay for what he stole. He must risk whatever punishment would be imposed. Even though he wanted her to do it for him, she required him to do it himself.

They went to the store together. While her son waited, she found the manager and explained the situation, lest the matter be merely brushed off as having little importance. The boy faced the manager, and in tears told what he had done. The manager emphasized the seriousness of shoplifting. Then the boy went through the checkout line and paid for the chapstick with his own money. By forcing her son to feel the consequences of wrong, a minor misdemeanor was transformed into an indelible lesson.

Parents must not be intimidated by their own imperfections. Verse nine makes an explicit contrast between earthly fathers and their

Heavenly Example. The Greek text calls them "fathers of our flesh," while He is characterized as "the father of spirits." God knew every earthly parent would be imperfect, but He gave them children anyway. He also gave them the authority and responsibility to train those children. Parents must never allow the imperfections of their flesh to immobilize them from discipline.

The chastening which human parents give is based on finite understanding: "They chastened us as seemed best to them" (v 10a). God expects this as normal. Parents must not be intimidated just because they do not know every detail of the situation. They can know enough to do their job properly. Finite understanding can apply the principles of God's Word and thus participate in the wisdom of the infinite.

Characteristics of Appropriate Discipline

God's goal in discipline is to enable His children to partake of His character. He chastens us "for our profit, that we may be partakers of His holiness" (v 10b). Parents pursue a similar goal. They discipline their children to reproduce the righteous character already developed in the parents. Wise parents help their children learn as teenagers some of the hard lessons they learned in their twenties and thirties.

During this training, the child experiences the unpleasantness of discipline. "No chastening seems to be joyful for the present, but grievous" (v 11a). The word used to describe discipline is "grievous," and this root word also describes Jesus' anguish in the Garden of Gethsemane (Matt 26:37,38). The excruciating unpleasantness of this term clarifies the basic intent of proper chastisement. It must be very unpleasant. Otherwise it is not discipline at all.

Children are naturally short-sighted. After being disciplined by her mother, three-year old Rachelle exclaimed, "I wish only Renee [her younger sister] and I lived here!" Proof of whether a child has really been disciplined (or whether the parent only went through the motions) is the final result which comes *later*. "Afterward it yields the peaceable fruit of righteousness to those who have been trained by it" (v 11b).

Proper discipline is no fun for the parent, but he perseveres because of the goals he has in mind. The progression in these verses illustrates the grandeur of these goals. He disciplines his child because he wants him to be a partaker of life (v 9b), bypassing the pitfalls and dangers that could shorten his life on earth (cf Eph 6:3). He wants him to understand spiritual reality and be a partaker of holiness (v 10b). Even this is not enough. He wants his child to have a life overflowing with the peaceable fruits of righteousness (v 11 b).

Appropriate discipline motivates the child to take special precautions against failure in the future. The pain is severe enough to produce an incentive for avoiding a repeat performance. He realizes his areas of weakness, and proceeds with new caution. "Therefore strengthen the hands which hang down, and the feeble knees, and make straight paths for your feet, so that what is lame may not be dislocated, but rather be healed" (vv 12-13).

He pursues right actions and thus promotes moral healing and strengthening in areas of past failure. Instruction helps the child to see the need for positive action. Discipline properly done motivates the child to take that action. This discipline helps him develop internal standards of right behavior.

Areas Needing Special Attention

Several areas of human depravity deserve special diligence to avoid future failure. It is so easy to get caught up in selfishness that genders strife with others. "Pursue peace with all men" (v 14a). Every child needs to be taught to avoid selfish conflict.

Lack of personal holiness is equally deadly. It is easy to put on a facade of righteousness, a mere whited sepulcher which hides dead men's bones and all kinds of uncleanness. Every child must learn to pursue holiness in its essence. "Pursue . . . holiness, without which no one will see the Lord" (v 14b). The pure in heart are the ones who will see God (Matt 5:8).

Bitterness against chastisement is one of the most common areas of failure. Children need to understand discipline as a necessary part of grace. Every person needs to look "diligently lest anyone fall short of the grace of God; lest any root of bitterness springing up cause trouble, and by this many become defiled" (v 15). Bitterness has long tentacles which reach beyond its owner to defile others. It is so easy for a child to react in bitterness, and spread that bitterness among his brothers and sisters. If a child responds in bitterness, the parents should tenderly instruct him regarding the seriousness of his response. They may also need to apply more discipline as a catalyst to facilitate understanding.

Failure to respond properly to discipline amounts to the sale of one's spiritual birthright. Godly parents intend chastisement to bring blessing: life, holiness, peaceable fruits of righteousness. Improper response to this chastisement repudiates the benefit of discipline in the hope of experiencing some short-term gratification. The child therefore is like a fornicator who perverts a blessing into a curse. Parents must help him avoid becoming a "fornicator or profane person like Esau, who for one morsel of food sold his birthright. For you know that afterward, when he wanted to inherit the blessing, he was rejected, for he found no place for repentance, though he sought it diligently with tears" (vv 16-17). Children must be taught that resistance to discipline will channel their lives into disaster. Parents should consciously use disciplinary confrontations to help their children delight in spiritual priorities.

General Perspective of Proper Discipline

The general purpose of God's discipline is to produce a better runner, one who willingly lays aside weights and besetting sins (12:1). To attain this, God disciplines us like sons. In His wisdom, He presented first the sternness of the Old Testament Law (12:18-21) to prevent us from misinterpreting mercy as leniency (12:22-24). Even though we enjoy the blessings of the New Covenant, the knowledge that our God is a consuming fire sobers us into obedience. We know His program will continue after everything else has been destroyed (12:25-29).

Parents who follow God as their model disciplinarian have similar goals and methods. Discipline is not an end in itself, a mere vent of parental frustration. The goal is a mature person who willingly discards anything hindering the achievement of higher priorities, even if those things are not wrong in themselves. Initial parental firmness in controlling the child makes him teachable and open to receiving wisdom. He learns that his parents are not to be trifled with, that they are not merely playing a game. He learns to choose values that will outlast the shaking of both heaven and earth.

Results of Neglecting Discipline

The life of the undisciplined child is like an untended garden. Soon it is overgrown with weeds, briars, and thistles. All kinds of disagreeable and unpleasant characteristics crowd out desirable character qualities.

When parents neglect to discipline their children, they are actually training them in negative behavior. The child learns that he can be dishonest and get by. He learns that he can whine and grumble and get out of work. He learns that greed has its rewards, and that sophisticated excuses bring benefits. The child is being trained in negative behavior. Such a child is wallowing in the tyranny of self, and therefore cannot be happy. His days are frustrated by joyless self-centeredness.

One of the most common ways parents neglect discipline is by disciplining inconsistently. This has several serious results. It makes discipline more work whenever it is attempted, and is more likely to engender anger and resentment in the child rather than respect. Since the discipline is inconsistent, the times the child "gets by" are essentially intermittent positive reinforcement of his wrong behavior. This reinforcement has a much greater effect than the discipline itself. Ultimately, the child extrapolates his experience into the hope of getting by while disobeying God.

The undisciplined child is insecure because he does not know where his boundaries are. He does not know what is acceptable and what is not. For days he will disobey his parents with impunity, and then suddenly be crushed when in exasperation they lash out at him for a minor offense.

This situation breeds resentment against the parent. The child wants his parents for the benefits they provide, but resents their authority. A resentful child thwarting parental authority is difficult and unpleasant to live with. The parent therefore begins to resent his presence. The child senses this resentment and becomes more belligerent and disobedient. This increased antagonism produces degenerative and accelerating cycles of resentment that flare up into hatred.

Such an environment is a seedbed for multiplied problems. These families experience severe problems unknown to parents who are diligent in rooting out evil before it is fully grown. King David's bitter harvest of compounded problems was the direct result of failing to apply God's solutions to earlier problems (2 Sam 11-18).

Wicked children are the final fruit of parental neglect in discipline, bringing a great curse upon their parents. "A foolish son is the grief of his mother" (Prov 10:1). The old age of such parents is one of grief rather than joy. "He who begets a scoffer does so to his sorrow, and the father of a fool has no joy" (Prov 17:21). Any momentary embarrassment associated with discipline is far overshadowed by the shameful result of disciplinary neglect: an undisciplined, wicked adult. "The rod and reproof give wisdom, but a child left to himself brings shame to his mother" (Prov 29:15).

The rebellion of the child may become so deeply entrenched that the parent is powerless to bring him under control. The writer of Proverbs warns all parents to be diligent in disciplining the child while his heart is tender and pliable, while there is hope for proper response: "Chasten your son while there is hope" (Prov 19:18). The clear implication is that the situation can degenerate into a hopeless case.

Proverbs 22:15 emphatically states that the rod of correction will drive foolishness far from the heart of the child. The same Hebrew root for "fool" and "foolishness" is then used in another emphatic statement in a later chapter. "Though you grind a fool in a mortar with a pestle along with crushed grain, yet his foolishness will not depart from him" (Prov 27:22). The person who is not disciplined properly while he is young becomes set in his foolishness. No matter how severe the chastisement, such a person will not profit from it. He will only become more resistant and belligerent. The comparison of Proverbs 27:22 and 22:15 shows that the rod will not be effective if the parent waits too long.

When a parent realizes he has failed in fulfilling his responsibility to properly discipline his child, the first step toward a solution is to repent. Parents have not been left in the spiritually futile situation of merely having "problems" or "weaknesses." The fact that the parent has sinned is the key to victory. Sins can be confessed, forsaken, and forgiven. God's grace can be applied to provide a solution. Mere "weaknesses" are intractable.

After receiving God's forgiveness, the parent should confess his sin to his child and ask his forgiveness for selfishly neglecting discipline. If the rebellious child is willing to live at home and submit to the force necessary to teach him proper attitudes and behavior, there is yet hope. Otherwise the parent has no recourse but to ask God in His grace to do what is humanly impossible: bring beauty out of ashes by sending the shattering disciplines of life to bring the erring child also to repentance.[7]

Results of Diligent Discipline

Diligent discipline brings great joy to the family. The Scriptures call this the peaceable fruit of righteousness (Heb 12:11). Instead of degenerative cycles of resentment, this family experiences affirmative cycles of delight. The disciplined child knows his boundaries and is happy in them. He knows his parents truly care for him. His response in obedience increases their delight in him. He feels this affection, and naturally responds with a greater delight in his parents. Obedience is a normal joy, not an oppressive burden.

Children who have experienced proper discipline know its importance in having a happy family. They see undisciplined children as miserable and unhappy. Our friends had a ten-year-old son who knew the security and contentment resulting from healthy discipline in the home. His mother made him responsible to watch the three-year-old child of a friend—a child who continually misbehaved and exhibited unwholesome attitudes. The boy discussed the problem with his mother, and explained: "That child is an unhappy kid! What he needs is discipline. Discipline is the key to happiness!" Then with horror on his face, he realized his statements might need to be applied to himself. "What am I saying?" he exclaimed. Healthy home experience was the seed-plot for insight.

As an experiment, I once asked my four oldest children to write lists of what they thought were the five most important principles for raising healthy, happy children. Their comments are included here, as they illustrate their perception of the importance of discipline in enabling children to be happy.

The five-year old: "1) Spank them when they are naughty. 2) Obey right away. 3) Children can't have as much candy as they want." (She couldn't think of anything else.)

The seven-year old: "1) Discipline. 2) Don't let your children have everything they want. 3) Love your children. 4) Don't let your children get by with bad things. 5) Don't be mean to your children." (On this last point, he at first used the word "harsh" and then crossed it out and substituted "mean." I asked why. He thought a child may sometimes be very persistent and need harsh discipline. Child abuse was equated with being mean.)

The nine-year old: "1) Discipline. 2) Must not have a TV 3) Teach them the Bible. 4) Teach them to be polite. 5) Teach them to pray."

The eleven-year old: "1) Teach them about the Bible. 2) Discipline them carefully. 3) Get them interested in books, music, or/and art rather than T.V. and computer games. 4) Emphasize the togetherness

---

[7]Fugate, *Child Training,* p. 75

of the family and having each person do his part. 5) Make the most of their abilities."

Parents who are diligent in discipline receive a great reward: the blessing of children who are filled with wisdom. "A wise son makes a glad father" (Prov 10:1). "The father of the righteous will greatly rejoice, and he who begets a wise child will delight in him. Let your father and your mother be glad, and let her who bore you rejoice" (Prov 23:24-25). For her diligence, the virtuous woman of Proverbs 31 is crowned by children who rise up and call her blessed (31:28).

Although disciplinary action is unpleasant for the parent, it is the key to increasing parental delight in his child. "Correct your son, and he will give you rest; yes, he will give delight to your soul" (Prov 29:17). This is a great contrast to the child who is left to himself (Prov 29:15).

The general tenor of Proverbs is that a child who is properly trained and disciplined will be a wise and good adult. This truth is stated explicitly: "Train up a child in the way he should go, and when he is old he will not depart from it" (Prov 22:6). This text has an uncomfortable implication: a child who chooses evil as an adult is proof that his parents did not train him properly. God is presenting this statement as a general pattern of truth. He is not saying there will be no exceptions. But the exceptions will be the exception, not the rule.[8]

Many parents are looking for ways to excuse their own failure rather than face what this text actually says. All kinds of exegetical gymnastics have been performed on this verse. Some say it means the child will eventually repent of his evil years and turn again to God in his old age. Others appeal to the original text and make tenuous arguments regarding the lexical nuances of a very flexible Hebrew preposition.

Some interpreters appeal to the Hebrew text which literally says, "Train up a child according to *his way,* and when he is old he will not depart from it." They admonish parents to observe carefully the natural bent of the child, and train him according to his gifts. Delight in his special talents, and help him develop those. Don't expect a slender, artistic child to become a football player. Don't frustrate your child by "trying to make a tomato plant bear pine cones," and then sadly wonder why he also rejects his spiritual training. Training a child according to his gifts is supposed to keep him from rejecting the ways of the Lord.

---

[8]The book of Proverbs is packed with general statements of truth. This does not mean that these statements are inflexible rules which never have any exceptions. For example, "When a man's ways please the Lord, He makes even his enemies to be at peace with him" (Prov 16:7). The life of the Lord Jesus and the blood of the martyrs exhibit clear exceptions to this proverb (Heb 11:36-38). Samson's parents were very much concerned about the details of his upbringing (Judg 13:8,12). Possibly Samson's profligate lifestyle is an exception to Proverbs 22:6. Certainly Deuteronomy 21:18-21 suggests an exception. Otherwise the parents should have been stoned.

The fallacy of this view is that "it" at the end of the verse must refer to the same thing as "way" at the beginning. If the first half of the verse refers to training in natural gifts, the last half must also—reducing the proverb to nonsense: "Train up a child according to his natural gifts and talents, and then when he is old he will not depart from those areas of endeavor." Such a statement is no proverb. The paraphrasers are trying to eat their cake and have it too. The standard translations have it right: it is best to understand "his way" as referring to *God's* way.

All of these alternative interpretations of Proverbs 22:6 ignore the obvious meaning of the verse in order to salve the guilt of negligent and disobedient parents—guilt which God intends for them to feel. The remedy for guilt is not exegetical salve, but confession and repentance.

Taken in its natural sense, Proverbs 22:6 is sobering to parents in terms of their responsibility before God, and is also a great encouragement to those who are serious about training their children. They are working in harmony with the laws of the universe. The overwhelming pattern is that proper training produces children who choose what is right.

The English word "train" translates the Hebrew verb *chanak*. This word means to dedicate or inaugurate.[9] Its usage here embodies the idea of starting a child on the path which he should go. The parent's task is to direct the child into a path which he would not choose if left to himself, but which he will choose if properly initiated and dedicated to the ways of righteousness. This is not just a single-event initiation, but a process permeating the entire life of the child.[10]

This does not mean a trained child is a mindless robot who has no choice. Suppose after carefully teaching your ten-year-old the value of money, you give him a choice: a sparkling red yo-yo, or a check for $1000 when he turns twelve. There is no question what the well-taught child will choose. That choice does not mean he is a robot programmed and dominated by his parents. It simply means he understands reality: a plain little piece of paper is worth much more than a colorful yo-yo ready for immediate action.

Many Christian parents fail because they have not diligently taught their child *how* eternal values transcend everything this present world has to offer. Any parent who disobeys God's commands in order to attain a higher standard of living is telling his child that temporal gain is more important than eternal values. When the child comes to make his own choice, he can make it only on the basis of what he knows.

---

[9]Harris, Archer, Waltke, editors, *Theological Wordbook of the Old Testament,* Vol 1, p. 301.

[10]The word translated "child" (*na'ar*) is especially appropriate for indicating extensive training over a period of time. In the Old Testament it can refer to individuals ranging in age from infancy to adulthood. Notice in particular the span of ages implied in the book of Proverbs (1:4; 7:7; 20:11; 22:6,15; 23:13; 29:15).

Parents who dedicate themselves to training their children will see them grow up knowing reality and making the only reasonable choice: the reproach of Christ is more valuable than all the treasures of Egypt.

Questions

Sometimes parents have specific questions about how to handle problem situations. Here are some suggestions.

What if my fifteen-month-old won't eat his food? Do not force him to eat, because he may be going into a growth slump, or he may be on the verge of getting sick. Do not confuse the issue by feeding him snacks between meals. Never let him skip vegetables and then eat dessert.

Should older children be spanked? The Scriptures set no age for when spankings must cease. For an older child, spanking carries with it an inherent humiliation which adds to the effect. Adults have testified that being spanked as a teenager was exactly what they needed.

Should the rod be used on infants? For children less than one year old, it is better to use your hand because by the time you get the rod the child will not know why he is being spanked. Avoid striking above the waist lest your child learn to flinch when your hand approaches.

Should the father spank the boys and the mother the girls? No, the parent involved in the situation is more familiar with the details and can deal with it immediately, and should therefore handle the discipline. An exception could occur when the wife is physically unable (late pregnancy, postpartum recovery). Then the husband should deal with the more difficult discipline cases.

Since we want our child to learn proper social behavior, wouldn't it be effective to isolate him for 2-5 minutes in his room because he bit a sibling? A five-minute dose of loneliness is not an effective deterrent for biting someone. Use God's prescription instead.

Isn't it better to use loving creativity rather than resorting to corporal punishment? Don't disobey God and then invent pious-sounding reasons for following your own ideas.

What about people who didn't discipline their children, and yet their children turned out right? Even now, those children may have less obvious character flaws that could have been corrected in childhood. Never use an apparent exception as an excuse to disobey God. Never presume on the grace of God.

What if you live in a foreign country where the culture disapproves of spanking? God's principles are transcultural. We must obey God and rely on Him. Incidentally, we live in that kind of culture here. Discipline in private.

Should parents always use spanking as their method of discipline? For young children spanking works best. It makes good sense to emphasize the method that works best for this strategic age. Sometimes other methods can be used, particularly as a natural consequence of the misbehavior. For example, if a child dawdles at the table, he misses dessert because he is not finished with his vegetables. However, the use of a physical rod is the gibraltar of effective discipline. Do not merely take my word for it. Read the book of Proverbs and believe what God has said.

Summary

There are many ways a parent is tempted to neglect discipline. He may misunderstand love, not realizing that he who neglects discipline actually hates his child and wants to see him destroyed. He may think his own example will be sufficient, or that certainly example coupled with instruction will be effective. Possibly the sins of his own past have made it difficult for him to discipline his children for similar failures. Ultimately, discipline is neglected because parents fail to face their moral obligation to obey God's command for child discipline.

Parents having a proper philosophy of effective discipline will diligently notice small symptoms revealing significant problems. They will utilize the "Opportunity Twos" to train the child in effective living while those lessons are relatively easy. Discipline will begin early, as soon as the child exhibits defiance against his parents' will.

Effective discipline will have a physical rod as its primary foundation. The use of this rod will make the discipline a noteworthy event. This event must match the offense, being both severe enough to be worthwhile, and yet not overdone in abusiveness or unreasonableness. Prayer is an important ingredient: asking God to work internally with the child's heart, while we work externally in making the lesson clear.

In all these things, God is our model Father, and therefore our model disciplinarian. Observing how He chastens us, and seeing His goals in chastisement, help us know how to properly discipline our own children.

The book of Proverbs makes the general pattern clear. Basically we can choose the kind of family we want. Neglect of discipline brings disaster. Careful discipline with instruction brings joy and peace.

Discipline is hard work, requiring diligence, persistence, consistency, and sacrifice. Sometimes when parents realize the failure of their past, they resolve to operate their homes in a Biblical manner. Then they are shocked when several sound spankings do not result in immediate transformation of their child's character. They have expected the walls of Jericho to fall after circling the city only once or twice. The Israelite warriors marched around Jericho once. The next day they marched around again. Day after day they marched around. On the final day they marched around *seven* times.

Model children are not available as instant results of stirring in magic ingredients. Model children are available when parents consistently obey God's directives in discipline, and therefore open the channel for His grace to be showered upon their family.

Your Choice: Despair or Delight

13

Developing Delightful Children

Everyone would like to have delightful children. Children who obey. Children who are polite and unselfish. Children who love each other. Children who are honest. Children who make wise decisions. Children who are fun to live with.

Fortunately, the guarantee of such children is not some rare magic potion available to only a select few. Delightful children are available to parents who really want them: parents who obey God's directions for the family.

This chapter assumes commitment to Biblical principles of family living, and is intended to give some practical suggestions on how to develop delightful children. These suggestions are not exhaustive and are not all universally applicable, but are a smorgasbord which parents may find useful in dealing with problems they face. These starting points can launch parents into their own creative applications of God's principles for their specific situations.

General Principles

Delightful children are not automatic. A laissez faire approach to child training will not work. The second law of thermodynamics states that things left to themselves go downhill. A child left to himself brings shame. He needs help from beyond himself to rise above his innate tendency to choose wrong. Parents must actively help their children to obey God.

Do not neglect your opportunities and privileges as a parent. Time slips away. Ten years from now, what will you wish you would have done today? Do it now!

In the Scriptures, instruction and discipline are intimately coupled. Instruction is made effective through discipline. Discipline opens the mind to receive instruction. Delightful children cannot be developed without discipline.

In every area of child training, parental example is crucial. There are at least three reasons why a parent will be unable to effectively teach a principle he personally violates. First, his own lack of integrity will dull his ability to articulate the principle. Second, his hypocrisy will create resentment and disdain in the heart of his child. Third, a disciple will ultimately become like his teacher (Lu 6:40), not merely like what his teacher says.

Often the child becomes a kind of mirror indicating where the parent needs to repent and grow in holiness. Each parent must deal with his own flaws as well as correcting the faults of the child. To excuse the wrong in a child because of similar wrong in the parent is to multiply disaster in the family.

Several assumptions make it possible to abbreviate the following discussion because these principles apply to each issue. 1) Parental example is the platform for teaching. 2) The parent should try to incorporate specific Scriptures relating to the given issue. 3) Parents should affirm their children's obedience to those specific Scriptures. 4) Establishment of right patterns in the home develops a distaste for wrong patterns.

Personal Character Development

The characteristics of all children center around two major areas: personal character and social development. Development of a delightful child begins with a focus on his character.

Heart For God

The primary ingredient of good character is a heart that loves God and obeys Him. Develop this by studying the Word of God with your children. Emphasize Bible stories, the great picture book of human existence. Focus on the lessons we can learn from the experience of Bible characters. Do not limit yourself to formal teaching alone. Relate God's word to the activities of life (Deut 6). Show your children how rich and exciting the Scriptures are.

Be involved in ministry yourself. Share the beauty of Christ with others. Involve your children with you in ministry: singing, witnessing, handing out gospel tracts, visiting the elderly. Many children never see one of the greatest evidences of God's existence: lives changed as a demonstration of His power (Rom 1:16).

Introduce your children to people whose hearts are focused on God. Invite missionaries to your home. Cultivate friendships with spiritually-minded families. Do not limit yourself to contemporaries. Read to your children from the biographies and autobiographies of great saints. Use Faith Coxe Bailey's *Young Rebel in Bristol* to introduce your children to George Mueller. Ten-year-olds can enjoy Courtney Anderson's *To the Golden Shore,* a comprehensive but excellent biography of Adoniram Judson. Teenagers should read *Shadow of the Almighty* by Elizabeth Elliot, and see how even as a young man Jim Elliot truly had a heart for God.

Wise Decisions and Responsibility for Actions

Wise decisions are based on a solid foundation of moral training. Teach your children wisdom by emphasizing the study of God's Word and obedience to it, especially the book of Proverbs. Teach your children to be afraid to disobey God. This is the beginning of wisdom, a sad commentary on many contemporary Christians who are unafraid to disregard what God says. Help your children understand how obedience to God's commands protects them from disaster, as illustrated by Proverbs 6:20-24. Older children can benefit by reading a chapter of Proverbs for each day of the month.

Let your children see how you yourself make decisions: observing surroundings, noting cause and effect, spending time in prayer, avoiding haste. Let them see how you resolve the issues you personally face. Let them pray with you in issues facing the family.

Show them how to think responsibly. When a mother does errands, she can ask her children: "Which one shall we do first?" She can also ask, "Why do you think I chose this one first?" One mother (whose husband was not a believer) explained to her children why she does her husband's errands first—to make sure they are done if time runs out.

Teach your children to learn from others. When your child behaves inappropriately, ask: "Could you see Mr. Smith [a spiritual person whom the child regards highly] doing this?"

Help your children learn from mistakes of others. Show them a newspaper article which describes someone getting hurt. Help them reason through the factors putting a person into a dangerous situation. Was a child molested because foolish choices (either by parents or the child) invited trouble?

Again, expose your children to good biographies. Let them see how others obeyed God and triumphed over evil. Let them see how evil behavior reaps sorrow and ultimately destroys one's character.

A child needs to know that he should not obey strangers. But if someone tells him to do something that is right, he should obey. His own conscience will teach him. For example, if in the church lawn someone tells him to stop mistreating a small boy, he must obey. He must also understand that if he ever has questions about whether to obey someone's command, he should come to you and ask.

Give your children tasks to do, and hold them responsible for doing those tasks promptly and correctly. Make irresponsibility more trouble than appropriate behavior. Make sure they understand the importance of being careful because accidents do matter. Require them to pay restitution for inconvenience and wrong against others (cf Ex 21-22). Consistently discipline infractions.

Allow your children to bear the consequences of their own decisions. A father can tell his child, "Put on your shoes and you may go shopping with me." If five minutes later the child does not have his shoes on, do not wait. Go shopping without him. Of course, if the child had a pattern of willing obedience, and simply could not find one shoe, the parent should have mercy and help him look for it. But if the child was habitually negligent about putting things away, let him stay at home and feel the disappointment of his own carelessness.

Some children are habitually inattentive. They never hear what their parents tell them. Make it worth while to hear. Clearly tell them once, and let them bear the consequences of not hearing.

Teach your children the importance of trustworthiness: wise decisions and proper behavior even when their parents are not present with them. Ingrain an attitude of loyalty—first of all to God, and then to the patterns the family has established. When questioned by a youth pastor why he did not participate in certain youth activities, one teenager replied handsomely, "First of all, I'm a Christian, and I don't think Christians should do that. Second, I'm a Drexel, and Drexels don't do that!" He knew the joy of both a moral foundation and family loyalty.

Obedience

Demonstrate your own obedience to the authorities who are over you and to the principles you teach. No mother can expect her children to obey her if she does not obey her husband.

Always insist on obedience, even if your request was not specifically a moral issue. When a parent gives any command, it becomes a moral issue for the child. Tardy or grudging obedience is not really obedience. Mothers could try this test for a toddler, "Take this cookie to Daddy, and then I will give one to you."

Parents must arrange things so they can be attentive to disobedience, and deal with it. A mother may be so harried with her home responsibilities that she fails to notice disobedience. She needs to involve her children more in the work so she can be sensitive to wrongdoing and correct it promptly.

Truthfulness

By definition, a lie is something done with the intent to deceive. This includes acting a lie. Conversely, a child who says something false merely because he had faulty information is not guilty of lying.

"Tales" told by children are not to be taken lightly. It cannot be passed off as mere "kidding" and of little consequence. "Like a madman who throws firebrands, arrows, and death, is the man who deceives his neighbor, and says, 'I was only joking' " (Prov 26:19)! Parents should never condone or participate in any "practical jokes" or surprises that involve lying.

Children best understand the seriousness of lying by seeing what God says about it. Satan is the father of lies. Anyone who lies is obeying Satan. All liars have their part in the lake of fire (Rev 21:8).

The seriousness of lying is emphasized by the amount of space Paul gives in discussing it compared to other sins in Colossians 3. Why is this such a serious matter? It is one of the biggest problems in the church, bigger than anger, wrath, or slander, even though these are more obvious. Many people are not really honest.

Paul gives the following reasons for not lying: 1) you have put off the old man with his deeds (Col 3:9). 2) You have put on the new man (3:10). 3) This new man is renewed in the knowledge of the Creator (3:10). 4) There is no distinction of people in this new man (3:11).

5) Christ is all in all. Thus, anyone who lies to his brother is lying to Christ (3:11; cf Acts 5:4).

Tell your children stories to show them how lying gets a person into deeper and deeper trouble. New lies are needed to cover up old ones. Remembering how to make all those lies fit together eventually becomes impossible. Tell about the Watergate scandal. More than his conduct, President Nixon's lies finally cost him the White House. Those who lie to escape danger are faithlessly presupposing that God is not able to deliver them. Read Corrie Ten Boom's *The Hiding Place* to help your child see the contrast between Corrie's lies and her sister's honesty.

Train your children to tell the truth regardless of consequences (Prov 12:19). It may occasionally be appropriate to withhold punishment for a misdemeanor when a child tells the truth about it (especially if he volunteers his confession without having been caught). This cannot be the pattern, however, lest the child get the idea that honesty means automatic acquittal. Know your child. An alert parent can discern whether confession springs from a desire to cleanse a guilty conscience, or merely from a desire to escape punishment. In general, a child should receive a double penalty in a situation involving lying: one for the misdeed, and one for the lie.

Gratitude

At times the Lord in His graciousness gives us answers we are not even seeking. As a beginning parent I decided that the general method of dishing out dessert to children was unreasonable. Often a child would get a piece of cake practically the same size as the one given to a grown man who had eaten four times as much meat and vegetables. I realized that for balanced nutrition, children should have only a small sliver of cake.

As I followed this approach I noticed a serendipity benefit: gratitude in the children. They were grateful for a small piece of cake. They were grateful for the opportunity to clean the crumbs out of the cake pan. This grateful attitude spilled over into other aspects of life as well.

In a similar vein, gratitude is enhanced by giving *small* gifts at birthdays and Christmas. Large gifts breed materialism. Focus instead on doing things for one another, making gifts for each other, ministry to others. At Christmas we should be teaching our children to express their gratitude for the greatest Gift by giving gifts to Christ, rather than hankering after what they will get. One year our children purchased clothing for suffering Christians in eastern Europe. They have also enjoyed baking cookies or bread to give to our hosts when we go Christmas caroling as a family.

Gratitude can also be enhanced by making your children aware of the needs of the world: millions of people go hungry. If your family sponsors a child in a poor country, the support activity will be an automatic monthly reminder for gratitude.

Establish a pattern of habitual acknowledgment of others. Mothers have a great opportunity to express gratitude when they receive a wilted bouquet of dandelions from a toddler's grubby hand. "Please" and "thank you" should be part of normal household atmosphere, not just good manners for guests. Children should be encouraged to make thank-you notes for gifts or other benefits received from friends. Everyone loves to receive children's art.

Make Ephesians 5:20 practical: "In everything give thanks." Help your children understand how to do that. We do it by an act of the will, even when we don't understand why things happen as they do. We realize the situation could be much worse. Our appreciation of blessings often grows in their absence: water tastes especially good when we are really thirsty. We know God allows unpleasant experiences to refine our character and to give us the ability to comfort others in trouble (2 Cor 1:4). We thank our sovereign God for allowing *temporal* disappointment in order to bring *eternal* gain.

Contentment

Contentment in the children is founded in an atmosphere of parental contentment. Avoid the stranglehold of things. Beware of TV ads for toys and games, ads engineered to create a lust for more and more. Live simply and frugally. "Godliness with contentment is great gain" (1 Tim 6:6). Help children to savor what they have by giving them small gifts and small dessert portions.

Sometimes grandparents inundate the grandchildren with gifts—not only at Christmas, but also birthdays, holidays, or just any occasion that can be made into an opportunity for giving gifts. Big gifts. Expensive gifts. What can be done to curtail the detrimental effects of this situation without alienating or wounding the grandparents?

Talk to the grandparents and point out how excessive things actually breed discontent and greed in children. Ask if they could express their love by giving a few small gifts while quietly making an investment fund in behalf of the children—a fund that could be accessed for non-consumables (such as education or housing) when the child is mature.

Be cautious about indulgent grandparents taking children to the store and letting them pick out what they want. Suggest the giving of books, educational toys, tickets to special events such as music concerts. Encourage grandparents to give of themselves: take the grandchildren on walks, read stories to them, tell about themselves when they were children. Little ones never tire of such things. Help grandparents understand that they will experience much greater joy by maximizing their interaction with their grandchildren, rather than by showering them with things.

Make what you do together as a family the greatest attraction of your home. Let your children experience life's greatest joys—not in things, but in God, other people, achievement, creativity.

Creativity

Creativity is a native endowment of the child. The parent's job is to foster and develop that creativity. Firm requirements of obedience enable a child to focus his creativity on useful projects rather than on finding out whether his parents are telling the truth.

Beware of things which hamper creativity: television, addictive arcade type computer games, affluence. Without access to television, children are naturally motivated to read, invent games of their own, and interact constructively with their siblings.

By example and instruction, show your child how to use his brain instead of your wallet. My eight-year-old son wanted a camera. Instead of buying one, I worked with him in building a pin-hole camera. The necessary simplicity of the result automatically clarified basic principles of camera operation.

A parent who teaches his child many things sets the stage for new levels of creativity in his child. The child has many more ideas to work with. Give your children deliberate opportunities in the creative arts.

Art is one of the easiest creative expressions for the toddler. Begin by surrounding him with children's books filled with realistic pictures. This may mean going to used book sales. Sadly, the drawings in most contemporary children's books are vastly inferior to those published thirty or forty years ago. Our children gained their concept of good art by a heavy exposure to art that is really good.

Give your children blank paper instead of coloring books. Have your children explain the pictures they have drawn. Show interest and delight in what they have done.

Help the older children encourage the younger ones. When our son Roland was small, he was discouraged with drawing. He saw his attempts as atrocious compared to what his older sisters could accomplish. We helped the girls praise his pictures for what they really were: beautiful creativity for a child his age. With that encouragement, Roland's art began to flourish.

Teach your children to play a musical instrument. Teach your children to sing. Singing together as a family is a wonderful activity. Learning to sing together in four-part harmony is work, but it pays great rewards: fellowship, teamwork, companionship, effort. Each person must sing his part with the right pitch, the right vowel, the right dynamic level, the right rhythm. Each part is different, but vitally necessary. The result is a sculpture in sound, beauty that cannot be accomplished by individuals alone. Besides, skill in music opens doors into spiritual ministry. It provides even more advantages than "the wonderful lessons learned in football"—without the liabilities.

Crafts and woodworking can provide opportunities for older children. Fathers would be wise to invest in a few tools for repairing simple things around the house. Help your sons learn how to fix things.

Diligence

In general, people need to be *taught* how to work. All of us have a certain amount of innate laziness. Children need to learn that laziness brings inconvenience. One way to dramatize this fact to a sluggardly child is to have a day when everyone "does nothing" (including Mother).

Allow children to make choices, and require them to live by those choices. I know of a family whose children help with the work associated with a large garden. When one child complained about not wanting to help with the beans, the father gave him the freedom to quit and go play, "But remember, when we sit down for supper, you will have to go hungry. The choice is yours." Such an arrangement is very Biblical (2 Thess 3:10), even though it sounds strange to ears saturated with the follies of socialized laziness.

Many adults are sloppy in their work because they never learned as children to work efficiently and carefully. Children should be required to redo an entire job if it was incorrectly done. If dishes are not washed clean, the child should do dishes again after the next meal. A child needs to know that you expect good work. If a child is not thorough, tell him, "Clean your room, and when you are done I will check it." Sometimes an older child can participate in the process by checking the room for you.

Require a child to bear the brunt of her own carelessness. If she has a pattern of putting wrong ingredients together when baking, freeze her sloppy cake and let her have a piece of it whenever the rest of the family eats a properly prepared dessert.

Sometimes children have a habit of dawdling. They fritter away hours at a task that should require only minutes. An effective approach is to set a time limit. Punish them for being late. Help them understand why diligence is more enjoyable than slothfulness. If results are slow in coming, begin setting time limits without warnings. Remember, the goal is not merely to get the job done. The job itself is relatively unimportant. The goal is to establish a pattern of diligence.

For children who dawdle at the table, let them miss dessert if their plates are not empty by the time dessert is served. If dawdling persists beyond the time allotted for the meal, put their food in the refrigerator and have them eat it cold at the next meal. Children rapidly learn it is more fun to eat promptly than to begin a meal with cold leftovers.[1]

Perseverance

In teaching a child perseverance, it is useful to review the factors in your own failure to persevere. Did you fail to give the task high enough priority? Did the job seem overwhelming?

---

[1]In general, I prefer not to spank a child for faults related to mealtime. The trauma of the spanking is so disruptive to the digestive process that it can become counter-productive to spank a child so that he will eat his vegetables. If the proper use of the rod in other situations has clearly established parental authority, I think alternatives are preferable for mealtime.

Help your children learn how to work through situations. Train them as they clean up a messy room. Break the task into easily handled small jobs so they can see immediate progress: pick up the toys, put away the clothes, straighten the bed, dust the dresser. A big mess is ordered by focusing on small segments.

Give a child a task which you are sure he is capable of finishing. Don't allow him to stop until it is satisfactorily completed. Let him know he will miss lunch if he doesn't get finished in time. Such incentives rarely need much repetition.

Commend your child for completing a job, even though you might not give him an "A" for the result (do not destroy the lesson by being excessively particular). Teach your child not to be "weary in well doing." Help him see that Satan wants him to grovel in discouragement. Establish patterns of laying aside every hindrance, and persevering because we joyfully anticipate the result (Heb 12:1-2).

Neatness

Neatness is not automatic. A child must be taught how to categorize and sort. "Put your papers in the top drawer. Put your trinkets in the bottom drawer." Set a limit on how much stuff he may keep. Let him have a "treasure drawer" where he can save his special treasures. When that drawer gets full, have him decide what to discard.

Let the children help you keep the house neat. Older children can easily pick up after the one-year old. When children are old enough to appreciate the value of money, a system of "fining money" marshalls their sharp little eyes to help you. Let them collect a penny for articles the others leave out of place.

Cheerfulness

Parents should never tolerate whining, complaining, or begging. If a child uses such tactics, the parents should automatically refuse the request. Susanna Wesley had a policy of never giving her children what they cried for. Frequently, children who are fussy are just tired. Send them to bed for a nap. Children quickly learn that wrong attitudes are counter-productive.

Sometimes a parent can imitate a child's whining tone to help him see how unpleasant it is. Require the child to speak properly, and then commend him when he gets it right.

In the frantic scurry of the day, it is very easy for a busy mother to "tune out" the whining component she hears and ignore it. Husbands must be sympathetic and help their wives to attentively take the time during a busy day to administer correction. Ultimately this saves time because it makes the household run more sweetly and efficiently.

Have a policy of expecting cheerfulness as right and normal. Continual adherence to this standard will produce an atmosphere which the older children will not want to see disrupted by grumbling from the younger ones. They will then help you train the others.

Self-Control

All of us experience sorrow and disappointment. Children need to learn how to cope with sadness. A parent can help a child who has accidently broken a favorite toy, "I know this happened, and it makes you sad. I understand your feelings. You may be sad for thirty minutes. Then you need to be happy."

Parents should not tolerate wild screaming just because an insect landed on a child's arm. Teach them that this is the equivalent of crying "wolf, wolf" when there is no wolf. Incidentally, some mothers need to learn this lesson themselves.

When a child is disciplined, he should cry softly (not loudly and rebelliously), and this cry should continue for only a short time.

If your child has difficulty with anger, help him see the root causes of his anger: selfishness, greed, jealousy. Help him solve these root problems. Teach him that lashing out in anger only increases his sorrows.

Self-Acceptance

Many people are correct in having a poor self image, because their selfishness makes them despicable. It is utter folly to try to convince someone of "self values" which he knows are not true. This is merely the false religion of positive thinking. Christ provides the solution to a poor self image: be a servant. The servant becomes great according to God's definition. Greatness is the key to self-acceptance. Servanthood is the key to greatness. Therefore, servanthood is the healthy way to build self-acceptance. Those who are truly great need not worry about "poor self image."

In the family, self-acceptance begins as a by-product of the total home atmosphere. An atmosphere where the parents love each other. An environment of loving teaching and consistent discipline. A home where parents delight in each child as a person and a friend.

Self-acceptance continues as the child learns to be a servant. Help your children experience this kind of greatness when they are very young. Tell your toddler, "Would you please get me a tissue?" He will experience great joy and fulfillment in serving you.

Social Development

Many people have social problems because of their character deficiencies. Many aspects of social maladjustment are corrected automatically by solving character problems.

If a child exhibits problems in his social relationships, spend some time thinking about his character. Focus first on making those internal changes affecting every relationship. Then concentrate on those things which we more specifically call "social graces."

Courtesy

Respect and courtesy are based on an environment of politeness. Spouses must treat each other and the children with graciousness when alone at home. Children must never be allowed to respond to their parents with back-talk. Always insist on polite behavior. Properly trained children contribute to a gracious home atmosphere.

One of the places to begin is in table manners. Establish politeness as normal. All requests are accompanied by "please." No one leaves the table without being excused. Everyone chews food with his mouth shut, and no one talks with food in his mouth. Dawdling and silliness are not permitted. Children are required to eat a small portion of each food served. Unless vegetables are finished, dessert is forfeited. Everyone waits to eat dessert until all are served (this promotes the joy of fellowship rather than merely the pleasantness of the dessert).

Children do not dominate the conversation and thus gain an exaggerated impression of their own importance. Instead, they learn to participate in meaningful discussion guided by their parents. Establishing these patterns makes mealtime a cherished privilege, not a chaos to be endured. It is an opportunity for family fellowship and spiritual growth. Mealtimes are a major component of proper home atmosphere.

Require your children to practice the courtesy of not interrupting one another. When a younger child is telling a story, do not permit an older child to interrupt even though he can tell it better.

Sometimes disrespect evidences itself in impatience. Whenever this occurs, make the impatient one wait longer. Obviously his patience needs exercise. One who barges ahead at the door can retrace his steps and enter properly after the others.

If a child is rude, unkind to his peers, or demands his own way, let him go to his room and spend time alone while the other children have fun together.

Children need to understand that your family does not tolerate disrespect to parents, older people, or the handicapped. Emphasize the Golden Rule.

Love For Siblings

The problem of conflict between siblings is as old as humanity. Greed, jealousy, and resentment explode into fires of hatred. This selfishness is intensely destructive: obvious disaster to others, a blighting canker to self. Teach your child the folly of sibling friction by showing him its terrible results in Biblical history.

Cain's jealousy of Abel set the stage for murder, departure from God, and the founding of a debauched line of God-haters.

Jacob's greed for Esau's blessing motivated his use of deceit. God's laws of sowing and reaping caused him to wander as a stranger, to be cheated into marrying a girl he did not love, and to be deceived by his own sons.

Joseph's brothers harbored such deep resentment that they sold him into slavery, not knowing they ultimately would bow their knees to the one they despised.

The jealousy of Miriam and Aaron against Moses halted the entire Israelite camp for a week while they waited for Miriam to be healed of God's judgment of leprosy.

In order to establish his rule over Israel, Gideon's son Abimelech murdered sixty-nine of his seventy brothers.   The disasters of his wicked regime were finally halted by a woman who threw a millstone off a wall and crushed his skull.

David's brothers falsely accused him when he obeyed his father by going to the Valley of Elah. Their animosity was a salve for their own incompetence in cowering before the blasphemy of Goliath.

Teach your child how to deal with jealousy and resentment by instructing him about God's ordering of the universe. He deliberately made people with different gifts and gave them different opportunities. God's view of equality is not absolute, but relative to the needs of a given task. The three families of Levi were given the job of moving the tabernacle. Moses provided two carts and four oxen for the family of Gershon, four carts and eight oxen for the family of Merari, but none for the family of Kohath who carried the holy things on their shoulders (Num 7:6-9).

Help your children to rejoice in the benefits brought to the family by a sibling's talents.   Teach your children to focus on developing themselves where they are weak, rather than being jealous of gifts which God has given to another. Help your children understand God. Teach them to love God's will, and to take disappointments as part of God's good providence.

Use specific Scriptures to confront attitudes of jealousy and resentment. Simple obedience protects children from escalating rivalry (cf Prov 6:20-24). "This is my commandment, that you love one another as I have loved you" (Jn 15:12). God clearly defines love and informs us that any wonderful deeds done apart from love are unimpressive in His sight (1 Cor 13). "Be kind to one another, tenderhearted, forgiving one another" (Eph 4:32) is a command, not just a good suggestion.

Parents can also take specific actions to avoid outbreaks of jealousy and resentment.   Remember, the child is immature and particularly susceptible to the temptation of jealousy.

A young child faces unique adjustments when a new baby arrives in the family.   Cataclysmic change interrupts his familiar routine. Someone else has usurped his mother's attention. Guests exclaim over the new baby and bring him gifts. Suddenly, the older child feels left out and alone, wishing for the good old days. Alleviate this pressure by giving him a special gift when the baby is born. Involve him in the joy of serving the new baby.

Teach your children to be glad when another person gets what they wanted. Have the child visualize himself as the one benefitted while others grouch. Let him see how unhappy this makes everyone. When one child receives something special, help him to learn the joy of sharing it.

Sometimes a child resents his siblings because he knows his parents have not been consistent in disciplining them. He feels like he has been treated unfairly, and that the others get away with all kinds of mischief. Absalom's hatred of Amnon festered for two years because King David did not deal with Amnon's incest.

Some of the sibling friction seen in the Scriptures had its roots in parental favoritism. Isaac liked Esau's venison while Rebecca loved Jacob. Jacob showered special favors on Joseph who was the son of his favorite wife. Parents should beware when they feel themselves gravitating toward any one of their children. It is natural for a parent to be drawn toward one personality more than another. When this occurs, however, the parent should deliberately build more bridges between himself and the other children. Parents must avoid favoritism. Do not always take the same child with you when you go shopping.

At the same time, avoid an inordinate focus on equality. Every child does not need a new pair of shoes just to keep everyone equal. Parents who meticulously try to make sure they are treating every child exactly alike doom themselves to frustration. Needs and opportunities are different. Even the attempt for absolute equality will backfire: the selfishness of the child causes him to judge his parents as always being unfair to *him.*

Unselfishness

It is natural to be selfish. We all need to be taught unselfishness. The first ingredient of such teaching is the example of the parents. Selfishness can raise its ugly head in myriad situations. I know of a father who served himself butter at the table while his family ate margarine which was cheaper. His selfishness bred resentment in the children.

A child needs to understand facets of unselfishness commonly overlooked. A mother should make her children aware of how the father is working hard to unselfishly provide for his family. This provides an opportunity for gratitude to be expressed. Frequently our children spontaneously thank my wife and me for "the good meal" they have just enjoyed: my wife for preparing what I have provided.

Parents can create an atmosphere of unselfishness by doing little things that mean so much to a child. Our family enjoys trying new foods. If at work someone brings in cake or cookies for the workers, I have a choice. I can either eat my portion immediately, or I can wrap it in a napkin and let each member of the family have a tiny taste. This attitude readily bears fruit as the children experience the joy of sharing in the same way.

Children need to hear what the Scriptures say about unselfishness. Christ is the perfect Example. He came not to please Himself, but to please others. Philippians 2 is the classic statement of His selflessness.

Help your children understand that they are merely stewards of their possessions. Everything belongs to God (Psa 24:1). Ask, "Would

God want you to share His toy?" Ultimately, unselfishness is embodied in the Golden Rule: Treat others the way you would like to be treated.

Create an environment of sharing and friendship. Then specific ownership is not so important. Make it worth the children's while to share and play happily. Don't waste time with detailed arbitration of every sibling dispute. Simply require them to stop their game or put the toy away. They soon learn it is more fun to share than to have their games terminated. Insist on attitudes of gentleness and kindness.

At Christmas, have a special family project which centers on sharing with someone in need, rather than having the children focus on what they get. Encourage the children to make gifts for one another. In our home, the children focus on the joy they experience in giving, not receiving. It is a special pleasure for an older child to give a beautiful toy (which they have outgrown) to a younger sibling for whom it is a supreme delight.

Teach the older children to be a blessing to the younger ones. They need to guard those who are weak, and watch out for their safety. Prevent older children from taking advantage of younger ones in unfair trades of treasures such as stamps or money.

Older children need to do things that the younger ones enjoy. Sometimes they should read a story to a little sister instead of doing what they would personally prefer. Let older children experience the joy of helping the younger ones play and have fun.

Encourage competitive games requiring the older children to make concessions for the little ones. In general, the oldest could win every game with his superior physical and mental development. Instead in games of tag he must learn to allow himself to be caught, and to permit a toddler to exuberantly escape. He tags carefully to avoid knocking over a small child. He learns that unselfish fellowship is more fun than the game itself. Children who experience this joy in their own family will not continually beg to go play with friends exactly their age.

The younger ones need to learn unselfishness as well. They need to respect the wishes of the older ones by not messing with their things.

Younger children must learn to accept the assistance of older siblings. Frequently a two-year-old will stubbornly insist that only his mother feed him or dress him or read him a story. He needs to learn to appreciate the help and kindness of his siblings. Sometimes he will need to be spanked before he relinquishes his selfish determination to always have his mother care for him.

Younger children also need to learn to take good advice when it is given by an older sibling. Even small children can recognize good advice. Sometimes they refuse merely because it came from the mouth of another child. Parents need to guide this interaction carefully. The older child should not be permitted to be bossy or to tyrannize younger ones. But the older child should learn to properly exercise authority for the good of a younger one. A two-year old should be spanked for resisting a five-year old who is trying to prevent him from running into the street.

Home Responsibility

For too many children, home is simply a grand hotel run by Mom and Dad. The children are the freeloading guests who consume food, relax in bed, and enjoy entertainment while the parents do the work. The results are irresponsibility, selfishness, and laziness.

Capitalize on the fact that young children love to help. They think it is fun to sweep, dust, or set the table. A mother should welcome her little ones who want to help in the kitchen, even if they spill some flour, or make a mess of her counter-tops. Remember, the goal is not to get work done as fast as possible; the goal is developing a relationship with your children and helping them to learn to work with you. Having them help will take longer initially but will pay dividends later. Even so, the time will come when the novelty wears off and they will no longer think it is fun. Then the parent needs to firmly insist on chore performance as normal routine. Later, the older ones will help you train the younger ones.

Begin early in teaching your children home responsibility. As soon as a single, simple command is understood, the child can learn responsibility. "Put the book on the shelf."

It is easy for two-year-olds to fold washcloths and pick up clothes. With help, they can make their beds. Arrange your cupboards so they can reach the dishes needed for setting the table.

Before Rosalyn turned three, she got dressed with the help of an older sister. She helped set the table, picked up her toys, and helped entertain the one-year old.

Roland at age six could do additional chores. He could make his bed, dust and vacuum his room. He cleared the table and washed dishes. He emptied trash cans into the garbage can. He daily placed clean towels on the bathroom racks. He helped do the weekly dusting and cleaning. He sorted wash and folded wash. He peeled potatoes and helped weed the garden and pick the vegetables.

Renee at age eight and Rachelle at age ten had additional chores. They helped fix meals. They baked cookies, cake, and bars. Rachelle baked bread. They hung wash to dry. They prepared garden vegetables for canning and freezing. Rachelle mowed grass.

Remember, it is a privilege to be part of a family. Every child should experience the joy of being a contributor to his family, not a parasite. Children who early learn to enjoy home responsibility are learning about reality: happiness is based on service, not indulgence. They learn the joy of working together.

Dating

American Christians have short-changed their children by turning them loose in their teen years to make a wild guess on who would make a good companion for life. The teenager is rapidly changing and developing. He is becoming an adult, beginning to formulate his goals in life, understanding his gifts, thinking about how to serve God.

It is folly to plunge such a person into an intense emotional romance. Interrupted by romantic preoccupation, he does not give sufficient attention to his life goals and aspirations. Not having solidly formulated his life purpose, he cannot adequately evaluate his romantic relationship. Since neither issue is given adequate attention, the tendency is for the couple to mature in opposite directions after marriage. Sadly they grow apart.

Most people agree that teenagers are too young to marry, and yet they persist in promoting the folly of teenage dating. Therefore marriage is implicitly held off "until later." The result is intensification of emotional involvement, with a neglect of the issues involved in marriage. By the time an appropriate chronological age is reached, emotions totally dominate any thinking. A careful, rational decision based on the facts is practically impossible. *If teenagers are too young to marry, they are also too young to date.*

From the very beginning, cultivate in your child a desire for strong relationships with his parents. This desire is natural, but is often crushed by parents who push their children away to a baby-sitter, parents who are not interested in what they consider petty or incessant questions, parents who love to "get away from the kids." Never tease your child about dating or marriage. Such teasing does not make early dating less dangerous, and it builds a barrier between you and your child.

The question of life companionship is the most critical issue of social relationships your child will ever face. Teach your child that marriage is *for life,* with no "second chances" for poor choices. Teach important principles and priorities early. If parents wait until their offspring are ready to begin dating they have waited too long. Establish an atmosphere of godly attitudes about life companionship.

Teenagers should be involved in group activities, providing interaction with many different people and personality types. Their parents should coach them on the issues involved in marriage. Once the child is old enough to marry, the parents should actively guide his courtship experience. Parent-child interaction and trust can save many heartaches.

Parental Excuses

No one likes to admit failure. We all want to be successful. Whenever we fail, we secretly hope the failure was actually the fault of someone else, or was caused by something totally beyond our control. Many times when we see failure looming ahead on the horizon we begin to make excuses, hoping to somehow make ourselves feel better.

Sadly enough, excuses actually pave the highway of failure. Don't succumb to them. The basis for excuses is an improper interpretation of facts. Face your problems honestly, in the light of God's Word, and in the power of His Spirit. Change direction instead of looking for a convenient scapegoat. Included here are replies to some common excuses regarding the family.

Discipline will damage my child's personality. Apart from discipline your child will indeed be damaged. God did not leave Adam and Eve undisciplined in the Garden of Eden. Without His disciplinary intervention, they would have become absolute monsters in their depravity. So will your child.

My child is strong-willed. No parent should ever complain about having a strong-willed child. The stronger the will, the greater the opportunity. Our world needs men and women who are inflexible in their adherence to truth and righteousness. Our world needs saints who will not be tossed about by every wind of doctrine, every frivolous spiritual fad sweeping through the church. Our world needs people who are not swayed by the crowd in a mindless pursuit of wrong. Our world needs people who have determined to obey God absolutely.

How do you build something that will last? Do you choose pine or oak? Using oak is more work, but the result is not easily broken. When I see my newborn exhibit a strong will, I welcome this great opportunity to channel his will into unswerving obedience to God.

My child is hyperactive. Frequently this is merely psychological cover-up terminology for parents who have never taught their child to obey. Too often, these parents avoid their responsibility by giving the child a drug to calm him down. Their actions solidify the damage.

My child is just aggressive. An aggressive child needs to be taught proper behavior. Channel his aggression into something useful.

My child just has a temper like his grandfather. Heredity is no excuse for unbridled sin. All of us inherit a sinful nature from our parents. What if the grandfather was a murderer? We would never excuse a child who followed in his steps.

My child is just going through a stage. In reality he is just learning how to mask his real problem by semi-socially acceptable behavior. Later the same problem will erupt in a different form, but with a vengeance. Deal with the problem now, while it is easy. Transform the "Terrible Twos" into the "Opportunity Twos."

My child has so much energy he can't sit still. It is not a question of energy, but of the will. Do an experiment. Give him a gift of ten dollars for holding still for thirty minutes, and prove it to yourself.

My child doesn't mean to be bad—he just forgets. Make it worthwhile for him to remember.

My child's temperament is the cause of the problem. Use the Biblical directives God gives for this kind of child: obedience and honor are required for all children, regardless of temperament (no special cases). Parents contribute to their child's problems by not requiring obedience. Such parental irresponsibility is difficult for even "normal" children to handle. Many "psychological" problems would disappear if the child were simply loved, taught, and disciplined instead of labeled as locked into an unfortunate genetic makeup.

Other kids were a bad influence on my child. If your child was hanging out with the wrong kids, he was part of the bad influence.

You just don't have the problems that we have had. No one is ever qualified to give advice to parents who are failures, and who want to excuse themselves rather than learn. If you don't have children, they reject you for lack of experience. If you have only toddlers, they feel you don't understand later stages. If you have a ten-year-old, you somehow escaped the bad teachers in their school. If you have no teenagers, you haven't even faced anything yet. If your teenagers are upright, you were lucky not to have a pastor like they did. "The sluggard is wiser in his own eyes than seven men who can answer sensibly" (Prov 26:16).

You are not qualified to say these things. After a seminar session an overweight old man growled at me, "I'd like to hear your seminar thirty years from now when your children are grown and have families of their own!" I asked why, but he just stalked off without answering. After the next session he approached me again: "How old are you, anyway?" "Forty-three," I replied. "How old are you?" His caustic reply: "Seventy-eight! You have a lot to learn yet!"

Later it was no surprise when his pastor told me his home life was wretched. He was one who treated his wife terribly, and was not on speaking terms with his own son. One of the oldest of delusions is to hope to escape truth by trying to discredit the truth-bearer.

Experience is not a prerequisite for speaking God's message. God sent Samuel, a young inexperienced boy, to tell Eli how he had miserably failed in his family, even though God knew Samuel's own sons would be wicked men. To succeed in the family, we must obey God's message—a message of invincible authority which provides solutions to problems that otherwise are absolutely intractable.

Is the Standard Too High?

God's standard is indeed high. His ways are solutions, not mere suggestions. We can choose. Shall we follow our own ways, or God's? A happy family is not purchased by money, intelligence, or education. A happy family is available through obedience.

Sometimes when people hear the things taught in this book, they wonder if the standard is too high. How could children be happy in such a "stern" environment? Actually, the environment I have proposed is not so much sternness as freedom and joy in the context of clear boundaries and righteous expectations. Such home life is the key to childhood happiness.

Years ago we encouraged our daughter Rachelle to keep a journal where she records her thoughts. Her description of her parents in this journal reveals the kind of attitude she has toward them. The following verbatim quotation was written when she was eleven years old.

Father is thirty-six years old and will be thirty-seven on June the twenty-sixth. He was born in Harrisonburg, Virginia as a preemie who had to be fed every two hours. His grandmother, Clara, lived with his family until she died when he was twenty-six. She was very sweet and taught him many things. He grew up in Shenandoah Valley.

Now he is a man. Here is how he looks. He is somewhat short, 5'7", and is very trim. He has dark, slightly wavy hair that is thinning and dropping out. He has a ruddy, round face and dimples that do not show because most of his cheeks are covered with a thick, rich reddish-brown beard. One part of his upper cheek has reddish sores on it. This is from a disease called shingles. He has hazel eyes which do not see as clearly as they should, and he wears dark-rimmed spectacles. He looks like a king.

He reads the Bible a lot and can explain it in an interesting way. He explains boring math and science things in a very interesting way! He plays games with us children a lot! He's good at them, too! He is quite eloquent and vehement at times. He has a quick temper. I love him.

Mother is thirty-five years of age and will be thirty-six on July the fifteenth. She was born in Lancaster, Pennsylvania on July the fifteenth, 1950. She was married to Father in August of 1972, at the age of twenty-two. She is a very noble, kind, mother. Descriptions fail me. I fear that for a detailed description you must turn to your Bible, Proverbs thirty-one, and read it.[2]

Behavior when no one is looking is the acid test of training, the ultimate demonstration of whether principle has been internalized by the child. Rachelle has given us complete freedom to read her journals (except for sections which she marks "private"). One day I discovered an interesting incident which she recorded at age ten, and I include it here as a final example.

Well, my favorite haunt now is the basement. Boxes! What beautiful, strange and mysterious things they contain! Endless things to look at and examine. One thing I found yesterday was an old journal. Father was twenty when he wrote it. I didn't know that. I thought that it was some old notes for a school talk. I opened it to about the middle.

December 29, 1969, I read. I glanced down the page. There were not many particularly interesting things, something about Father saying that he wanted to do what God wished about marrying Mother (which I *did* think interesting). I shut the book. Just then Mother called me.

That afternoon, I went downstairs again and got the journal. I opened it to the first page and read: NOTICE. THIS JOURNAL IS A PRIVATE AFFAIR. IN IT ARE RECORDED PERSONAL WISHES, THOUGHTS, AND ASPIRATIONS, IN ADDITION TO CONFIDENTIAL CONVERSATIONS. I REPEAT. PLEASE READ NO FARTHER.

I was dreadfully disappointed, as well as feeling a little guilty for seeing some, and my feelings were reeling inside me. There were lots of reasons not to heed it.

"Father wasn't my father then. I don't have to obey.

"Father's probably changed his mind for a private journal, as he has changed his mind with other things.

"Father doesn't need to know.

---

[2]Rachelle's Journal, April 2, 1986.

"I'll really be missing out if I don't know these things."

Then the other side spoke. I knew that the first reason was not completely honest, and the third reason was just plain trash.

"I like to be trusted.

"I like to please Father, and respect his wishes, even if he made them when just a boy.

"I like to respect *anyone's* wishes in this respect.

"Also, I think that to *not* read it would be what is right."

So the good won. Although I yearn to read it, I shall not, for the reasons listed above, for that was the right thing.[3]

Conclusion: Power to Fulfil God's Standards

Sometimes when parents see God's high standards for the family, they feel overwhelmed. They wonder where to start. They see so many deficiencies in themselves, so many failures in the precedents already established, so many negative influences rushing in upon their family. How can they ever meet God's expectations?

The answer? Mere humans cannot meet these standards. God's standards can only be fulfilled through supernatural power. Ultimately, success in the family will never be realized unless parents look to Christ in faith, asking Him to live His powerful life through them. Holy living in the family is part of the great salvation package which Jesus provides through His death and resurrection. The Apostle Paul gives a concise explanation of this glorious salvation in Romans 5-8.

God gave His instructions so we could know right from wrong. These instructions also show us our own sin—how far we have missed the mark. Romans 5 describes our plight in terms of racial heritage. Adam is the head of the race of sinners. Jesus is the head of a new race of saints. Adam's one act of disobedience plunged the entire race into doom, under the condemnation of death. Jesus' act of obedience in going to the Cross was God's master stroke in eternity. It enabled us to switch races—escape the doomed race, and through the resurrection of Christ to be incorporated into a new race which will reign in life (5:17). This is not merely a future hope, but something to experience in the present.

As an example, suppose I as a white American were weary of being an American and wished to become Japanese. To accomplish this I could renounce American citizenship, travel to Japan, eat Japanese food, wear Japanese clothes, follow Japanese customs, and study Japanese under a native tutor. However, even if I worked at it diligently for many years, I would never be mistaken for a Japanese native. My skin, hair, and eyes are the wrong color. My accent would be imperfect. My thought patterns would be rooted in the West instead of the East.

However, suppose I could die, and then be born again from a Japanese mother. The situation would be markedly different. I would

---

[3]Rachelle's Journal, December 12, 1985.

naturally learn correct speech and accent from her. I would naturally like Japanese customs, and would think in Japanese patterns. Everyone would recognize me as ethnic Japanese.

This example helps explain God's grace as outlined in Romans 5-8. As long as we are merely in the Adamic race, we are doomed to helplessness under the power of sin. Christ became a man to die in our place. By being united with Him, our "old man" (all we were in Adam) was crucified with Christ 2000 years ago, and we are privileged to be raised together with Christ to walk in a powerful new life (Rom 6:4). God's grace allows us to switch races by being born again.

Most Christians find it relatively easy to believe in justification by faith alone. They simply accept God's statement that Christ's sacrifice on the Cross was sufficient to take away their sins, and that they are therefore forgiven. No amount of walking on crushed glass or lying on beds of nails could ever procure any favor from God in obtaining forgiveness. It is only by faith in Christ's finished work.

Unfortunately, however, many of those same Christians try to accomplish sanctification by works. They imagine that trying harder and praying more will somehow enable them to meet God's holy standards. They doom themselves to the frustration of Romans 7 because they have essentially embraced only part of the salvation package. Salvation in Christ is a total solution, both justification and sanctification. Justification deals with the sins of the past. Sanctification deals with the problem of sin in the present. Just as we look to Christ in faith for forgiveness, we must also look to Christ in faith for the power to live a holy life, the power to actually meet God's standards.

In Christ, God provides the answer to the problem of indwelling sin. The Law could not make people good; it could only condemn them for being wicked. Therefore God sent His Son in the flesh to condemn sin on the Cross, so that *"the righteous requirements of the law might be fulfilled in us* who do not walk according to the flesh but according to the Spirit" (Rom 8:4, italics mine). God does expect His standards to be obeyed. He is not interested in pretending we are righteous when He knows we are not. He has provided Christ's work in death, burial, resurrection, and ascension to enable us to meet His standards. The book of Hebrews goes into great detail about the ministry of our heavenly High Priest who gives us power over sin, not merely forgiveness from sin.

This applies particularly to the family. As a parent, I confess to God that of myself I am undone, unable to live the way God wants me to live, falling far short of His standards. Then, by faith in what He has said, I thank God for His action on the Cross 2000 years ago, action providing the way of escape from the doomed race in Adam. I thank God for union with Jesus Christ which baptized me into His death and united me with Him in resurrection. By faith, I ask Jesus to live His resurrection life through me, providing the power to live a holy life.

This is not a "once-for-all" request. Sometimes I fail to appropriate Christ's power. Then I come back to Him, asking for forgiveness, and again asking Him to live His resurrection life through me.

Let me illustrate how this understanding has been a great blessing to me personally. I have had a real struggle with anger. I would get angry with my wife or with my children, and then have to ask their forgiveness. It was so distressing to fail again and again. But when I began to understand God's full provision for power over sin, I confessed my helplessness to Christ, and by faith asked Him to live His resurrection life through me.

Sometimes family singing practice in preparation for seminars would be frustrating: one child would slouch, another would bump someone in the ribs, another would begin to snicker, someone would miss notes because he was not paying attention. One day as we were practicing music together, I suddenly realized that in the midst of a very exasperating situation I was responding the way Christ wanted me to respond. Not because I was holding my anger in check by brute strength, but because Jesus had answered my cry of faith, and was living His life through me.

A whole new joy and love for Christ welled up within my soul. I knew Jesus was alive. Not merely because I believed the Gospel accounts as the inspired Word of God, but because Jesus enabled me to live a life which by hard experience I had found impossible. I experienced a taste of Paul's glorious testimony: "I have been crucified with Christ; it is no longer I who live, but Christ lives in me; and the life which I now live in the flesh I live by faith in the Son of God, who loved me and gave Himself for me" (Gal 2:20).

God wants every parent to fulfill His standards of righteousness in the family—not by focusing on self, but by looking in faith to Christ to live His glorious life through him. When this happens, the family becomes like a city set on a hill, a beacon calling the people of our world to come and taste and see that the Lord is good, and that His ways bring peace and joy.

Bibliography

Bauer, Walter; Arndt, William F.; and Gingrich, F. Wilbur. *A Greek-English Lexicon of the New Testament and Other Early Christian Literature.* 2nd ed. revised and augmented by F. Wilbur Gingrich and Frederick W. Danker. Chicago: The University of Chicago Press, 1979.

Brown, Colin, ed. *The New International Dictionary of New Testament Theology.* Vol. 1. Grand Rapids: Zondervan, 1971.

Brown, Francis; Driver, S. R.; Briggs, Charles A. *The New Brown-Driver-Briggs-Gesenius Hebrew and English Lexicon.* Christian Copyrights, Inc., 1983.

Bruce, F. F. "Women in the Church: a Biblical Survey." *Christian Brethren Review* 33 (1982):8-9.

Calvin, John. *Commentaries on the First Epistle to Timothy.* Translated by Wm. Pringle. Grand Rapids: Baker Book House, 1979.

Elliot, Elisabeth. *These Strange Ashes.* New York: Harper and Row, 1975.

Fleming, Jean. *A Mother's Heart.* Colorado Springs: Navpress, 1982.

Fugate, J. Richard. *What the Bible Says About . . . Child Training.* Garland, TX: Aletheia Publishers, Inc., 1980.

Handford, Elizabeth Rice, *Me? Obey Him?* Murfreesboro, TN: Sword of the Lord Publishers, 1972.

Harris, R. Laird; Archer, Gleason L., Jr.; Waltke, Bruce K. *Theological Wordbook of the Old Testament.* Vol. 2. Chicago: Moody Press, 1980.

Heth, William A. and Wenham, Gordon J. *Jesus and Divorce: The Problem with the Evangelical Consensus.* Nashville, TN: Thomas Nelson Publishers, 1985.

Jeschke, Marlin. *Believer's Baptism for Children of the Church.* Scottdale, PA: Herald Press, 1983.

Kent, Homer A., Jr. *The Pastoral Epistles.* Chicago: Moody Press, 1958.

Kuhn, Isobel. *Ascent to the Tribes: Pioneering in North Thailand.* Chicago: Moody Press, 1956.

Lambdin, Thomas O. *Introduction to Biblical Hebrew.* New York: Charles Scribner's Sons, 1971.

Ludwig, Charles. *Susanna Wesley: Mother of John and Charles.* Milford, MI: Mott Media, 1984.

Meyer, F. B. *Abraham.* Fort Washington, PA: Christian Literature Crusade, 1978.

Morris, William, ed. *The American Heritage Dictionary.* New York: Houghton Mifflin Co., 1969.

Pride, Mary. *The Way Home: Beyond Feminism, Back to Reality.* Westchester, IL: Crossway Books, 1985.

Ray, Bruce A. *Withhold Not Correction.* Grand Rapids: Baker Book House, 1978.

Robinson, Haddon W. *Biblical Preaching.* Grand Rapids: Baker Book House, 1980.

Spurgeon, Charles H. *The Treasury of David, Vol 2.* Fincastle, VA: Scripture Truth Book Co., 1984.

Stauffer, J. Mark, ed. *Our Hymns of Praise.* Scottdale, PA: Herald Press, 1958.

Stillman, Nigel and Tallis, Nigel. *Armies of the Ancient Near East.* Worthing, England: Flexiprint Ltd., 1984.

Stitzinger, Michael F. "Genesis 1-3 and the Male/Female Role Relationship." *Grace Theological Journal 2* (Spring 1981):23-44.

Trapp, Maria Augusta. *The Story of the Trapp Family Singers.* New York: Scholastic Book Services, 1949.

Wigram, George V. *The Englishman's Greek Concordance of the New Testament.* Grand Rapids: Zondervan Publishing House, 1970.

_____. *The Englishman's Hebrew and Chaldee Concordance of the Old Testament.* Fifth Edition. London: Samuel Bagster and Sons, Ltd., 1890.

Yadin, Yigael. *The Art of Warfare in Biblical Lands.* Vol. 1. New York: McGraw-Hill Book Co., Inc., 1963.